MY ALTERED

T0267837

"An illuminating autobiographical explora[tion] [of] researcher Rick Strassman's early life and firsthand experiences with altered states of consciousness. . . . This sensitive and self-revealing examination of how these powerful compounds affected Dr. Strassman's personal evolution and his insights into the potential impact of psychedelics make a valuable contribution to our understanding of human consciousness and the potential for new and valuable psychiatric treatments."

CHARLES S. GROB, M.D., PROFESSOR OF PSYCHIATRY
AT THE UCLA SCHOOL OF MEDICINE

"In his gripping, painfully honest memoir *My Altered States*, eminent psychedelic researcher Rick Strassman delves into the risks as well as spiritual potential of psychedelics. As capitalists seek to monetize these remarkable substances, Strassman's book provides a much-needed counterpoint to the hype and hoopla."

JOHN HORGAN, SCIENCE JOURNALIST AND
AUTHOR OF *THE END OF SCIENCE*

"Brave, honest, real, self-critical, deeply personal, and well-told, Rick Strassman's account of his formative years casts compelling light on his subsequently pioneering career in psychedelic science. A necessary contribution."

JEREMY NARBY, COAUTHOR OF *THE PSYCHOTROPIC MIND*

"Rick Strassman's memoir is a gift defined by both raw honesty and a distinct literary beauty. He shows us how scientific exploration itself can be an altered state, guiding us deeper into practices like meditation, psychedelics, and psychoanalysis. Get ready for a wild ride, including a telepathic one on a flying carpet."

JEFFREY J. KRIPAL, AUTHOR OF *HOW TO THINK IMPOSSIBLY*

"If you want to know what shaped the mind of one of the most important and influential psychedelic scientists of the last century, I can't recommend this book highly enough."

ANDREW R. GALLIMORE, PH.D., NEUROBIOLOGIST AND
AUTHOR OF *REALITY SWITCH TECHNOLOGIES*

"The doyen of DMT studies finally begins to share his personal experiences with psychedelics—as well as his personal history—in this wise, intimate, funny, at-times disturbing, always heartfelt memoir. It covers his life up to the time he joined a Zen Buddhist monastery while on leave from medical school in his early twenties. I highly recommend this book."

TAO LIN, AUTHOR OF
TRIP: PSYCHEDELICS, ALIENATION, AND CHANGE

" . . . Having the mind and the courage . . . you're such an important part of the psychedelic history of this country because what you did is you legitimized a very important thing."

JOE ROGAN, FROM A CONVERSATION WITH RICK STRASSMAN, M.D.,
REGARDING HIS CONTRIBUTIONS TO PSYCHEDELIC RESEARCH
ON THE *JOE ROGAN EXPERIENCE*, EPISODE #1854

"This book is a magnificent treat, offering page-turning accounts that are as fascinating as they are engaging. . . . Beyond the usual altered states, Strassman explores unconventional and rarely recognized types of shifted consciousness with elegance and wisdom gained from years of reflection. . . . *My Altered States* is a mind-expanding treasure, illuminating the depths of human consciousness with a rare and captivating brilliance."

DAVID JAY BROWN, COAUTHOR OF
THE ILLUSTRATED FIELD GUIDE TO DMT ENTITIES

"*My Altered States* successfully bridges psychopharmacology and psychotherapy in a coherent whole that will satisfy the initiated as well as the lay reader who, like Dr. Strassman, seek to tap into the deepest mysteries of the mind."

TADEO FEIJÃO, M.D., PRESIDENT OF THE
UNIÃO DO VEGETAL (UDV) GENERAL DIRECTORATE

"Rick has taken on the daring task of writing about how various substances have affected his consciousness. He does so by immersing us into his own soul and circumstances in an honest, elegant, and engaging style that also triggers self-reflection. This book is a gem."

LUIS EDUARDO LUNA, PH.D., COAUTHOR OF
INNER PATHS TO OUTER SPACE

MY ALTERED STATES

A DOCTOR'S EXTRAORDINARY ACCOUNT OF
TRAUMA, PSYCHEDELICS,
AND SPIRITUAL GROWTH

RICK STRASSMAN, M.D.

Park Street Press
Rochester, Vermont

Park Street Press
One Park Street
Rochester, Vermont 05767
www.ParkStPress.com

Park Street Press is a division of Inner Traditions International

Cataloging-in-Publication Data for this title is available from the Library of Congress

ISBN 978-1-64411-979-2 (print)
ISBN 978-1-64411-980-8 (ebook)

Printed and bound in the United States by Lake Book Manufacturing, LLC

10 9 8 7 6 5 4 3 2 1

Text design by Priscilla Baker and layout by Kenleigh Manseau
This book was typeset in Garamond Premier Pro with ImaginaryFriend BB and
Futura Std used as display typefaces
Artwork by Merrilee Challiss

To send correspondence to the author of this book, mail a first-class letter to the
author c/o Inner Traditions • Bear & Company, One Park Street, Rochester, VT
05767, and we will forward the communication, or contact the author directly at
rickstrassman.com.

Scan the QR code and save 25% at InnerTraditions.com.
Browse over 2,000 titles on spirituality, the occult, ancient
mysteries, new science, holistic health, and natural medicine.

To Ken Nathanson, 1951–2023

"Unreal"

Troubles overcome are worth telling.

YIDDISH PROVERB

CONTENTS

Part II
FINDING MY WAY

PREFACE

RESEARCH IS ME-SEARCH

I HAVE BEEN RECORDING my altered state experiences since my late teen years, as well as remembering and reconstructing ones that occurred earlier. While most resulted from consuming psychoactive substances such as psychedelics, cannabis, and alcohol, others resulted from meditation and psychoanalysis. Circumstances beyond my control led to others—childhood abuse and later a serious mood disturbance in my early twenties.

As with many academics, "research is me-search." That is, I found these states to be so compelling—either positively or negatively—that they inexorably steered my career into psychedelic drug research. I have also sought to integrate altered states into my worldview, behavior, and psychospiritual growth. This led to the study and practice of meditation-based Zen Buddhism for over twenty years.

This, then, is a memoir of altered states of consciousness, from "before birth" to the closing of a Zen monastery's gates behind me twenty-two years later. It is a portrait of a young seeker born into a certain time and place, with certain abilities and disabilities. There are stumbles and revelations, dead ends and vast panoramas, joyful moments and abject terror, messianic optimism and soul-crushing despair. Ultimately, however, there is no final redemption, no tidy ending. It is simply an account of my efforts to become free, and in so doing, hoping to make the world a better place. In this context, altered states of consciousness have played a crucial role in the project of my life.

In presenting these accounts, I rely on skills I have developed and honed throughout my life, involving myself in traditional and reliable paths of inner exploration. One such discipline is psychoanalytic psychotherapy, which I began as a child in an effort to resolve my speech dysfluency. In medical school, I had my first course of long-term treatment with this type of psychological therapy. And in my thirties, I embarked upon a four-year classical psychoanalysis with sessions occurring up to five days per week, lying on the couch. In addition, during my psychiatric training and academic career, I studied and taught psychoanalytic psychology and psychotherapy. And while treating psychiatric patients in academic, community, and private settings, I employed psychoanalytic principles and methods as much as possible.

In my early twenties, I began practicing and studying Zen Buddhism under the supervision of a long-standing Western monastic order. I underwent lay ordination, founded and helped run an affiliated meditation group, and maintained close relationships with clerical and lay members of the community for over twenty years.

Later, I returned to my Jewish roots and immersed myself in the Hebrew Bible's language, spirituality, and philosophy; that is, foundational Judaism. After eighteen years of study, this project resulted in *DMT and the Soul of Prophecy*,[1] a comparison of the biblical prophetic state of consciousness with that which the naturally occurring psychedelic DMT brings about.

Finally, I draw on hundreds of psychedelic drug sessions I supervised during my years of research with DMT and psilocybin in the early 1990s at the University of New Mexico School of Medicine. I describe in depth these pivotal studies—which initiated the renewal of American clinical research with psychedelics—in my book *DMT: The Spirit Molecule*.[2]

Thus, I bring to bear a variety of explanatory models with which to interpret my own altered states. I will discuss these models when they help clarify general principles that extend beyond simply what happened to me any particular day. These include concepts like set, setting, intention, and dose; the nature of the unconscious; brain networks and psychopharmacology; and metaphysical considerations of the relationship between the worlds of spirit and matter.

These exegetical remarks appear after every narrative—except for the final chapter—in the "Reflections" section. My intention in including this material is to both describe how certain experiences came to pass, as well as their meaning.

As a memoir, these events—and my attempts to understand and integrate them—partake of a literary quality. Therefore, this work joins that of others who have described effects of a variety of mind-altering substances. These include Charles Bukowski and alcohol,[3] Albert Hofmann and LSD,[4] John Lilly and ketamine,[5] William James and nitrous oxide,[6] Sigmund Freud and cocaine,[7] William Burroughs and heroin,[8] Thomas De Quincey and opium,[9] and Jacques-Joseph Moreau and hashish.[10] It also ventures into the autobiographical literature about altered states accompanying mental illness, such as Jung's *The Red Book* and Jamison's *An Unquiet Mind*.

Merrilee Challiss's remarkable artwork captures each chapter's most meaningful emotional and consciousness-related features. It therefore is essential to this memoir, visually expressing more than words alone are able. Each image epitomizes an episode's mood—such as fear, joy, pain, ecstasy, confusion, hilarity, despair, or equanimity. In addition, they evoke the characteristic properties of the altered state under discussion. For example, regarding psychedelics, novelty and meaningfulness; with alcohol, disinhibited behavior; and with meditation, enhanced focus and concentration.

When reading any memoir, questions arise about the character of the author. Who am I as the protagonist? What influenced me to venture so far afield so often? What was I looking for and why? What did I find? What are the themes that run through these accounts? What unites them—if anything? Have I succeeded, and how; or have I not, and why?

These are deeply personal accounts, and I admit to some anxiety sharing them. Several do not portray me in an especially flattering light, and I make no attempt to paper over their "warts and all" quality. Hopefully, you will attribute these to my inexperience, naïveté, or misguided intent rather than malignant motivations or intractable psychopathology. In addition, several chapters describe my responses to external events over which I had little control, rather than taking one or the other mind-altering substances. In these circumstances, all I could do was react with the resources I had.

Nearly all of the experiences in this book occurred with others. In order to preserve their anonymity, I change names, gender, occupation, and other personal identifiers, as well as dates, places, and locations.

EXPLORING ALTERED STATES OF CONSCIOUSNESS

FIFTY YEARS AGO psychologist Charles Tart proposed definitions of an "altered state of consciousness" that have undergone little change in the intervening half-century. An altered state of consciousness is "a qualitative alteration in the overall pattern of mental functioning, such that the experiencer feels his consciousness is radically different from the way it functions ordinarily"[1] and "a unique, dynamic pattern or configuration of psychological structures"[2] differing from the baseline state of everyday normal waking consciousness. Examples are meditation, alcohol and drug effects, prolonged hyperventilation, hypnosis, psychosis, deep sleep, anesthesia, dreams, and delirium.

Our drive to experience altered states of consciousness may be as fundamental as those for sex, food, and companionship.[3] Young children spinning themselves to dizziness shows how early this drive to alter subjective experience appears. Altered states like dreaming and psychoses that occur involuntarily suggest that these changes in consciousness are an essential feature of the human mind-brain complex.

These altered states are intensely private, existing in our own minds. While we can describe and discuss them, it is not (yet) possible for anyone else to share the exact same subjective experience. And even if that were possible, our reaction to and interpretation of that experience would be uniquely ours. This is why reading accounts of others' altered states is so compelling. We look for similarities and differences between ours and the writer's. How well does he or she capture the details and essence of such episodes? How does he or she understand and apply them? Do such accounts confirm, negate, or otherwise affect how we understand and interpret our own altered states?

SET, SETTING, AND CAUSE

Three fundamental factors determine every altered state brought on by drugs or other stimuli. These are *set*, *setting*, and *cause*. This last factor includes a drug, method, or psychometabolic disorder like schizophrenia or hypoglycemia. In terms of cause, there is also the "dose"—the amount of the mind-altering substance, the intensity and duration of performing a mind-altering technique, or the intensity and duration of the endogenous disturbance.

Set

Set is our mental, physical, and spiritual condition when we enter an altered state. Our mental set includes long-standing personality, habits, and coping style. Suggestibility—the degree to which our social and physical environments influence our state of mind—plays a significant role, too. Our intellect also contributes—education, vocabulary, and abstracting ability. Sensory function, as well—visual, auditory, and other perceptual organs' acuity and sensitivity. Our genetics also affect our reactions to any mind-altering intervention; for example, a personal or family history of, or vulnerability to, mental illness.

Mental set also includes our current state of mind. Are we anxious or relaxed; angry, happy, or sad; satisfied or not with love and work? Previous experiences with the particular cause affects our expectations, too, and this in turn will influence our reactions to their effects. A previous nightmarish or beatific encounter with LSD cannot help but color how we approach an upcoming day with the drug. Similarly, one's reaction to psychotic symptoms in schizophrenia will differ over the course of the illness, depending on set and setting issues. Is this the first or the twentieth time hallucinations have occurred? Is the person around supportive family or in a hostile crowd of strangers? Even without previous experience, our set includes what we hope and/or fear will or will not happen during the altered state.

Why do we want to experience an altered state? This is our *intent*, and there are a multitude: pleasure, curiosity, problem-solving, escape, spiritual development, enhanced sociality, psychotherapy, and creativity. We may have darker motives, too, such as wishing to manipulate or harm, or to reinforce destructive beliefs or patterns of behavior. Or, is our decision to enter an altered state simply spur-of-the-moment?

Our physical health is another element of set. Are we well or ill, rested or fatigued, fed or hungry? Are we taking any medication—psychiatric or otherwise—that may interact with the altered state itself or the method of attaining it? How about drugs: alcohol, cigarettes or nicotine, opiates, cannabis, or stimulants such as cocaine, methamphetamine, or amphetamine? Are we under the influence of, or recovering or withdrawing from, any drugs?

One's spiritual state is also important. Do you believe in a spiritual level of reality? If so, do you believe in God, angels, or demons? What is your relationship to the spiritual world? Do you engage in spiritual practices such as meditation, prayer, yoga, chanting, service, or study? Do you belong to a spiritual/religious community? If so, and if there is a teacher/leader, what is your relationship with him or her?

Setting

Setting is everything else, the "not-you" part of the experience, the outside world. There is the physical setting: indoors or outdoors, rural or urban, daytime or nighttime, alone or with others, silent or with music. There is also the social or interpersonal setting, including the set of those around you. Are they strangers or people you know; friendly or hostile; therapist, researcher, or spiritual teacher? What do those around you know and think about, for example, psychedelic drugs? Will they understand what is going on with you, and are they available for support or camaraderie? Are they in the same altered state as you?

Cause

Countless drugs alter consciousness. Alexander Shulgin, father of modern psychedelic psychopharmacology, categorized mind-altering substances into three groups. The ↑ drugs are stimulants like caffeine and amphetamines; the ↓ compounds are sedatives like alcohol, opiates, and benzodiazepine tranquilizers; and the ✳ substances are the psychedelics. The ↑s and ↓s modify just a few mental functions, like energy, alertness, or mood. The ✳s, on the other hand, affect every element of human consciousness: body image, perception, thought processes, mood, and sense of self. Psychedelics include "classical" substances like the following.

LSD	Lysergic acid diethylamide or "acid"
Mescaline/peyote/San Pedro	Peyote and San Pedro are psychedelic cacti whose active ingredient is mescaline
Magic mushrooms/psilocybin	Psilocybin is responsible for the psychedelic properties of magic mushrooms
DMT	Dimethyltryptamine
Ayahuasca	An Amazonian psychedelic brew that contains DMT
5-Methoxy-DMT/"toad"	5-Methoxy-DMT is the active ingredient in the venom of the Sonoran Desert toad, *Bufo alvarius*

And there are "nonclassical" drugs that produce similar effects to classical ones.

Ketamine	A general anesthetic that produces psychedelic effects at subanesthetic doses
Salvia divinorum/salvinorin A	Salvinorin A is the active ingredient in the diviner's mint *Salvia divinorum*
MDMA	3,4-Methylenedioxymethamphetamine, a "psychedelic-like" methamphetamine derivative with primarily emotional effects
High-potency cannabis	The primary psychoactive compound is tetrahydrocannabinol (THC)

There are many techniques and practices—for example, breathwork—that produce altered states similar to those resulting from drug ingestion. This term usually refers to prolonged intense hyperventilation, as in "holotropic breathwork."[4] It may also include breathholding.[5] Mind-altering yoga *pranayama* breathing techniques have been in existence for millennia. In terms of these practices, the "dose" refers to the intensity and duration of engaging in such methods.

At other times, we have less control over the altered state we enter. Those suffering from psychoses like schizophrenia or severe mood disorders also perceive, feel, and think in ways similar to those brought on by mind-altering drugs or practices. We all dream, and some of us have had near-death experiences—both of which possess highly altered mental contents.

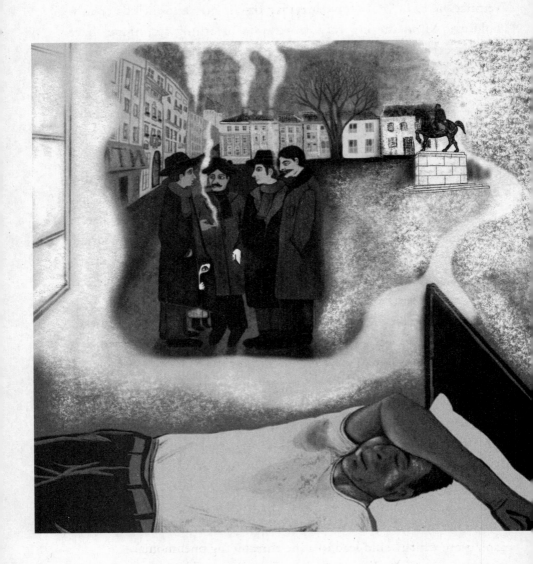

PROLOGUE

THE BEGINNING

COLD SWEAT DRENCHES MY BODY, soaking my clothes. I am lying on a single bed in my friends' guestroom. The midday June sun pours through the south-facing windows. But, despite the open windows, the air barely moves, and the heat is stifling. Am I reacting to the heat or to the drug? I'm under the influence of a novel compound related to psilocybin. It appears safe in animals, but no more than a dozen people have taken it. Preliminary reports are that it is an effective psychotherapeutic aid.

Arturo sits on the edge of the bed and gently wipes my forehead, cheeks, and neck with a cool wet washcloth. I shiver. He briefly rests his open hand, palm down, on my chest and breathes in a slow, deep, and loud manner, hoping I will imitate him. Doing so may help me relax. I have used the same method when I am with someone who is having difficulty during a psychedelic experience.

Nevertheless, my chills concern him. He reaches for the light blanket at the foot of the bed, unfolds it, and covers my chest.

"Am I sick?" I barely whisper.

"You're doing fine," he murmurs, but his sharp eyes keep watch. If it looks as if I am going to vomit, he will quickly turn my head to prevent aspiration, which could lead to a life-threatening pneumonia.

Eyes closed, dimly aware of my friend's comforting presence, my mind's eye gazes at the unfolding vision.

From a distance of several dozen yards, I see my father's father Selig standing in a small circle of friends—all men, all in their early

1

twenties. Fifty years before my birth, I see myself—about six years old—peering out from under his coat, standing pressed against my forbear's lower body. The perspective changes, and now I am in the mind of the little boy. I see and feel my grandfather's thick woolen outer garment protecting me from the cold blasts of autumn wind. The smell of cigars permeates his clothes and makes even more familiar the comfort of my cocoon. I adjust myself in this new space, and Selig accommodates my movements, shifting his legs to provide me more room. The movement causes the coat to open slightly, and it loses some warmth. I pull its edges closer together, just below my eyes. My steamy breath, which the coat captures, helps keep the chill off my face.

I look out toward the great square of Lvov* looming above us. Black shadows spread from the massive stone buildings visible in all directions—government, finance, high-end retail. Pale cobblestone extends to the horizon. Beneath my feet is a darker paving stone.

The four men stand in a close bunch to ward off the penetrating gusts punctuating the sunny day. Handsome and healthy, they are either clean-shaven or sport only small tidy mustaches. None wears the sidelocks characteristic of their Hasidic† brethren, whom they see as unenlightened, living in the past.

I feel safe within the confines of my grandfather's coat; however, the anxiety in the men's voices presses against me. I don't understand the language, but they are communicating dread, a sense of growing threat. I hear the word *pogrom*‡ and Selig's friends' eyes widen. I shiver and bring the coat edges even closer. Selig once more adjusts to my movements.

---

*Also, Lviv, Lemberg, Lwów. The largest city in Ukraine, founded in the early first millennium. Various powers have controlled it throughout history: Russia (the Russian Empire, as well as the USSR), Poland, Germany, and the Austro-Hungarian Empire.

†A stream of Judaism that began in eighteenth-century Eastern Europe. Their emphasis on direct spiritual experience over scholastic learning—in essence, a spiritual revival—produced a rift within European Judaism. Their traditional dress and hair caused them to stand out and prompted contemporary secular Jews to shun them.

‡A Russian word meaning a popular uprising against a community's Jewish members. Civic and religious authorities provoked, condoned, or ignored these deadly outbursts.

The friends share their fear, helplessness, and uncertainty. I telepathically understand what they are asking each other.

"What will we do?"

They direct their question in Selig's direction and lower their gaze
toward me.

"Where will we go?"*

The weight of the drug-induced vision flattens my prone body. Panic
stirs as I begin sinking into the bed. I jerk upright before I descend
much further, startling Arturo.

My guide quickly regains his composure. "Are you all right?" he
asks quietly. He is aware of my regressed vulnerable state and is on high
alert. You never know what people are going through, he thinks. Or
what they might do.

Sitting with my legs extended in front of me, I hang my head low,
neck at almost a right angle to my spine. I am drooling and shake my
head from side to side, then laugh. Sour sweat trickles from my under-
arms and down my sides.

"Wow," I muster. "This is intense."

"You're doing fine," Arturo murmurs soothingly. While his day job
is an economist at a major bank, he's been learning and practicing psychedelic psychotherapy for several decades. He has been around, and
I trust him. There are medical professionals in the group today, too,
which reassures both of us.

"Here. Have some water."

For a moment, the intense cold hurts my mouth. I swirl the liquid
around and noisily spit it back into the glass without swallowing any.

I stare at the incandescent water, puzzled and uncertain.

"Lay down again, okay? I am here for you." Not waiting for my

---

*My grandfather left Ukraine around 1908. In a 1918 pogrom in Lvov, local Ukrainians
and Polish troops killed about one hundred Jews over several days. During World
War II, over 100,000 Jews died in the Lvov ghetto and in the camps to which Nazis
sent them. The worst violence occurred in 1941, when Nazi-led Ukrainian forces killed
about six thousand Jews over two months.

response, he places one hand on my chest and another against my mid-back and guides me slowly back down.

Ten years before my birth, I lift my eyes, dully pondering a sky as deep blue as on that day in Lvov. It must be autumn here, too, I realize. A powerful wind likewise reminds me of the afternoon with my grandfather and his friends. Gusts blow the chimneys' smoke away from the vast mud-filled plaza where I stand. I lower my gaze to the horizon beyond the camp. The panorama—infinite fields and forest—is terrifying. No matter how close, it is impossible to reach. Now or ever.

I sense my nearly frozen feet in shoes buried in mud. I blink and tremble as a shockwave of wind assaults me through my threadbare striped pajamas. I almost lose my balance. A twenty-foot-high fence stands about thirty yards away. Squinting against the sun, I narrow my view and observe similarly shivering men all around. Rhythmically shifting their weight from one foot to the other, they stir the mud. Others lean against wooden barracks, watching. Weak, cold, and numb, a unique horror seeps into me—a dread filling my body, mind, and soul.

I bolt up again, looking around the little room. Pulsating air shimmers malignantly like an evil insect's slowly beating wings.

"Where's the barf basin?" I eke out.

Arturo deftly grabs a bright red plastic one-gallon bucket sitting on the floor nearby.

"Here," he says and sets it between my legs on the bed. I retch but nothing comes up.

"Lay back down, brother. Whatever it is, it's big and you need to go through it."

Tears pour down my cheeks. "How could this be happening?" I sob.

"Don't worry," he says. "It is happening." He adds, "And it'll be fine."

I lie back down on my own this time.

Immediately, I return to the camp. "Oh, God, what is this?" I moan. I am exhausted. My will has given out. I no longer desire existence nor experience, but my flesh is stubborn, in the habit of life, and holds on.

I see a mound of naked and emaciated bodies on the other side of the fence. Most, but not all, have stopped moving. The next moment, I am near the bottom of the pile, and see only blackness. My neck bent painfully, I taste something salty and thick, and retch. I am afraid to swallow, and my nostrils are clogged. Then nothing.

I become nothing. Now, I am nothing. Before, I had existed, but not as the actual Rick Strassman. There is no actual Rick Strassman. Neither I nor anyone else could identify me because I have not yet come into existence, I have never existed. But how do I know this since I am nonexistent? How can I compare myself to existence and realize my nonexistence? I have nothing to compare to anything else. I do not know that I am nothing, that I am identical with nothing. No difference exists between me and nothing. But I am also everywhere. Since

I do not exist, I am nowhere. But nowhere is everywhere because both are infinite, and one necessitates the existence of the other. Nowhere encompasses everywhere, everywhere is where I am not. I am potential and thus exist everywhere. At least for now, though, here I am, unaware of my nonexistence.

I am in a closet full of white light and face a closed door in front of me. White light all around. I want to merge with it, to become it. First, though, I realize the light must incinerate me and I yield to the fire. Reduced to weightless, silvery-gray ash, I stop identifying even with the all-consuming fire-light. For the next two hours, I skim along the border between emptiness and the light.

My reverie ends suddenly when something strong and hard clamps around the sides of my skull.

Twenty-seven-year-old Charlotte Strassman, hallucinating after an injection of scopolamine,* marvels at the sight. A dreamy blissful smile on her face, pupils replacing her irises, she wonders aloud, "Why are there radios floating through the air?" She grabs at one and her hand passes through it. She laughs. The masked and gowned obstetrician picks up the forceps from an adjacent tray. His gloved hands slide them into my mother's vagina. Soon thereafter, at 4:04 a.m., I take my first breath, my head flattened on both sides.

Reflections
PAST LIVES

In my early thirties, I began taking part in a psychedelic research group consisting of physicians, psychologists, and other white-collar professionals. There were two purposes motivating us. One was to characterize the effects of new compounds. Underground chemists sent us

---

*A drug obstetricians commonly used in former times to put women in labor into a "twilight" state of forgetful amnesia. "Scoping" prevented laying down any memories of a painful childbirth. It is the same compound responsible for many of the effects of jimsonweed, also called datura or locoweed. Those under its influence may be completely unaware that the reality with which they are interacting is entirely hallucinatory.

samples of these drugs to "bioassay" them; that is, take the substance and carefully note its effects. We then sent its inventor our reports. This information helped the chemist relate the drugs' pharmacology in animals with its psychological effects in humans. This is the field of "structure-activity relationships."

Did the new drug produce an effect that was, for example, more or less visual than the parent compound? Was it primarily emotional or intellectual? How long did it last? What were the side effects? Thus, our project contributed to understanding the pharmacology of consciousness, would inform development of newer drugs, and might even discover a unique psychotherapeutic tool.

The other function of our group was to work more in depth with better-known substances—such as MDMA and LSD—psychologically, spiritually, and interpersonally. We believed our character and training qualified us to uniquely understand, communicate, and apply information from the psychedelic state. This often took the form of extensive emotional sharing and self-disclosure in an atmosphere of utmost trust.

I entered two people's lives during my drug experience that day. One was a six-year-old boy in Ukraine in the first decade of the twentieth century. Another was an adult in a European concentration camp in the 1940s. How did this happen? In the absence of confirming the objective reality of these experiences, we are left to speculate.

We could interpret the visions' contents psychologically, as if it they were dreams, even though they felt much more real. In contrast to usual dreams, the contents of the visions demonstrated a greater coherence and temporal continuity. In addition, I maintained a more stable sense of self. I was not confused; rather, I clearly perceived and interacted with the visions fully aware, observing and remembering the unfolding events with great accuracy. In this way, psychedelic experiences share features with lucid dreaming.[1]

But why this particular vision and not another? As always, it comes down to set and setting.

Perhaps the subtle undercurrent of anti-Jewish sentiment I felt in the group that day triggered an association to my emigrant grandfather. Even after decades living in the United States, he still looked like an Orthodox Jew from the "old country." The psychedelic drug intensified feelings I was already dimly aware of and was trying to minimize. It also heightened my mind's ability to create emotionally meaningful linkages and images using psychic material already at my disposal—my knowledge of anti-Semitism and the Holocaust.

We may also interpret the visions using contemporary neuroscientific models. Functional brain imaging demonstrates that psychedelics loosen connections within brain circuits mediating our sense of self. This allows input from other circuits that the "self" normally keeps suppressed. Forgotten memories emerge, repressed feelings become conscious, stress and conflict take visual form, and new relationships appear between past memories and the present.

Are there "nonscientific" and "nonpsychological" explanations for the visions? That is, could I have truly been conscious of long-deceased individuals' experiences?

Reincarnation and past lives figure prominently in Eastern religions. My Zen teachers took this as an article of faith, a fundamental principle of the tradition. However, we did not discuss mechanisms of action of reincarnation; that is, how it worked. Instead, the importance of past lives related to how they influenced our present one.

While the Hebrew Bible lacks explicit mention of past lives or reincarnation, later developments in Kabbalah incorporated these ideas into their theories and practices. This may be the result of the diffusion and accretion of other religions and cultures into more traditional Judaism.

Without requiring belief in the existence of transmigrating souls, the metaphysics of Maimonides—medieval Judaism's greatest philosopher and theologian—provides an explanation for past life visions. His system was built on Aristotle's theory of the Active Intellect—an invisible repository of information surrounding the Earth. In contemporary terms, it is a field of information. The "sublunar sphere" is the location of the Active Intellect, a sphere whose center is the Earth, while the moon's circuit defines its outer surface.

The Active Intellect's content is incomprehensibly vast: everything that has ever happened, is now happening, and may happen in the future, at every possible scale. The medievalists believed one could attain a certain proximity to the Active Intellect and thus access its contents. One's time and place, heredity, psychology, and experience combined to determine the unique specific information one apprehended.

Aristotle defined two mental faculties constituting the mind. The Intellect or "rational faculty" was the location of concepts, ideas, and notions. Everything else resided in the Imagination or "imaginative faculty"—emotions, bodily sensation, perception, and the sense of reality. One became aware of the Active Intellect's information through the function of the Imagination, which garbed this material in visions. Then, one's Intellect extracted information from these "imaginative" experiences—converting them to verbal thoughts, concepts, and notions.

In my case, we could propose that the psychedelic drug acted to stimulate my Imagination and allowed greater access to the contents of the Active Intellect. In that day's particular setting, my set steered me toward seeing and feeling the experiences of people from an earlier generation. These were individuals with whom I shared a close affinity—historical, emotional, spiritual, and biological. I then recognized and understood what I was seeing using my cognitive and intellectual functions.

This episode reinforces the value of "letting go" in difficult psychedelic moments. I had learned this from previous drug experiences, primarily by relaxing areas of bodily tension. In the years between college and joining the research group, regular meditation practice strengthened my ability to let go, to remain relaxed and attentive despite painful or frightening experiences.

Suffocating and drowning in human excrement at the bottom of a pile of concentration camp prisoners—either dead or in death's throes—sinking into seething mud, what could I do? I let go. Then I lost any individuality, my sense of self, a differentiation between me and anything else.

These memories, whether resulting from our Imagination conflating with the Active Intellect or increased functional connectivity in the brain, are sometimes eerily accurate. For example, a drug-induced vision of an episode of chocolate cookie–induced anaphylaxis when I was a toddler turned out to be true.

However, psychedelic memories do not always correspond to real events. My birth certificate does not mention forceps delivery, and it lists Seconal, a barbiturate sedative, not scopolamine, as the anesthetic. Either I projected these memories onto what happened or else the records are inaccurate. My guess is that the former is the case. Unconsciously, I may have felt the need to make my birth experience more traumatic than it was to support a self-image consistent with where I found myself that day in my friends' guestroom.

Finally, this account highlights the importance of the psychedelic "sitter" who supervises drug sessions. A good sitter assists in maximizing benefit and minimizing harm. The term refers to two closely related functions. One is to take the role of a babysitter, dealing with the comfort and safety of one's charge. "Sitting" also relates to the person's state of mind while managing others' intense experiences—a light meditative state, the result of "sitting meditation." It is an alert and receptive mind that simply pays attention to ongoing experience.* A good sitter lets someone "have their own trip," going through whatever they need to. At the same time, he or she can respond at once if the situation calls for it.

Arturo had taken and administered many and diverse psychedelic

---

*This is similar to what Freud called "evenly suspended attention," which skilled analysts bring to bear in listening to their patients.

substances, so he knew, in a general sense, what I was going through. He was attentive yet nonintrusive, helpful when necessary. He encouraged me to accept the experience, not push it away; to move forward and through it, not get stuck in fear. He shared his belief that the best outcome came from letting go. This provided hope when all seemed lost.

PART I

NATURE AND NURTURE

INTRODUCTION TO NATURE AND NURTURE
Early Childhood

THE FOLLOWING CHAPTERS recount several types of altered-state experiences. One category is memories of actual altered states that occurred during childhood. An example is my discovering meditation in second grade. Another type includes visions of childhood experiences that I witnessed during an altered state as an adult. These may be memories of real events. While I do not devote a chapter to this particular experience, I mentioned it in the previous chapter. In it, I relived one day on a psychedelic drug as an adult an allergic reaction I had to a chocolate cookie as a toddler. Later on, my mother verified the truth of that memory. Reexperiencing my forceps delivery in the previous chapter, however, "The Beginning," may straddle the line between real and imagined.

Some "childhood visions" I saw during an altered state in adulthood are unlikely to have occurred in real life. Rather, they are like dreams whose contents represent a condensed symbolic representation of one's mental state. A case in point is my vision of suffering sexual abuse that appeared while meditating in "Prayer Wheel." Here, the vision's contents and associated emotions corresponded to how I felt about my relationship with my parents when I was an infant. In addition, a vision may convey normally suppressed thoughts and emotions linked to being part of a larger historical and cultural universe without actually having undergone the events in question. The chapter describing past lives and deaths in "The Beginning" describes my sense of what it must have felt like for my ancestors in Eastern Europe during a particularly deadly phase of anti-Semitism.

THE EARLY MIND

What is our nature and how have others nurtured it? As these chapters deal with infancy and early childhood, I wish to briefly introduce models that help us address and understand these issues.

Infant *temperament* is the earliest precursor of adult personality. It's what the baby is like, its attributes or characteristics. While differences exist among classification systems, temperament usually falls into four broad categories: (1) warm, optimistic, social; (2) relaxed, apathetic, slow-moving; (3) analytical, quiet, nostalgic; and (4) irritable, quick to react.

Temperament is congenital, present at birth. It is the product of a confluence of multiple biological functions: hormonal, immunological, gastrointestinal, cardiac, and nervous system/brain. If you include past lives, our new body resonates with that previous consciousness, which now influences and is influenced by a new set of biological parameters.

Attachment style is the intermediate stage between infant temperament and adult personality. It is a general pattern of interactions between the infant/toddler and caregivers. The newborn has its unique temperament, and this temperament mediates its interactions with the world. And the most important interactions are with people. The responses the infant elicits in those around it feed back onto the child, encouraging certain responses and discouraging others. As with temperament, attachment style classifications vary, but four types that researchers regularly cite are (1) secure, (2) insecure, (3) avoidant, and (4) anxious. We sometimes come across (5) disorganized.

The quality of the "fit" between caregiver and infant influences this behavioral shaping, especially its emotional aspects. If the fit is good, the degree of stress is manageable for the child; otherwise, fundamental attachment interactions—such as feeding, discipline, and bedding down—become traumatic. For example, an insecure infant may respond well to a highly attentive and doting mother, while a secure independent one may find such a parent uncomfortably intrusive.

Adult *personality* is the final result of the process that begins with biological temperament and then interpersonal attachment style. Now, structures and processes are in place and modifying them is less likely. Contemporary psychology research has characterized five factors constituting adult personality: (1) extraversion, (2) agreeableness, (3) conscientiousness, (4) neuroticism, and (5) openness to experience.

Psychoanalysis also proposes a model of personality with roots in infancy and toddlerhood. For example, newborns and infants progress through psychophysiological stages: oral, anal, and genital. In each, the psychic–life force, or *libido*, concentrates upon and develops within one set of biological structures and functions before moving on to the next. Later, young children's interactions make their way through more-or-less hardwired interpersonal milestones; for example, the "Oedipal phase."* Adult personality finally forms—healthy or disordered to various degrees, including obsessive, hysteric, depressive, narcissistic, schizoid, and borderline.

Maimonides—the thirteenth-century rabbi, physician, and philosopher—suggested that character is what God gives us to overcome. This doesn't mean we must change our character, whose essential building blocks of temperament are biological. Rather, the idea is the following: We are what we do by choice, and not who we are by nature. We can modify our behavior—behavior that our inborn traits make likely—for good or ill. For example, we may be stingy by nature, but we can learn to practice generosity, thereby neutralizing a negative temperamental disposition. By virtue of our generous behavior, we become a generous person, even though our nature remains the same.

---

*Generally occurring between three and five years of age, at which time Freud believed aggressive competitive impulses emerged toward the same-sex parent. By dispatching that parent, the child would have the opposite-sex parent all to himself or herself. When one's upbringing is consistently caring, these fantasies gradually transition into wishes to be like the same-sex parent and seek out one's own opposite-sex mate. See "Clarissa" for a fuller explanation of this phenomenon.

ϟ

My temperament at birth was social, inquisitive, and intensely engaged. At the same time, I was irritable and quick to react. I was alert and responsive, restless, curious, and easily frustrated. If I didn't like something, I knocked it over. If I didn't get my way, I cried and threw a tantrum. These temperamental features also resulted in unpleasant sensitivity to sounds such as noisy eating or breathing. My parents' personalities were less than ideally suited to deal with my temperament, leading to an attachment style with significant insecure and anxious features.

The flip side of this elevated reactivity was my responsiveness to positive influences, such as friends and teachers, as well as the beauty of the natural world. Finally, I possessed strong powers of concentration, both regarding objects in the external as well as internal worlds. While time and inner work modified these early temperamental features, attachment styles, and personality, the broad outline of my adult character and behavioral style was, like most of us, apparent at an early age.

1

FLYING BABY

I HAVE ALWAYS ENJOYED BEING HIGH, but how far back does "always" go? The answer comes to me surprisingly late, in my early sixties.

A month after my sixty-second birthday, my life takes a turn for the worse. Two near-fatal infections and two failed relationships, both within a year, prompt my beginning a course of weekly psychotherapy that lasts more than four years. I am committed to finding out how things have gotten so off course.*

Once the acute phase of psychotherapy is over, my therapist and I begin to dig deeper. As my sickness resulted from an ill-advised trip to visit a woman I met online, examining these events gradually segue into discussing my former marriage, stepchildren, and divorce. The death anniversary of my stepdaughter reminds me of having so few photographs of life with my family. At the end of our marriage, my ex seemed to have taken every photo.

"Why did she take them all?" I ask rhetorically.

"What photos *do* you have from then?" Merle asks in her casually incisive manner.

"Good question," I reply. "I haven't looked in a long time."

Returning home, I search for photos I might have tucked away in an obscure corner. I find a manila envelope in the back of a drawer of

---

*For a more or less humorous fictional rendering of these events, see my 2019 book, *Joseph Levy Escapes Death*.

an ancient file cabinet, behind the "House refinance" folder. I open it and out spill dozens of mostly black-and-white photos. One catches my eye. On its back is my mother's handwriting, "September 1952. Rick, 8 months." I was born in February, so the date or my age is inaccurate. I wonder what she was thinking.

I am lying on my abdomen on a blanket on the lawn in our back-yard, wearing a white T-shirt and a white diaper. My legs splay out frog-like behind me. I am stocky, healthy flesh, no visible bones. A full head of dark hair, neatly cut, short bangs covering a half-inch of my promi-nent forehead, which takes up half my face. I am lifting my chest, my head is four-to-six-inches off the ground, and my chin is parallel to it. My right arm fully extends behind me, and my left must be as well, but it's not visible. My right palm faces outward. I'm in the yoga cobra pose, but not using my arms for support or balance. This position requires great muscular exertion; however, it appears effortless. It looks as if I am flying, my arms behind me.

At the bottom of the photo is the shadow of the top of a head, reaching to within two inches of my blanket. It is a man's head, most likely of my father, the photographer.

The expression on my face startles and discomfits me. I put the pho-tograph down and take a short walk along my dirt road. I can't relate

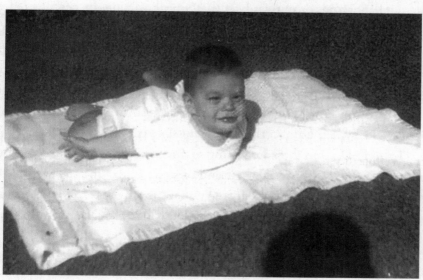

to my infant self. I let myself back into the house, sit down, empty my mind, and gaze into the face of my seven-month-old self.

He is staring straight ahead, focusing on a distant object at eye level. His face shows no strain, furrows, nor creases. My lips—the bottom one especially full—form a slight smile. The infant is transfixed, enjoying himself in silent motionless flight. He is paying attention with total concentration—not a glimmer of distraction or laxity. While flying, I also am basking in the presence of some kind of glory—absolutely satisfied, enraptured, focused, calm, and happy. It's an advanced level of happiness. I could not be any happier.

Now, looking at the photo, a powerful feeling of shame unexpectedly overcomes me. Ashamed because, blessed with strength, balance, concentration, and capacity for joy, why have I not become all I could be? Why didn't I do better? Or, have I attained my potential? How could I know? Did I grow into that image? Or did I grow into a distorted version of it? Who *is* that child? Did I disappoint my Maker, the One who granted me all those gifts? Because without God, nothing would have come of my parents' sexual relations. What were God's hopes for me? Have I been accomplishing them?

Leaving these ruminations aside, I realize how the pleasure of being high, flying, has been there from the beginning. Focusing inward on the outer horizon, or outward on the inner horizon—or perhaps more accurately, experiencing no difference between the inner and outer, body and mind. Here, in a microcosm, is the state that has served as my benchmark. It is one I have tried to reexperience, dwell in, re-create for myself and others, as well as articulate, teach, share, and write about throughout my life. Flight toward and communing with the distant object with which I am in the closest possible contact.

I also feel like an intruder staring so intently at this picture. I have no business trying to get inside the mind of someone having such a private wonderful experience. But it's my own mind, so why not? Yet it is foreign because it happened before I related to the world through words. In this infant, there is only seeing and feeling.

I imagine saying to him, "Wow! You're flying! You're flying!"

I would lift him, placing one hand under his chest and the other hand supporting his legs behind him, thus keeping him horizontal.

"Look at this! Look at this! Wow!" Flying through the air, showing him the sights. I imagine my hands on his body; that is, my body. It's strong, pliable, dense, and soft.

I wonder how my infant-self would respond to my presence.

Unbidden, I hear his little voice in my head, "There was nothing wrong with how things were. Why are you bothering me?"

Reflections
BORN THIS WAY

At seven (or eight) months old, my inherent biological temperament made up most of my psychological and behavioral repertoire. I was born with capacities for rapt attention and focus, and I felt immense pleasure exercising these functions. These character traits appeared early and have endured. While the specific objects of my attention have varied over time, the process and associated feelings have remained the same.

Over twenty years later, as I was beginning Zen training at The Temple, my work assignments were rarely glamorous. More often they were dirty and lonely: solitarily scrubbing toilets or pulling nails from junkyard lumber. The goal, however, was not simply behavioral; that is, "carrying water and chopping wood." Rather, it was the inner state, the joy that I could experience while doing something ordinary, even unpleasant. Attaining this inner state required applying all my attention to what I was doing. There was no room for judging, complaining, or comparing. These moments rekindled what I had forgotten I had already discovered as an infant.

Zen taught me that that kind of joyful attending doesn't have to be spontaneous. It was a state you could enter by fully attending to anything with both great exertion *and* relaxation. Doing so triggered a joyful reflex overflowing with meaningfulness. This was one of the most important tools I acquired at the monastery.

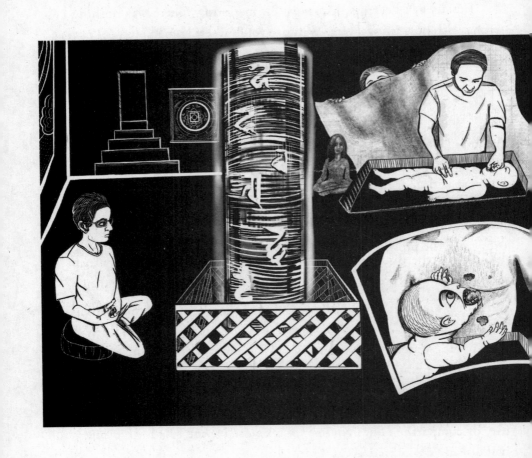

2

PRAYER WHEEL

IN THIS CHAPTER I recount a vision I had, when twenty-four years old, concerning my infancy.

I return to medical school after my stay at the monastery. Zen practice is new, but I fiercely cling to and nurture it. It is my lifeline after recovering from a crippling depression the previous year. I orient my life around the discipline: ninety or more minutes of meditation per day, regular scripture recitation and study, and ongoing correspondence with members of the monastic community. I reenter school in the class that follows the one I began with and make several good new friends. I find a psychotherapist with whom I begin a two-year course of psychoanalytic psychotherapy, and when my speech dysfluency affects my performance on clinical rotations, speech therapy effects significant improvement within a month. My grades are high, and I am favoring psychiatry residency training after graduation.

The summer before my final year of medical school, I attend a training program in Tibetan Buddhist psychology for mental health professionals. It's taking place at the Nyingma Institute in Berkeley, and our teacher is Tarthang Tulku, a young Tibetan lama with an increasingly large Western following. Because of his growing organizational responsibilities, this is the last summer he personally leads the class. We are a varied lot: between twenty and thirty Western academics, clinicians, and students.

The six-week course introduces us to the meditation practices and psychology of Tarthang's sect, the Nyingma.* We quickly establish a routine: morning class/instruction, practice, lunch, class, practice. Topics include Abhidharma psychology† and Tibetan history and culture. The lama teaches us a wide array of meditation techniques. Before dismissing us for the day, Tarthang gives us meditative homework. This weekend's assignment is to meditate in the prayer wheel room in the basement of the Institute.

I schedule a one-hour session for each morning. A fellow student joins me on Saturday. As we make our way down the stairs into the small, cool, dimly lit room, a powerful rumble fills the air, vibrating the floor and walls. The massive rotating prayer wheel—seven feet tall and three feet in diameter—is the biggest in the West. It weighs more than two tons and spins two to three times per second inside a simple gazebo-like structure. Three-foot-high lattice railings around this structure prevent getting too close. There are about six feet from the wheel to the walls, against one of which I rest my back. We are to use the energy of the massive spinning cylinder to amplify the power of meditation.

The environment requires getting used to, and I don't want to over-extend myself this first day. I work on relaxing into the wheel's power—a very deep relaxation—and gradually drop more and more resistance to the pressure it exerts.

The next morning, I enter the rumbling room alone and sit cross-legged on my black meditation cushion facing the wheel. My eyes gaze downward, lids half-open. The spinning cylinder generates a slight breeze that moves gently across my face. Subtle movements of light flicker across its intricately painted surface. I take several slow deep

---

*There are four main sects of Tibetan Buddhism, Nyingma being the oldest. Others are the Kagyu, Sakya, and Gelug.

†A psychological system analyzing the components of mind and their interrelationships. Abhidharma is one of three "baskets" of Buddhism. The other two are Vinaya, monastic rules; and Sutras, the Buddha's discourses. I borrowed from Abhidharma psychology in developing the rating scale we used to quantify the subjective effects of DMT in my studies.

breaths to relax my body and mind, which in turn increases the multi-perceptual effects of the wheel.

I love how I feel around it—excited and wary, a sense of danger and promise. I am fascinated by the cylinder, in love with it somehow. It is nearly a living creature, immensely powerful. But the thought crosses my mind: *Not infinitely powerful.* Nevertheless, I trust the intent of its builders and its keepers.

I pose the question, *Why am I so anxious?*

It's two queries, really: *Why do I stammer?* And: *Why does sex cause me to panic?* I know I am chronically anxious, but why these two symptoms? I intend to probe these questions with greater force and focus by channeling the prayer wheel's energy.

My awareness shifts. It expands, taking in much more, but also narrows to a fine point. I ask "Why?" and direct the question at my anxiety, which builds as I skate on the edge of a panic attack. The wheel's sound and vibration push me from the front as well as from the back, reflecting off the wall. I press onward.

"Why?" I whisper.

The cylinder's slight unevenness creates a strange higher-pitched warbling that harmonizes with the deeper rumbling notes.

Why?

I close my eyes and let the wheel's nearly overwhelming force enter me. With the aid of the wheel's power, I sense an opportunity, and decide to push for enlightenment instead of simply insight into psychological problems. This might be my chance. I know that attaining enlightenment requires tremendous effort, one that dispenses with every other consideration—comfort, sanity, even life. But I also know I must not want it nor try to achieve it. I hover, holding slightly aloof while pushing ahead with all my strength. I have help from the wheel.

Why?

Answering the question is how I will experience enlightenment. I won't let go. My mind digs into itself, using the question to dig. I feel a frown forming on my brow and relax my face.

WHY?

There is no solution, at least none I see, or feel, or think. I refuse to give up.

Suddenly I break into a madhouse of the psyche. It's a mental space whose essence is madness.

I am lying on top of a bassinet, naked, on my back, turned slightly to the right. I am small, six months old at most. My mother and father are there, talking, but I don't understand language. Nevertheless, I sense that the sounds they make convey scolding, punishment, and resentment. My father crams something that feels like a hand into my mouth and fills it.

He also is tugging at my penis. It is uncomfortable and painful. More than the physical pain is the psychological terror of being the helpless object of his sadism. While my infant self dimly recognizes his sad envy,* more immediate is an awareness of his pleasure in abusing me. I am pinned and cannot move. Feelings of violation fill my mind to bursting.

Steadying myself in the dark little prayer wheel room, I force my mind's eyes to stay open. I hear someone almost silently enter the room. I stay focused on the vision.

My mother is boxing me in by lowering and raising billowy white sheets, moving them around so as to cut off any escape. I am trapped, mouth and penis under assault. The sheets also hide the scene and no one knows. I want to stop the torture, but how can I, at six months of age?

In a frenzy, I attack my father with my mouth, ripping out pieces of flesh from his chest, tearing out hunks of his body with my teeth, killing him by eating him. I am increasingly horrified at these images.

---

*The goal of jealousy is to get something desirable that someone else has. In contrast, the goal of envy is to destroy that wished for object so that no one can enjoy it. "If I can't have that good thing, I'll make sure nobody does." One could speculate my father envied, among other things, my innocence, resistance to his control, and my mother's attachment to me.

The vision starts to lose its substance, and the pain and shock lessen. I open my eyes, lean back against the wall, adjust my breathing, and realign my posture. My analytic mind begins functioning, acting as a rudder, trying to translate into words what just happened.

How does this answer my question?

It's a miserable stew of feelings: anger, shame, humiliation, helplessness, pain.

Now what?

I remember a practice the lama taught us that week. Attend to the elements of the experience. Thoughts. Concepts. Images. Feelings. Who is experiencing this? Where does the experience come from? What is its nature? What underlies it? Don't react. Rather, inquire. Who? From where? What is its substance?

I'm exhausted and have to rest, and I empty my mind using my breath. I open my eyes and notice my friend sitting across the room. Seeing me stretch and move about, she gets up and sits down next to me. The wheel continues rumbling.

Reflections
"RECALLING" SEXUAL ABUSE

This is a fully psychedelic experience that occurred without a psychedelic drug. Therefore, it provides an opportunity to discuss endogenous psychedelics, ones that the body produces internally.

As an undergraduate, the similarities in descriptions between the effects of psychedelic drugs and certain meditation practices intrigued me. This overlap in features hinted at a biological explanation for non-drug highly altered states of consciousness. I wondered: If psychedelics and meditation produce the same changes in consciousness, do they also produce the same effects on brain function? That is, were the biological effects of meditation and psychedelics the same? If so, did meditation stimulate the brain to produce a psychedelic substance?

I oriented my clinical research career around this issue: the biological bases of spiritual experience. My search began with melatonin, looking for psychedelic effects of this pineal hormone. We knew little about the human psychopharmacology of melatonin in the 1980s, and some data suggested it was profoundly mind-altering. In addition, the pineal gland itself has long held an esteemed position in "spiritual physiologies" like those of the Hindu chakras and the kabbalistic Sephirot.* My melatonin research, however, revealed that this hormone's subjective effects were nonpsychedelic, only sedating. By then I had shifted my research direction to DMT, which is intensely psychedelic as well as endogenous.

DMT—N,N-dimethyltryptamine—is a chemical cousin of serotonin and melatonin. It occurs widely throughout nature, in hundreds if not thousands of plants and every mammal studied to date, including humans. Its synthesis in plants and animals begins with tryptophan, which enzymes then convert to tryptamine. Tryptamine then receives two methyl groups; thus, "dimethyltryptamine," or DMT.

Chemists first identified DMT in psychedelic plants from Latin America in the 1940s, and Szara's 1950s studies in Hungary established its psychedelic properties through self-experimentation. In the 1960s, researchers discovered DMT, bufotenin,† and 5-methoxy-DMT‡ in human body fluids. Early human DMT research focused on its potential role in endogenous psychoses like schizophrenia. Scientists thought that if schizophrenics produced too much DMT, or were abnormally sensitive to it, an anti-DMT medication might be an effective antipsychotic medication. My DMT studies also compared DMT effects to those of naturally occurring altered states of consciousness. However, my interest was in comparing its effects with nonpsychotic experiences like meditation and the near-death state in normal volunteers.

While the range of subjective effects of DMT is vast, two consistent themes emerged from our studies. One is that the experience is

---

*For an in-depth discussion of the pineal and consciousness, see *DMT: The Spirit Molecule,* especially pages 56–85.
†5-Hydroxy-DMT, a tryptamine compound with equivocal psychedelic effects.
‡An increasingly popular psychedelic secretion of the venom glands of the Sonoran Desert toad.

relational. It is full of content with which a fully intact personality interacts. The content may be bizarre in the extreme, and the personality may no longer feel as if it is in a body, but there remains a clear distinction between the "self" and the "other." The other characteristic feature of the DMT state is how convincingly real it feels. The experience is more compelling, true, meaningful, and convincing than everyday reality.

We now know that the mammalian brain makes DMT at high levels, comparable to those of well-known neurotransmitters like serotonin and dopamine. This suggests that there exists a DMT neurotransmitter system. DMT levels also rise in dying rodent brains, especially in the visual cortex,[1] and this points to a potential mechanism for the visions of the near-death state. Besides the dying process, we do not know what else stimulates endogenous DMT production in the brain. To the extent that mental practices and/or external stimuli alone, without drugs, result in DMT-like experiences, it makes sense that elevated endogenous DMT levels play a role in producing these effects.

In my fully psychedelic prayer wheel experience, endogenous DMT elevation provides a simple although unproven explanation. The state had all the features of a typical high-dose psychedelic experience: unusual clarity of mind, extreme emotions, physical sensations, and visions brimming with personally relevant contents.

My Zen meditation practice was becoming well-established by this time, I had been in nearly two years of psychoanalytic psychotherapy, and speech therapy was highly effective. I had matured while reacquiring confidence in my abilities. The Tibetan Buddhist institute was an inspiring, safe, and supportive setting that was ideal for exerting myself more fully in meditation, even toward the goal of achieving enlightenment.

We hear less about enlightenment in Buddhism than we do about mindfulness meditation, which helps promote general psychophysical well-being. However, Zen practice as taught by my teacher and community placed great emphasis on enlightenment—*kensho*—the great awakening. Daily practice—work, ritual, and especially meditation—could lead anyone who applies the right effort and focus to enlightenment. Thus, given the opportunity to amplify my meditation with the powerful physical, emotional, and sensory effects of the prayer wheel, I pushed for enlightenment.

As is often the case with psychedelics, however, I did not get the trip I wanted, but the trip I needed.

Did the content of my vision convey an actual historical event, a suppressed memory that emerged during the highly altered state? While possible, it is unlikely. However, I cannot rule it out. One of Freud's early theories—which he arrived at using the mind-altering method of free association as well as interpretation of the dream altered state—posited that a history of childhood sexual abuse in his female patients underlie their psychological problems. He later reinterpreted his patients' accounts as childhood fantasies, rather than memories, of sexual encounters with adults. Whether my experience was objectively true or not, never before had I felt so clearly, explicitly, and undeniably the dynamics between my parents and my infant self.

I previously discussed the importance of the "fit" between the temperament of an infant and its caregivers' personalities. My father and I fit poorly. He wanted quiet, I wanted to interact. He needed obedience, and I was defiant. He wanted a placid child, and I was rambunctious. In addition, he suffered from untreated depression and alcoholism.

The vision represented how my father's unhappiness pushed him to stifle my own life force—centering on my penis and my mouth, fundamental tools of communication and relationship. My own speech and sexuality became sources of anxiety and pain for me rather than of pleasure and communion.

As the vision progressed, I went on the attack, reflective of my twenty-four-year-old self's increasing autonomy and recognition of feelings, including murderous hatred. One could also adduce Freud's notion of "oral aggression"—due to deprivation of the most fundamental relational needs—directed inward and/or outward in the development of my stammer. That is, my speech defect caused me pain, as well as inflicted discomfort in those around me. In the vision, I turned the tables by using my mouth—the object of his hostility—to destroy my nemesis. All I could use was my physical mouth—not words—because I had not yet learned to speak.

My mother's role in this vision was more ambiguous. There was something ethereal, cloudlike, even choreographic in the billowing diaphanous sheets with which she prevented escape. Her acquiescence to my father's violence did not stop it and felt to me like complicity. The sheets also protected my father, and thus our family, from outside scrutiny and possible punishment, both of which would have reflected poorly on her as a wife and mother, as well as threatening the integrity of the family.

Finally, this account provides an example of how spiritual and psychological development differ yet impact one another. Psychological burdens make it difficult to attain enlightenment. And if a kensho—like any other powerful altered state—occurs in an unbalanced mind, that power may magnify one's psychopathology rather than heal it.

3

SPANKING

By the end of my first year of life, certain character traits have become clear: a powerful desire to interact with the outside world, abundant energy and perseverance, self-absorption, and resistance to outside control. These traits play a role in both triggering my father's violence toward me as well as how I cope with that abuse.

Kicking, with or without shoes on, is often effective when my father wants my busily crawling self to stop creating a noisy disturbance. I like banging things to hear how they sound. Or, bubbling saliva, I sprint-crawl around the room backward and forward. I tug at his pant leg to show him something of interest.

"Stop that!" he barks, simultaneously driving out a foot.

Sometimes I ignore the blows, or get angry at the attack and grab the vengeful foot. I might make indignant sounds to indicate protest. Leaning over to smack my upper body—shoulder, chest, back, sometimes my face—with a backhand is next. If I remain defiant, he lays me over his knee to spank me.

He strikes my bare butt, which he has exposed by pulling down my diaper, or the back of my upper thighs if the diaper is too tight or dirty. His blows sting, burn, and then penetrate more deeply. The flesh of these muscles—the biggest in my body—recoils reflexively.

Crying seems to end the spanking. I pretend to cry after he hits me only once or twice in order to shorten my punishment. This works for a while, but he soon realizes my strategy and beats me more for trying to fool him. Once, as I understand it, my father's two younger half-brothers—visiting at the time—intervene and pull me off his knee, concerned over the violence of the beating.

I try giving up resisting the pain. It is coming anyway, it will be here, and then it's over. Could I somehow enjoy it? Not exactly enjoy, but not resist. If I relax my body, the blows are less painful than if I tense. I try to transmute the pain so that it energizes rather than debilitates. However, my mental faculties are too undeveloped for this approach to succeed.

Maybe at least not cry, don't give him the satisfaction. That is difficult but sometimes I squeeze my eyes shut tight enough to prevent tears from falling and clench my lips so as to make no sound. No—that brings on more blows. Raising a cry is important to my father.

Finally, he sets me back down on the ground. If my mother is around, she places me in my crib, gives me a toy, tries to placate me. After all, what can she do?

Reflections
WORKING WITH PAIN

My father's use of physical punishment drew from several sources. His own mother died early in his own childhood, and he grew up angry, depressed, and resentful. He believed that if I hated him because of his violence, I would not grieve his death as he had after his mother's. His father also often used corporal punishment.

My father discovered alcohol at an early age and regularly drank to excess. This elevated his mood and increased his sociability, but also lowered his threshold for violence. His job was difficult, and marriage and fatherhood were not all that 1940s–1950s postwar American society promised. Laboring under these burdens, pleasurable relationships were rare and fleeting. In addition, his communication skills, especially regarding emotions, were deficient. Any type of emotional engagement was fraught.

I learned to decipher body language, interpret what my father was saying and how he was saying it, and the implications of the amount and type of eye contact. I became especially anxious speaking because of how he might interpret my words and tone of voice. This was a factor in the development of my stammer.

There were also times *I* decided to cross the threshold, unprovoked, simply to engage. My raising a ruckus pulled him out of his usually withdrawn state, and he had to attend to me. This dynamic had several purposes.

Some interaction was better than none. Maybe this time he would decide not to follow through with hitting and we would play together instead. Psychoanalysis calls this pattern "repetition compulsion," and in my case it has been an enduring feature of my adult life. In a repetition compulsion, one repeatedly engages in activities or relationships that are bound to turn out poorly. The more or less conscious justification for this behavior is the hope that this time the outcome will be better—either through a new as yet to be determined strategy and/or a miraculous change in the nature of the other person or circumstances.

There also were self-preservation elements; that is, I didn't want to lose touch with the enemy. At the same time, my survival depended on this man. Without him, I believed that the outside world would rush in, in a bad way. I didn't want him to forget about me.

Placing myself in harm's way played an additional role, as I wanted to see who would help. Am I completely alone in this painful situation? Why doesn't anyone come to my aid when I so obviously need it? This was a recurring theme in my psychoanalysis, as I discuss in the next chapter: "Tense Infant Analytic Session."

In this narrative, I describe an attempt to "transcend" the physical and emotional pain I experienced when my father beat me. However, in that setting and with my capacities, this was instead a defensive "dissociation"—a less healthy response.

I tried to dissociate my feelings from awareness; that is, I wasn't feeling angry, sad, or frightened. I was calm and relaxed. I also attempted to dissociate awareness from my body—I no longer felt physical pain. Finally, I tried to dissociate reality from the truth; instead, I believed that my father really loved me.

This early experience of dissociation as a means of "transcending" pain appears as a precursor to my later interest in altered states of consciousness. However, these experiences may only reinforce and strengthen dissociative reactions to emotional pain, rather than helping develop more adaptive responses.

Coming to terms with one's own abuse helps in working with someone else's and leads many people to become therapists themselves. In my case, I had to deal with the blurring between emotional closeness and pain. Learning to assess safety, while at the same time experiencing emotional closeness, with someone in a disorganized and potentially dangerous psychological state is a crucial component in psychiatric training. This was already a major focus of my own psychotherapy, and it contributed to my enjoyment and success working with psychotic patients. At the same time, prioritizing assessing others' state of mind over my own led to its own set of relationship difficulties over the years.

4

TENSE INFANT ANALYTIC SESSION

ONE DAY IN MY MID-THIRTIES, I enter my psychoanalyst's office. By now I'm in a rhythm, going five days a week. I joke with Dr. Metcalf—well, half-joke—about adding Saturdays. I manage getting away for nearly two hours every day from the university—an hour for the session and just under an hour of travel time.

It's like any other analytic day. Dr. Metcalf takes his position, sitting down on his well-worn leather chair to the left and behind the head of the couch. At the same time, I make my way to the firmly comfortable and similarly well-worn iconic piece of furniture and lie down. Usually I settle right in—take a few breaths; look around at the ceiling above, the wall to my right, and his foot to my left, and begin. However, today I can't get comfortable. My mind is blank but roiling.

"I don't know what's the matter," I open.

I'm making progress after two years of what turns out to be a four-year course of treatment. My academic trajectory is becoming clear. The melatonin research yielded no evidence supporting psychedelic effects, so I've shifted my focus to DMT and begun working on obtaining approval and funding for the study.

Analysis has also helped me cut through two Gordian knots in my interpersonal life. I have stopped pursuing women who have other boyfriends. And, I have withdrawn from a psychedelic drug taking group that has turned increasingly toxic.

I should be more relaxed. After all, that's what I have learned from my MDMA experiences. It's best to be relaxed, to let go, to feel no fear.

The silence bears down on me, and I suddenly feel my self-control slip away.

An extraordinarily uncomfortable high-voltage energy enters my body. I try diffusing it by fidgeting and shake my legs back and forth. I yawn, scratch the top of my head with both hands, turn my head from side to side, and clench and unclench my fists. I contract and relax my lower back muscles, creating an arch, which provides some relief. Tears form in my eyes and my nose becomes so congested that I can't breathe through it.

I remember a holotropic breathwork session* I had earlier in the year. While lying down, I forcefully and rapidly hyperventilated through my mouth off and on for a half-hour. The resulting altered state was surprisingly powerful, but I could stop it any time by resuming normal breathing.

This is different. It's come over me unbidden, and I am frightened. My fidgeting becomes thrashing, and I feel helpless and panicked. Why is this happening? What can I do? Will this stop before our time is up? How bad will it get?

My analyst shifts in his chair, quietly creaking the leather.

I mutely flop on the couch like a large fish on dry land. There's no way to express myself even if I could formulate a thought. What would I say? *Help me*? And how would my analyst help me? I slap my hands palms down against the couch. I don't know how, but maybe this will help ground me and/or let my analyst know I retain control over my body. Tears flow, my ears ring, I can barely see. Watery mucus bubbles around my nostrils and mouth as I try to breathe

---

*A method for attaining a highly altered state of consciousness using prolonged hyperventilation. Stanislav Grof, a psychiatrist with extensive research and therapeutic experience with LSD, developed this practice.[1]

through my nose instead of gulping air. The only thoughts I muster are, "Calm down! Control yourself! Slow down your breathing!"

The hour is winding down, and so is the episode. I am drenched in sweat, exhausted and disoriented. The room sparkles in an MDMA-like manner, but malignantly, like shards of dark glass. I look at my watch.

My analyst murmurs, "You must have been an incredibly tense child."

Heavy silence fills the treatment room.

He adds, "If you need extra time, you're welcome to sit in the waiting room." I'm thankful he doesn't say, "Our time is up." That would have been a routine close to an unexpectedly bizarre anything-but-routine session. I notice and greatly appreciate this evidence of his empathy.

Unsteady, I climb off the couch and carefully step into the waiting room. I sit in one of its four chairs and stare at the wall, collecting myself. Before long, I am driving back to the university.

Reflections
DISCHARGING STORED TRAUMA

Someone observing me during that analytic hour may have thought I was having an epileptic seizure. However, it was a "psychogenic non-epileptic seizure," one whose causes are psychological, not neurological. Earlier terms include "pseudo," "psychogenic," and "hysterical" seizure.

Hysterical or psychogenic symptoms—what we now call "conversion symptoms"—encompass the entire medical spectrum and include neurological, dermatological, and cardiopulmonary manifestations. The term *hysteria* harks back to the Greek word for "suffering womb." Classic Greek medicine believed that as these conditions were more common in women, they resulted from uterine malfunction; specifically, a displaced or "wandering" womb.

Psychogenic symptoms are dramatic attempts to keep unconscious memories and emotions out of conscious awareness. The success of

Freud's psychoanalytic movement was due in large part to the success of this model in helping resolve hysterical symptoms. Freud believed conversion of unconscious conflicts, feelings, and memories caused inexplicable physical symptoms—ones with no biological origin nor response to medical treatment. By accessing and coming to terms with the unconscious material underlying those symptoms, patients often got better.

My life was improving in the course of analysis. I was ending a long-standing pattern of establishing close ties with people who were exciting but dangerous, hoping that hopeless relationships would be fulfilling. A significant contribution to this problematic behavior was an under-current of putting myself in danger to see who would save me. It was an example of a repetition compulsion—which I described in the chapter "Spanking"—a dynamic with origins in my childhood physical and emotional abuse.

Thus, a recurrent theme in analysis was my wish for Dr. Metcalf to save me. I wanted him to tell me what to do, to rescue me from and punish tormentors to whom I inexorably and seemingly invol-untarily returned. That he didn't deliver me from danger was a regular source of anger and frustration. Once these self-destructive relationships receded into the background, we now turned our attention to my "wish for help." This was my path toward develop-ing the "transference neurosis," the focus of our next two years of treatment.

The "analysis of the transference" is key to successful psychoana-lytic treatment. "Transference" refers to the patient's attachment to their analyst, an attachment possessing the character and intensity of one's earliest relationships—most often with one's parents. In infancy, these relationships are nonverbal—sensory, emotional, and physi-cal. The body alone absorbs, feels, and reacts to these interactions. Somatically, we develop characteristic ways of responding to them without the mediating function of words.

The transference is a circumscribed microcosm, a condensa-tion of all past and present relationships projected onto the screen of the relationship with the analyst. What kind of help did I want from Dr. Metcalf? What did I believe he could provide? What help didn't I want? Why wasn't my analyst coming to my aid? Or was he? How could I tell? Did he help his other patients—or his family—more? Where did that craving for help come from? What other feelings and memories did that demand cover up or distort? What type of help was "reasonable" and what was "infantile"? These issues formed the scaffolding of the analysis of the transference neurosis.

The fully developed transference is a regressed state. It is one in which earlier and more primitive ways of thinking, feeling, relating, and behaving hold sway. It's as if one is a child again, living in the past, but now in the mind of an adult. Biological factors can produce regression, as in cases of delirium or dementia. Psychological factors also play a role; for example, in response to witnessing or experiencing overwhelming trauma. In the analytic situation, this regression is "regression in the service of the ego." A controlled regression that makes accessible previously repressed unconscious painful or anxiety-producing psychic contents.

Regressed behavior varies widely. People may become more demanding, needy, hostile, or otherwise act out of character. More severe forms assume behavioral manifestations, such as paralysis or blindness. In my case, I suffered seizure-like symptoms.*

I did not lie down on the couch that day planning to "regress in the service of the ego" to such a degree. However, it would not have been possible without the groundwork Dr. Metcalf and I had established over the previous two years.

The primary tool of psychoanalysis is "free association," speaking aloud whatever comes into the mind with no censoring or editing. By definition, this is a form of regression, freeing oneself from "adult," "polite," "considerate," and otherwise socially conventional communication. Therefore, I had already learned to practice

---

*I'm not alone in this. One of the most common diagnoses in epilepsy clinics is psychogenic nonepileptic seizures.

and work with a more primitive state of consciousness and style of interacting while lying on the couch in Dr. Metcalf's presence.

I trusted my analyst and the psychoanalytic process. While I did not know what the episode meant, I knew it meant something, something we would work on later. For the time being, I finally expressed—nonverbally, emotionally, and somatically—the profound inner tension under which I often labored.

Why a psychogenic nonepileptic seizure instead of, say, urinary or bowel incontinence, vomiting, paralysis, fainting, dizziness, or chest pain? The symptoms correspond to the unconscious contents; here, the muscular and respiratory frenzy best expressed the cumulative burden of my unanswered infantile pleas for help. In addition, my previous experience with holotropic breath work may have made more likely hyperventilating in that situation—priming the pump, so to speak.

I gained valuable psychedelic-related knowledge from that analytic hour. The deep level of regression I safely underwent in the presence of a supportive therapist made an enormous impact. Dr. Metcalf's response—calm, nonjudgmental, and delivered with gentle authority—reassured me. He could clearly manage situations like this. His interpretation also provided a crucial cognitive understanding of a nonverbal physical-emotional state. It was direct, to the point, and succinct; nevertheless, it felt unerringly accurate.

This, and less radical experiences during psychoanalysis, influenced how I later approached and supervised high-dose DMT and psilocybin sessions in two ways. First, I knew that helpless regressed states were bound to occur, and they certainly did. My safely navigating that psychoanalytic session helped me empathically and supportively respond to research subjects' deep immersion into similar territory. In addition, my analyst provided a model for nonintrusively supporting and guiding a highly vulnerable and dependent person under my care. Keep the talking to a minimum while watchfully letting your charge go through whatever it is they are dealing with.

A brief comment on the visual effects after I came to on the couch that day. They are not surprising, as visual alterations occur with hyperventilation. My previous drug experiences led me to immediately interpret those effects as "drug-like," and MDMA's mild visual effects were the first that came to mind.

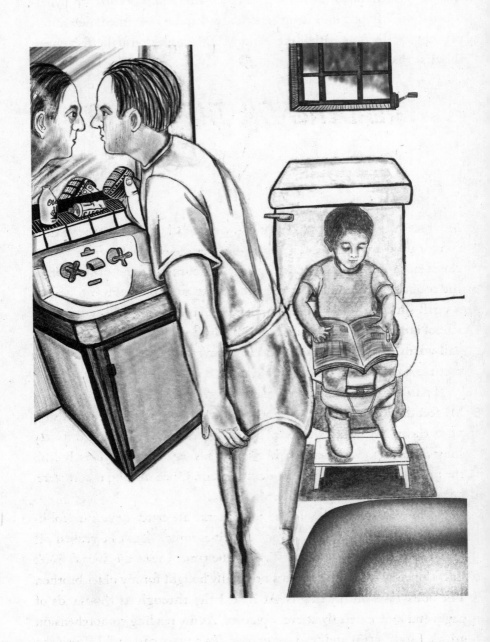

5

READING ON THE TOILET

My early childhood home has one small narrow bathroom. A combination bath-shower fills three-quarters of one wall, while a linen closet occupies the remainder. In the far corner of the other side of the room sits the toilet. Between the toilet and the bathroom door is a small sink with a mirrored medicine cabinet above it. My brother's school is earlier than mine and he's out the door just as I settle onto the still warm plastic toilet seat. My sister isn't in school yet, so when she uses the bathroom is more flexible.

I pull my jockey shorts down around my ankles and sit on the toilet. My feet do not yet reach the floor, so a little white plastic footstool supports them. My father stands at the sink, wearing a T-shirt and jockey shorts, shaving. My knee nearly touches his leg. He looks closely into the mirror as he uses a modern electric razor. Once shaving is complete, he generously applies Old Spice aftershave.

I am constipated. My bowel movements are hard, dry, and rabbit-like. We call feces "bunch," which describes mine. I can't be rushed off the toilet. Only time will tell. To pass the time, I read the World Book Encyclopedia, which my parents originally bought for my older brother. The book rests on my thighs. At first, I flip through its thousands of pages and look carefully at every picture. As my reading comprehension grows, I start again and read every page. Two years pass and I finish the last volume. Almost everything interests me: science, politics, history, religion, geography, anthropology. Arts are my least favorite, as it's difficult for me to understand what they mean—they commerce in images, not words.

It's a companionable setting in the bathroom—in retrospect, the most companionable of any early childhood interactions with my father. The drone of the electric razor reduces the anxiety I instinctively feel when we are physically close. And I must be left alone to properly shit, which my father readily accepts. Monopolizing the toilet causes him no inconvenience. Besides, there is a lot on his mind as he prepares for his workday at Hughes Aircraft, a forty-minute drive on the freeway. Shaving also spares him from engaging in small talk. If I don't understand a word, however, I ask, and he readily offers concise definitions while continuing his ablutions. He supports my bouts of concentrated reading, appreciating its value. It's also something that we share, as he spends most of every weekend reading science fiction while lying on the living room couch.

As I read, I gain new thoughts and learn new facts. I like how that feels. The outside world recedes from my awareness as I concentrate on reading. It's just me and the book. Quiet, serene, safe, and feeding my mind.

Reflections
THE SECURITY OF THE WRITTEN WORD

Words are like bodies; meanings are like souls.
MOSES IBN EZRA

Study is a tool to alter consciousness. It is also a tool to ground and direct altered consciousness. At an early age, I sensed these effects of study when sitting on the toilet engrossed in the World Book Encyclopedia. I was lucky to have parents who loved to read and who filled our home with books. They understood reading as a way to learn and become successful. It's how you got ahead. The activity itself also provided me with refuge from a forbidding family environment.

Fully engaging with the written word requires concentration and focus, similar to meditation. The text also becomes the object of awareness and therefore directs the development of the state. Reading *Mein Kampf*, Danielle Steele, or Spinoza in an altered state of consciousness—for example, on LSD—will produce different effects on your mind, both short- and long-term. Conversely, the nature of the altered state resulting from studying one or the other of these works will differ.

While I was training in Zen years later, an essential element of the discipline was reading books about Buddhism and Buddhists. Relating with texts in the company of other serious practitioners—monastic and lay—taught me how to apply the mind of meditation to study. That is, when reading, simply read. You've decided what to study, so now your job is to understand what you're reading thoroughly and deeply, to relate to it directly, applying all of your attention and energy to the task. As with meditation, this helps minimize judging, becoming angry, or daydreaming.

Applying meditative consciousness to study channeled more consciously and effectively my affinity for and innate love of reading and learning. It provided me with a valuable tool for changing my relationship with my medical studies when I returned to school after leaving the monastery. I was now able to set aside my criticisms of Western medicine, something that had contributed to the serious depression forcing me to drop out a year earlier. Now, my only task was to master the material, to read and study to the best of my ability.

Psychedelics and other mind-altering techniques can augment the effects of study and their integration into one's daily life. They amplify and make more meaningful preexisting notions and beliefs. Therefore, what you fill your mind with—the latest social media phenomenon, physics, or the Hebrew Bible—will determine the content and interpretation of any psychedelic experience. They can modify emotional reactions to what you are reading, making it easier to work with. Psychedelics also may transform concepts and ideas into perceptible—for example, visual—form. This provides an extra dimension for arriving at novel solutions to questions we are wrestling with. Altered states may also stimulate original associations between ideas and imagery and thus lead to enhanced creativity.

How then does one decide what to study? Using the altered states platform, one looks for a synergistic relationship between what you study and the altered state. That is, how consistent is what you are reading with the most compelling ideas and feelings from your psychedelic or meditative experiences? Does your study stimulate similar feelings of truth and value? Conversely, how do those ideas and concepts enhance your understanding of those altered states? Do they make more sense? Do they make integration of such experiences into your daily life easier and more fruitful?

6
LEARNING TO MEDITATE

Ours is among the tens of thousands of young families who pour into Southern California after World War II. The public schools struggle to keep up with the influx of children. I'm in second grade but our class has too many students, and construction of the new school to which I'll be transferring is behind schedule. I end up in a stopgap situation: a classroom in a school located between my current and future ones. It's only for a couple of months, but I'm unhappy with the disruption. Beginning first grade was anxiety-ridden. My mother walked me through the gates the first couple of days while I cried, sad and afraid. That memory is still fresh, but I'm too embarrassed to ask my mother to walk me into this school, too.

I assume the role of class clown. Being a wise guy. Other kids think I'm funny, but the teacher doesn't. One day, Mrs. Smith stands in front of the class and shows us a picture of a pastoral scene. There's a meadow, trees, a barn, and peaceful grazing cows.

"Those cows have no brains," I snicker.

It's the last straw for Mrs. Smith. "One more wisecrack and you'll go to the corner!"

This time I chortle. "Wisecrack!"

I look around. Some kids laugh, others look worried, several avert their gaze.

Mrs. Smith glares at me and points to the far corner of the room.

She barks, "Go to The Corner!" She then adds for good measure, "And you sit there until you decide you can behave!"

The teacher grabs me by my upper arm while the class, hushed, watches us make our way back to that dismal spot.

Fear and curiosity mingle. I've seen her banish other kids to The Corner. It's in the shadows, the furthest reaches of our little universe. Within minutes, the kid begins to sob and cry, pleading to return to the group's comfort.

I wonder what's it like back there. All alone, next to the clanking and hissing radiator. I'm proud, too. I'm an outcast, I reflect. A tough guy. A rebel. I make my own rules and live by them. I'm excited to forge my way into the unknown. It's the path I've chosen, my own actions have imposed this situation upon me.

"Where should I sit?" I ask calmly, unnerving Mrs. Smith.

"There!" she says. "And don't come back until you're good and ready!"

Uncertain about that criterion for readmission, I ignore it and sit on the floor, cross-legged, facing the wall. The radiator is to my left, and my head comes up to the top of it. I make sure not to get too close but near enough to soak up its warmth.

This isn't so bad, I think. I look around and examine where I am. Drops of water drip off the bottom corner of the radiator into a small catch bowl on the floor. The sound—plink, plink—comforts me. There is nothing else except blank walls to my right and in front of me. Satisfied with my survey of this tiny self-imposed prison, I settle into gazing straight ahead at the wall, which is two feet away. I relax, feel calm. My anger, fear, and loneliness lessen. I'm happy. It's quiet. I don't have to perform, behave, listen to the teacher—someone who will be out of my life soon enough.

How long can I do this? I ask myself.

It's been long enough for Mrs. Smith. Exasperated, she calls out in my direction. "Are you ready to join us?"

I am, but then again, I'm not. I'm fascinated by this discovery.

Reflections

REWARD FROM PUNISHMENT

As a seven-year-old second-grader, I chose the path of disruptive behavior when facing the stress of changing schools. Although I sought novelty as a child, I also needed secure routines. I couldn't control where I went to school, so I tried to exert control over the new setting.

Mrs. Smith chose withdrawal of human contact as my punishment—one that young children find especially painful. However, I entered a pleasant meditative state instead.

My temperament lent itself to sustained concentration and focus. These became active, as a reflex, and the results—feeling calm and happy—replaced my emotional distress. Sitting cross-legged helped, as did dim lighting and the sound and warmth of the radiator. The setting conduced to a relaxed state of body and mind. I became more fully aware of my physical space. Shifting my attention from anxiety to curious observing was surprisingly rewarding.

The tranquil state I describe here brings to mind my attempt to achieve equanimity in the face of physical abuse, in the chapter "Spanking." Those earlier attempts were in response to extreme duress, from which I desperately yet unsuccessfully sought escape. In this chapter the circumstances were less dire and even provided comforting elements, and I was therefore more successful.

PART II

FINDING MY WAY

INTRODUCTION TO FINDING MY WAY
Young Adulthood

THE ACCOUNTS OF ALTERED STATES of consciousness in this part occurred between seventeen and twenty-two years of age. They begin with leaving home for college and end with my entering a Zen Buddhist monastery five years later. The narratives encompass dramatic highs and lows: From laughing uproariously on LSD watching people eat fried chicken to lying in a sodden gutter drunkenly bemoaning breaking up with my high school girlfriend; from blissfully merging with all existence to fears of eternal madness; from falling in love at a Bach concert on LSD to falling on my head while drunkenly dancing naked on a pool table with a stripper at a fraternity party; and from the messianic elation of formulating a manifesto of healing the world to a near-psychotic melancholy that necessitated a leave of absence from medical school. While the excesses of these tales stand out, it's also possible to discern the deeper trends defining the direction my life was taking.

I initially suffered a short-lived bout of school anxiety as a young child, which dissipated in the face of my success as a student. I got good grades, my teachers liked me, and I was athletic and popular. Despite healthy self-esteem related to school, my identity was fragile, and my sense of worth was low. This had its origins in my experience of violent abuse. I could not understand why my father hit me, and my inability to stop him increased my distress. Why couldn't I make it better? My essence felt defective, yet I was competent. So, who am I? Good or bad? Defective or whole? These are common issues among those with backgrounds of physical and emotional abuse. Herein also lie some of the drives impelling my brush with messianism; that is, for me to fix things in my life, I would fix the world. I would benefit both directly and indirectly by achieving this goal—I'd heal and be healed.

Another thread running through these recollections is putting myself in harm's way while in an altered state. This is the evolution of another pattern with its origins in infancy. That is, a fear of danger resembled the fear of being hit, re-creating certain aspects of those events. Maybe this time I would master my fear, or the situation would magically become safe. Of course, I was not conscious of these wishes at the time. They were unconscious. In addition, that fear reminded me of closeness, albeit dangerous, with my father. There was also the never-ending search for someone to save me from danger. This harkens to my mother's ineffectively shielding me from abuse. Similarly unconscious, as I got older, I hoped that someone would step up and help me, that I was not alone in this.

While growing up, I developed a love of chemistry. Instead of reading the World Book Encyclopedia on the toilet now, my favorite bathroom books were tomes like the Time-Life series on chemistry. I especially loved learning about the elements: what they looked like, the history of their discovery, their properties and uses. The most fascinating elements were those producing dramatic effects—burning, exploding, smoking, smelling, and producing bright colors. Gradually, fireworks and explosives came into focus. I checked out from our local library every book on their manufacture. Our nearby drugstore had a "chemistry corner" where I bought ingredients for gunpowder and basic pyrotechnics. Not satisfied with the quantities available nor overall inventory, I wrote to the chemical supply house in Chicago that supplied our drugstore and received a thick catalog. I ordered and began receiving regular half- to one-pound quantities of my standard as well as more exotic chemicals, no questions asked.

Close calls with neighborhood kids reduced my social circle but, undeterred, I continued producing all manner of dangerous substances. I was especially proud of the ones that ignited when coming into contact with water. One Halloween in high school we terrorized multiple neighborhoods by urinating on and thus igniting an array of fireworks. Blowing a hole in the pitcher's mound of the baseball diamond in our nearby park was the culmination of my pyromaniacal adolescence. I planned to major in chemistry in college, with the goal of developing my own line of fireworks.

I was an ugly duckling in middle school and never dated, although I had crushes on several girls, including my cousin. Once shedding my dental braces and exchanging my thick eyeglasses for contact lenses, my popularity among girls rose significantly. In my senior year of high school, my girlfriend and I were voted the cutest couple in our graduating class of over eight hundred. Throughout this relationship, though, we remained virgins.

I also ran track—the 100- and 220-yard dashes, and the 4x100-yard relay—with moderate success. However, a highlight of my athletic career was my teammates choosing me as the varsity team's captain. In this role, I gained comfort working alongside non-Jewish and less academically accomplished classmates.

I left my family and hometown to attend and live at a nearby private college. While The College was top-flight, Stanford University was my first choice.

All manner of drugs and alcohol were available at The College. As I lacked any previous experience with them, I rapidly made up for lost time. My early drinking experiences were unpleasant, and after discovering cannabis and psychedelics, I began using both regularly. My first two years of college were full of new experiences of chemically induced altered states. Not all were positive, and regular psychedelic use made focusing on schoolwork difficult.

I transferred to Stanford as a junior where I could concentrate on academics. I regained a sense of competency by excelling in my studies. I discovered the fields of consciousness and the biological bases of behavior, learned Transcendental Meditation, and took a class on Indian Buddhism. I also fulfilled my dream to perform neuroscience research in a premier laboratory.

An LSD trip between my junior and senior years showed me my life's mission, but the path itself was obscure. In this altered state, I conceived and wrote a manifesto for saving the world with the psychedelic experience. Buddhism, psychoanalysis, and psychopharmacology were the three pillars upon which I hoped to construct a thorough approach to human nature and a method for widespread healing. Lacking a practical avenue through which to pursue this goal, I developed hypomanic symptoms soon thereafter. Almost immediately upon entering medical school, my messianic state turned into a serious depression. I could not adapt to the academic demands nor the New York City environment. I dropped out and returned to California before finishing my first year.

I attended several Buddhist retreats, and after locating a supportive, understanding, and inspiring Zen monastic community, enrolled in their lay resident training program. I wondered if withdrawing from the outside world would lessen my suffering. While at The Temple, I learned to shift the balance between imagination and action toward more action. Zen practice offered a practical model that at the same time aspired to the most elevated spiritual ideals. Thankfully, my depression remitted at the monastery, and I returned to medical school. Therefore, it feels fitting, after recounting the altered states that ultimately led me to The Temple, to end this book with its gates closing behind me.

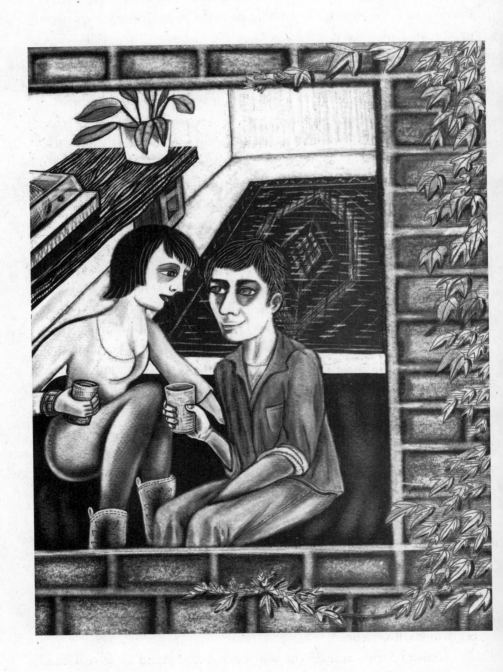

7

TERRY AND BEER

EARLY AFTERNOON, DAY 2 at The College, a white unmarked van pulls up and parks in front of The Dorm. A grizzled fifty-year-old man climbs out of the cab and wheezingly makes the short trip back to its rear double doors. He coughs up the ramp into the cargo area and loads two aluminum kegs onto his dolly. There's a splint on his right wrist. He maneuvers the kegs down the ramp onto the street, jerks the loaded dolly up over the curb, and sets them onto the sidewalk.

Jim, the senior resident advisor who gets me stoned for the first time several months later, calls out, "Where's the hardware?"

I'm familiar with kegs. In high school, I needed to store water for my garage chemistry laboratory. A friend's father owned a scrap metal yard, and we found an empty serviceable keg to which we welded a faucet. However, today's pump, valve, hose, and spigot—all the items necessary for getting beer out of a keg—are new to me.

"Pressurization" comes to mind. It's science in action. Pleasantly reminiscing over my home lab, I turn to one of my new dormmates and say, "It all comes down to science."

"Yes," he replies, but looks puzzled. After a moment, it seems like my comment sinks in. Regardless, he brightens and adds, "Right. Let's get drunk with science."

A crowd forms around the now-open keg. I stand close so I can watch how to get at the beer.

Someone laughs behind me, "Like flies to shit."

I turn to identify the speaker but can't. Instead, I notice Terry and we make eye contact. She smiles and moves toward me and the keg.

"Finally," she chuckles. "The beer's here. I'm so thirsty."

Terry is exotic. At nearly six feet, she's slightly taller than I am. She wears cowboy boots and a wide silver bracelet with turquoise inlays. She's all arms and legs, and when she strides forward, her pelvis somehow precedes her. Tanned smooth skin, short thick dark hair, her flashing brown eyes fix on me with a steady, slightly amused expression. I'm uncomfortable with her direct gaze and look away.

"Pour me one, would you?" she asks me and moves closer.

Terry's relaxed and friendly. I am tense and uncertain. I can't place her accent.

I try to break the ice. "Where are you from? You have a weird accent."

"And I can tell that you've never seen cowboy boots. At least on a girl."

Was I staring at her feet? I stand uncertain, hands by my sides. How do you pour a beer from this thing?

Terry steps up, efficiently gives the keg a couple of vigorous pumps, takes hold of a red shiny plastic cup, and fills it. She hands me the beer, overflowing with foam.

She smiles at me. "Have you ever worked one of these things?"

"Not exactly like this."

She next fills her cup and lets out a satisfied sigh. "There we go."

She lifts her beer toward me and says gaily, "Cheers!"

Up to this moment, I have taken only a few sips from one of my parents' Olympia or Schlitz beers. I didn't like the bitter bite and wondered how they and their friends could enjoy drinking it. None of my high school friends drank. We were role models: athletes, members of the student government, and got good grades. Alcohol wasn't on our minds.

My single experience with a drunk high school friend confirmed my avoiding alcohol. Lee arrived drunk one night at a football game.

His silly grin, feverishly bright eyes, and transformation from shy and diffident to garrulous was discomfiting, and we shunned him the rest of the evening.

Terry and I bang together our cups full of foamy beer. Some sloshes out as they collide. We laugh. The beer is cold. Slightly sweet, musty, and biting. Better than I remember, especially the sweetness.

Soon, I feel a surge of excitement and exclaim, "That's refreshing!"

It moistens my mouth, dry from nerves. I wonder if this is what happens after you drink beer. The second cup is sweeter, and this one I drink as quickly as Terry does. Strangely, I am more relaxed while also feeling energized and stronger. I'm less anxious in this new crowd, less concerned about what others think of me. It's not an increase in self-confidence as much as not caring about what people think, almost devaluing them. I don't care if I say the wrong thing or the right thing because I don't care about those who may judge.

Conversing with Terry becomes surprisingly easy. I make her laugh. After the painful break up with my high school girlfriend the month before, I began to feel attractive again.

More students mill around the keg in front of The Dorm, a no-frills two-story building that even then is over sixty years old. It sports a nondescript gray stucco exterior and three west-facing entrances: one at either end and one in the middle. The keg is directly below my second story room occupying the building's northwest corner.

Terry flashes me a startlingly bright smile and I turn away, not sure how to respond.

"It's too crowded here. Let's go back to your room," she suggests.

Her request catches me off guard, as does the perfectly natural manner in which she makes it. A confusing flood of feelings mixes with the alcohol, and my mind drifts. I can't process her request. What about Dulce?

Dulce and I had broken up earlier in the summer because of our very different visions for the future. I am finally free of my family and excited about the endless possibilities and destinations. More than anything, I want to leave home. Dulce wants to continue living with her parents while training as an actuary—following in her father's footsteps—marry, and begin raising a family. While my best childhood friend and I were taking a two-week road trip before starting college, she had begun dating the son of her parents' best friends. My jealous anger at her upon discovering their relationship validated her assessment that I was not a suitable partner.

I see Terry expects a response. Does she want sex? I'm a virgin.

I finish my third beer and assess my state. My speech is different. I'm slurring words. This is "drunk"? I touch my lips and cheeks. They are rubbery and becoming numb. The potato chips I am passing into my mouth feel and taste strange, no longer appetizing. There is a cool lightness in my head, as if there is more air in my skull, above the eyes. Happy, too. And a little stupid, as in not seeing clearly what is in front of me—mentally that is—lacking a clear sense of my circumstances.

Am I betraying Dulce? Well, I think, she's betrayed me.

"Okay," I finally reply. We take each other by the hand. Hers is huge and nearly swallows mine. I look down at her feet and notice they too are bigger than mine. I think "Amazon" and hear myself chuckle.

We walk up the single flight of stairs, turn left at the landing, and enter my corner room. We sit on the bed. It's as if Terry must retract her limbs in order to accommodate the small bed. She sits a little stooped, feet on the ground, her knees, oddly elevated, come up to nearly chest level. I can't look directly at her. Instead, I stare at her arms and legs.

Looking around, she stands, makes her way to the window, and opens it. Sounds from the party drift upward and into the room. I join her and we look down at a growing crowd coalescing on the sidewalk, the keg directly in the group's center.

"Looks like fun," I say. Maybe it does, maybe it doesn't; I can't really make an informed opinion. People are loud and their emotions exaggerated. I regret what I said, nevertheless, wondering if Terry might think I want to be there with them rather than here with her.

She takes my hand, and we return to the bed. This time, she sits cross-legged on it, her eyes gazing at me expectantly.

We talk.

She opens. "Where did you grow up?"

"In the San Fernando Valley. It was fun. I ran track and was captain of the varsity team. I was a good student but missed being valedictorian because of a B in physics." Unable to help myself, I add, "My girlfriend and I were voted cutest couple in a class of eight hundred kids. She was the class secretary-treasurer." I wonder if talking about Dulce will put Terry off. It might make things easier. If she thinks I have a girlfriend, I will have an excuse for not having sex with her.

"Oh."

I don't expect this response. It's as if that monosyllable—instantly, unexpectedly, and strangely—cracks a façade overlaying my sense of self. Built up over the years, my Los Angeles identity—the people, schools, summers at the beach, movies in Hollywood, all of my accomplishments—quickly pales. The value and meaning of my life's successes and accomplishments suddenly fade. Terry's reaction shines a harsh light on deep-rooted barely conscious insecurities. A weight descends onto my shoulders.

I try shaking off the beer's effects and alarming wave of self-doubt. I ask, "Where did you grow up?"

She laughs only a little self-consciously. "My father is a state senator, and he leveraged his political connections to accumulate wealth. We live in a high valley in the mountains of northern Idaho on a fifty-thousand-acre working ranch."

I don't ask what a "working" ranch is. How does that differ from any other kind of ranch?

She continues. "We grew alfalfa and had five hundred head of cattle. I was raised around cowboys and drank and partied with them. I ran some of our heavy machinery and took care of our animals. I started riding a horse when I was five."

Terry looks fondly at the well-worn boots covering her giant feet while describing the awards she garnered as an athlete-scholar at her elite private boarding school.

I wonder, How big is an acre?

She continues, "I guess I grew up privileged. I really wanted to get into The College, and my dad knows people on their board. I feel a little funny about that part."

I don't tell her that The College was my second choice.

I am a second-rate guy at a second-choice school. Terry is a first-rate girl at her first-choice college. And in contrast to me, she loves and admires her father. I feel the gap widening between us.

I try to bridge it.

"When I was growing up, I body-surfed a lot. My friends and I worked on our tans at the beach. On weekends we went into Hollywood to watch new movies. After a movie, we'd go out for a hamburger or pie and ice cream. Sometimes milk." I pause. "There are some great burgers in Los Angeles—Hamburger Hamlet . . . Bob's Big Boy . . ."

Gaining a head of steam, talking about restaurants I like, I add, "Have you ever had an Orange Julius? It's my favorite after-beach drink. I spent a summer trying to duplicate its formula. Malt played a role— that's as far as I got."

"Oh." Terry looks around the room, as if there must be more to my room—or to me—than first meets her eye. Maybe she's missing something and needs to look harder.

As I gaze at her uncertainly, I feel her pull away.

Who is this woman? Where do I stand in her universe?

My breath is souring from the beer. I look down at the floor and see the nearly empty red plastic cups holding our stale beverages. No longer cool, sweet, crisp, or refreshing.

I lean over to kiss Terry the Amazon privileged politician-rancher's daughter. Her mouth tastes like mine. She's strong, as are her mouth and tongue. I touch her small breasts through her shirt. I feel kind of silly, doing what's expected, a social reflex. I am acting like a man. Forget about Dulce! Here I am! Away at college, making out with a rich, beautiful, confident, competent—albeit nearly alien—woman. I've made it. I'm free.

What else can I do besides foreplay? Despite a nine-month relationship with Dulce, we were never even naked together.

Our kissing intensity rapidly tapers off. An image intrudes into my mind: a metal hubcap falls to the ground and spins noisily. The clattering frequency rises as it approaches rest, at which point there's a dramatic silence. We look at our watches at the same time. It's eight thirty.

Terry rises from the bed. She stretches and unwinds her unnaturally long limbs. Then yawns.

"Well, I think I'll be going. It's been a long day. It was nice talking."

I'm relieved. "Okay . . . I think. That's fine. I'm usually in bed by nine anyway."

She yawns again, I open the door, we step out into the hallway, and walk the few steps to the stairs. I watch her descend and emerge from The Dorm. After brushing my teeth at the communal bathroom at the end of the hall, I return to my room and look out the window. Terry stands on the sidewalk next to the keg, casually holding onto a senior classman's arm. She throws her head back laughing, holding a cup of beer.

At breakfast in the cafeteria the next day, I quietly sit next to the fellow she was with and overhear him say, "Wow. That Terry girl. She's a wild animal in bed."

Reflections
ALCOHOL: FIRST TASTE

Charles Bukowski describes his first time getting drunk:

Never had I felt so good. It was better than masturbating. I went from barrel to barrel. It was magic. Why hadn't someone told me? With this, life was great, a man was perfect, nothing could touch him . . . We sat on a park bench and I chewed the gum and I thought, well, now I have found something. I have found something that is going to help me, for a long long time to come. The park grass looked greener, the park benches looked better and the flowers were trying harder.[1]

Each of us has his or her altered state of consciousness of choice, and frequently this is one that a particular substance or class of substances produces. For many of us, it's alcohol. Bukowski's waxing on about his first experience with wine is rapturous and borders on the psychedelic.

By the time I entered college, I had never been drunk, smoked cannabis, nor taken a psychedelic. In contrast to my instant affinity to cannabis and psychedelics, it would not be an exaggeration to describe my first experiences with alcohol as nightmarish. Subsequent chapters narrating early drunken bouts will prove my point. Perhaps my genetic tendency toward alcoholism created an unconscious aversion to the drug. What if I had begun drinking earlier, found it to assuage my insecurities, or enjoyed it more? I too may have suffered a premature death from alcoholism, a fate that befell my father less than ten years later.

There are many types of "alcohols." In alcoholic beverages it is *ethanol*. Alcohol increases the effects of GABA—gamma amino butyric acid—the most abundant inhibitory neurotransmitter in the brain. GABA slows down firing rates of neurons and thus dampens overall brain activity. The benzodiazepine antianxiety and sleeping medications like Valium and Halcion similarly enhance GABA's effects.

Alcohol rapidly passes through the stomach and small intestine, into the bloodstream, and then into the brain. Inhibitory brain circuits, like those located in the frontal lobes, are more sensitive to inhibition by GABA than are stimulatory circuits. Therefore, alcohol's inhibitory effects on inhibitory brain function result in a stimulant-like effect. This indirect stimulation occurs before more general depressant effects predominate: decreased pain sensitivity, slurred speech, unsteadiness, slowed thinking, and sedation. With continued intake, inhibitory effects mount and lead to loss of memory, coma, and death. However, in some people a sense of stimulating effects persists through the drunken state by maintaining an "optimal" rate of drinking.

Endorphins also play a role in alcohol-induced elation, and naltrexone—an opiate/endorphin blocker—reduces these pleasurable effects. In addition, dopamine contributes to these positive feelings by activating a brain center called the nucleus accumbens. Nucleus accumbens activation is also how cocaine and amphetamines elevate mood and increase energy.

Psychoactive substances, especially those that reside in plants, seem to possess a particular spirit. "Spirit," here, as in "soul," its essential attribute. No better example of this is alcohol, where we explicitly call distilled products like gin and vodka "spirits."

That evening, I sensed in myself and others the nature of alcohol's spirit. It magnified emotions like sociability and self-confidence. It also lowered my inhibitions. This latter effect may be prosocial and/or anti-social, as certain inhibitions are necessary for peaceful human interactions. It also produced a certain emotional and cognitive lability, rapid shifts in my appraisal of myself and others that lacked the usual mediating function of self-reflection. I did not care about others' reactions to me as I became more outgoing and confident, but just as quickly felt painfully awkward around and judged by a woman I had just met.

This description of drinking beer with Terry reinforces the importance of set and setting in determining the outcome of any drug-induced altered state. At first, the excitatory effects of the beer helped me become more outgoing in an anxiety-laden situation. However, it also released more deep-rooted fears that my higher brain centers, so to speak, had been keeping out of consciousness for most of my life. Remember, this is the first time I had ever been "intoxicated." What I call a "façade" in the narrative was not a case of "faking it." Rather it was becoming suddenly aware of the prospect that my life lacked a center of gravity.

This episode also highlights my willingness to try a drug in order to find out what it's like. Such actions aren't especially noteworthy. However, my attempt to objectively assess alcohol's subjective effects intimates my later scientific studies of mind-altering substances.

8

KITTENS

THE NEXT MORNING, I feel the aftereffects of the beers with Terry. I'm irritable. The sun pouring into my room hurts my eyes and the voices of people using the nearby bathroom grate my nerves. I nap most of the afternoon. Sitting down with my dormmates that night for dinner, my mood is low. As we begin eating, our resident senior advisor Jim invites our table to a keg after dinner. It's at his fraternity's cabin in the mountains behind The College.

"Right on!" Woody bellows, his suspenders nearly falling off his shoulders. "More beer!"

I say, "I don't know. I'm not feeling so great."

Stu says, "Don't worry. The best cure for a hangover is more beer."*

I don't know about hangovers but agree to come along.

Jim drives the fraternity van that carries about ten of us young men. He turns left onto a dirt road, and we cross a small bridge, park, and make our way along a short trail to the cabin—a small run-down wooden structure perching on the slope of a side canyon. It's a good twenty-foot drop to the bottom. Each of the cabin's two rooms is small, not much larger than my dorm room. Dust-covered, threadbare beds and couches litter both. No one has been here for months. Someone starts up the

---

*To the extent that alcohol withdrawal contributes to a hangover, providing additional alcohol reduces its severity. However, this only postpones withdrawal.

barbecue—which, happily smoking, supplies a steady stream of hamburgers, hot dogs, and baked potatoes. A fresh keg provides beer. The canyon loses sun quickly and pitch blackness suffuses the enveloping wilderness. The temperature drops abruptly, and we retreat inside.

Everyone fills his cup and drunkenly awaits what's next.

Woody and Jim position themselves facing each other in the kitchen, beers in hand.

"Ready?" Woody challenges our senior resident advisor.

"I sure am, you pussy!" Jim roars back.

"One! Two! Three!"

On "three," each downs his beer as rapidly as possible.

Woody wins. Jim requests a rematch and wins. Jim also wins the tiebreaker. Victorious, he lowers himself into an overstuffed chair, raising a cloud of dust. A fit of coughing passes, and he returns to his primary task—maintaining a watchful eye over his young charges.

Woody isn't finished. He looks around and challenges the group. "Who's next, you pussies?"

I'm not familiar with college life—drugs, alcohol, sexual exploits. Nevertheless, I've always been competitive in academics, sports, and dating. This is something I might win. There is a basis for my optimism as I drank soft drinks out of cans faster than any of my hometown friends. I know how to guzzle carbonated cold drinks. In addition, I am smarting from the awkward encounter with Terry last night. I felt like a loser. Tonight, I can win.

Bravely and hopefully, I turn to Woody, "I'll take you on!"

"OK, you pussy!" Woody laughs confidently.

We fill our red plastic cups and take our positions.

"Ready, set, go!" Woody says, handicapping himself a half-second.

I watch his Adam's apple bob up and down as he chugs the beer. I lose this round but gain valuable information. Don't breathe, and keep your throat open. Pour, don't swallow. The next round is a tie.

I win the third round.

Woody takes a break and sits down. I survey the room, confident now, searching for challengers. I forget about my hangover and my earlier reluctance to attend tonight's gathering. The beer is cold, wet, and refreshing. If I keep the beer flowing, it continues tasting fresh and I maintain a positive state.

These are my new friends. Dorm mates. My drinking prowess impresses them. I'm energetic, strong, unstoppable. I let out a big "Hurrah" after finishing a cup.

Tom walks up to me, says, "Hey, Rick. You might want to slow down."

"No way, man. This is great. Do you see how fast I can drink beer?!"

On a roll, I call out, "Where's the next one??"

How many beers do I drink? Six, ten, fifteen? I stagger out to the overhanging deck and direct my urine down into the canyon.

I've never peed outside before. This is a first! All these new experiences!! I turn around and reenter the cabin. It's quiet and dark. How long have I been outside?

Stu lies on one of the couches and groans, "There's no way we're driving back into town. We are way too drunk."

I take in the setting. Where will I sleep? There's nowhere to lie down in the living room. Am I even sleepy?

The room begins to spin. I grab onto the back of a moldering couch to steady myself and nearly fall.

Someone chuckles in the darkness. "Not feeling so good? Ha ha. You shouldn't have drunk so much." It sounds like Tom.

I lurch from one piece of furniture to the next, my head pounding, and come to a door. Opening it, I look into the blackness of the sunroom. Incredulous at my luck, I see an empty large bed in the middle of the room, covered with blankets. This will do. I don't care where I sleep. I've got to sleep. I fall face first on top of the pile of blankets, stirring up another cloud of dust.

I rest my head on a ragged pillow. Suddenly, I vomit on the bed, a hot steaming mound of barbequed meat and potatoes. That's better.

I wake up and raise my arm to look at my watch but can't read its face. Something rustles by my head. Several things. Painfully, I raise my eyes and make out two kittens mincing around, inches from my face.

Tracking their movement triggers waves of nausea and vertigo. I quickly lean over the edge of the bed and eject onto the floor another torrent of acidic bilious vomit. The kittens, startled but curious, jump down to take a look. They sniff, gingerly extend and quickly withdraw paws, and, satisfied, jump back onto the bed. They sniff at my face, drenched in sweat.

More kittens appear and I fight for space. This is their bed. Everyone is elbowing everyone else. When I close my eyes, the bed spins under me. Opening them, nausea prevails. Hours of nonstop vomiting, vertigo, and batting aside kittens. The sky begins lightening, heralding hope that my situation improves.

I hear movement in the next room. Creaking floorboards, pants zipping. Groans, laughs, curses.

I am too sick to move. Tom and Ambrose come into the room and pull me up and out of the sodden bed. It's painfully bright and I can only squint. Speaking requires too much effort and hurts my head, so I try not to talk. Everyone climbs into the van. Shortly, we are back at The Dorm.

Reflections

ALCOHOL, EXUBERANCE, AND COLLAPSE

In the preceding chapter, "Terry and Beer," I commented on the stimulant-like effects of alcohol. That is, the depressant effects of alcohol first depress inhibitory brain functions, which result in feeling more energetic and alert.

In this narrative, there is an additional factor: drug effects are greater the faster its blood levels rise. This is why, for example, snorting or smoking cocaine produces a greater high than the oral route of administration, even with comparable blood levels. Conversely, on the way down from their peak, the same blood levels do not produce the same effect as they do on their way up. So, if you continually raise drug levels, you will continue to get high—in alcohol's case, stimulated and elated. However, when levels rise too high and adverse effects accumulate and intensify, intake ceases, and levels in the body drop. Stimulation falls and sedation predominates.

Engaging in a drinking contest that night at the cabin, my energy, mood, and confidence remained elevated as my blood levels continued to steeply increase—until toxicity ensued. In addition to the gastrointestinal effects, I blacked out, which is also more common with heavy rapid drinking. Such drug-induced amnesia results from the breakdown of the transfer of short-term to long-term memory. I "lost time" standing on the deck and did not remember the winding down of the party.

These first two encounters with alcohol on consecutive evenings did not recommend the drug. Nevertheless, the brief positive changes in mood, confidence, and sociability were real, and hinted at the possibility that drug-induced altered states existed with more benefits and fewer drawbacks.

9

CLOUD SPEAKERS

TAP, TAP, TAP. I listlessly look over at my dorm room door. The quiet but persistent knock rouses me from the black hole of my calculus homework. I don't get calculus, and I don't want to. I'm too mad at it to exert any more effort. I hate things that stymie, let alone defeat, me.

I'm not expecting anyone but welcome the interruption. It's Friday night at The College, a cold damp November evening, and people are gathering. The sun set hours ago, and the campus, nestled against the foothills, lies under a blanket of smoggy fog. Adding to the haze is smoke rising up from fireplaces in the highly coveted casitas that many seniors live in. Light pours out of nearly every room of my dark stone dormitory and provides respite against the gloom.

My little second-story room is warm and bright. An accordion-style steam heater hisses cheerily. A bare overhead bulb, two floor lamps, white walls, and white linoleum floor make for a shadow-free environment.

I lean against the back of my white plastic chair, raise my arms over my head to stretch, and get up. It's less than three steps from my similarly white plastic desk to the door. I open it. Standing there is the resident senior advisor Jim.

In exchange for room and board, and over the objections of his no-longer live-in girlfriend, Jim from Iowa oversees the only all-male residence on campus. It's the main dorm for athletes, and I landed there because of my track background. Eighty of America's most promising young men live here under Jim's watchful eye.

He's clean-cut, about my height but stockier, and sports short blonde hair. He played football for a year but, after a couple of injuries, decided it best to quit. He's friendly, soft-spoken, upright, and wholesome, a steady hand steering this sometimes raucous boat. We like each other, but a culture gap doesn't make for easy communication. It's a long way between my Los Angeles Jewish sarcasm and Jim's Midwestern Protestant directness. Since freshman orientation, we've exchanged brief greetings but little more. This is the first time he's come by himself to my room. Tonight, he looks especially relaxed.

He doesn't say anything, and I break the silence. "Hi, Jim."

Jim's smile, already broad, broadens further. "Hey, Rick. Can I come in?"

"Sure."

He steps across the threshold and makes his way to the other white plastic chair that almost touches the right side of the desk. I return to my seat and push aside the pile of math problems. Problems caused by math. I look across the desk at my senior advisor. In addition to his grin, Jim's eyes are red and puffy.

He straightens himself in the chair and begins with mock solemnity, "I understand you've never gotten stoned."

"You mean smoke marijuana?"

Jim nods.

My heart pounds. "No."

Jim says with pride, "If that's the case, as your senior resident advisor," he pauses for effect, "it's my duty to introduce you to marijuana."

Marijuana!

All my friends in the dorm smoke weed, having started in middle or high school. I don't know anything about it, and have avoided it, removing myself from smoking circles when they form. Sharing joints is unsanitary, and as an athlete I don't want to harm my lungs. My parents are both chronic smokers, as are their friends. Smoking has always looked like a bad, nasty habit.

⚡

One summer day when I was sixteen, I first saw someone smoking a joint. We were assistant counselors at a Jewish day camp where I had been a camper several previous summers. Ron invited me over to listen to Cream on his stereo and watch him play his electric guitar. He closed his bedroom door behind us and pulled out a glass jar full of green leafy marijuana, rolled himself a joint, and puffed away as we listened to Eric Clapton. I was curious but also alarmed and vaguely insulted when he offered me the joint. Marijuana was illicit, and he wanted me to join him? I brusquely demurred. He took off his sunglasses only once while we were in his room, and his eyes were red and puffy. At the same time, he seemed happier and calmer.

Jim leans forward, rests his hands on the shiny white desk. "You're lucky," he murmurs conspiratorially, "I've got hash. Blonde Lebanese hash."

I recognize the word "hash." It's a very strong form of marijuana, but I'm uncertain about specifics. Ambrose—whose New England trust fund bankrolls him and our friends' steady supply of beer and all manner of drugs—talked about blonde Lebanese hash just the other night. I wonder if this is from the same batch. I couldn't understand his description of its effects because he compared it to marijuana's.

Jim continues, "It's easier to smoke than grass, and you don't need as much. Even better, you're almost guaranteed to get high the first time. That's not always the case with marijuana."

I listen intently.

"Have you ever smoked anything?" Jim asks.

"I took a puff off my dad's cigarette once and didn't like it. I was seven or eight. I tried again with one of Woody's cigarettes a few months ago. That's it."

Jim nods avuncularly and reaches into his shirt pocket. "I've got a little pipe that works great." He pulls it out. "Hash tastes better than cigarettes. It's easy. Trust me. I'm your senior advisor." His smile elevates his cheeks, which nearly cover his eyes.

I have no plans tonight. Tomorrow I can sleep in.

I scrutinize my mentor and his drugged glee. Why does he look so happy? Happier than usual, that's for sure. I'm rarely happy at The College. I miss my childhood friends and ex-girlfriend Dulce and may fail calculus.

"Okay," I say. "I'll try it."

Jim sets the flat dark wooden pipe on the desk. It's about four inches long and fans outward from a narrow mouthpiece to about an inch wide at the bowl end. A fine wire screen fits snugly just below the rim of the bowl.

Jim's hand revisits his pocket and pulls out a small aluminum foil packet that he places next to the pipe and carefully unfolds. Resting in the middle of the foil is a one-inch-square flat chunk of dull waxy solid, yellowish-tan, about one-half inch thick. A thin layer of fuzzy yellow dust covers the hash. Jim's movements stir a tiny breeze that carries a sweet, pungent, and spicy smell, and I inhale deeply. Like cinnamon plus amber. And something else I don't recognize.

"Beautiful smell, isn't it?" Jim declaims.

I ask, "The color. Is that why they call it blonde?"

Jim nods and repeats, "You *are* a lucky guy."

He rummages through my wastebasket and pulls out a sheet of paper marked with angry mathematical scratchings. He lays it face down, thankfully, on the desk and breaks off a pea-size bit of hash onto it. Rolling it between his right thumb and forefinger, he crumbles the hash into a neat fluffy pile. He carefully fills the bowl with the powder as he hums a vague Led Zeppelin tune, lightly compresses the powdery material with his forefinger, and nods with satisfaction.

He hands me the pipe. "This is it."

While I examine it, Jim looks around and asks, "How about some music?"

I gently set down the pipe, get up, and take the few steps to my stereo. The components sit on a board suspended between two cinder blocks on the floor. Amplifier, turntable, and receiver. Headphones rest on the floor under the board, and albums fill most of the remaining space below the components. I'm proud of my system, having paid for it myself from my summer post office job. I crouch in front of the electronics, turn on the amplifier and turntable, and sift through my albums.

"Santana okay?" It's Latin American, like marijuana—I think.

"Right on," Jim says.

I return to my desk chair, facing my guide.

"It's easy," Jim reiterates. "Put this end into your mouth. I'll light a match and hold it close to the hash. Then slowly inhale. Don't overdo it. I know you ran track and have strong lungs."

He stretches his right leg out in front of him, reaches into his pants pocket, and pulls out a box of small wooden matches. Riffs of Santana waft through my room.

"Watch me," he advises. Jim lights a match, puts the mouthpiece between his lips, and positions the flame above the bowl. He takes a long, deep, slow inhalation. The flame descends and touches the hash, which begins to glow and smoke. After inhaling fully, he holds his breath, chest expanded. After five seconds or so, he coughs, cheeks ballooned, expelling a cloud of white smoke. His cough sounds like a bark. He stills himself, quickly regains his composure, and leans back against his chair.

"So, that's how you do it," Jim tells me. He stirs the hash, exposing the unburnt material. "There's a lot left." He smiles.

The twenty-one-year-old Iowan hands the pipe to the seventeen-year-old Angeleno.

I put it in my mouth, holding it with my right hand. I incline forward, and Jim holds a freshly lit match over the hash. I inhale tentatively, haltingly, as I ask myself, *What will this be like?*

The flame doesn't move.

"Pull in harder," Jim says. "Draw the flame down."

I take a more forceful drag. The flame drops into the bowl and the top and edges of the hash glow. Just like when Jim did it.

Interesting. Pretty, too.

"Attaboy," Jim says softly while his eyes fix on the bowl. "Take as much in as you can, but slowly."

I hold my breath after filling my lungs and exhale deeply, loudly, exaggeratedly, as I've seen my friends do. Smoke leaves my mouth. It feels cool in my lungs, not hot. I'm surprised. I imagine the smoke there, cloudy white.

Jim nods. "That's good. Take another one like that."

The advisor's expression turns thoughtful. "Wait. First, I'll have one more." He takes another large toke, and after exhaling, stares ahead silently. He blinks and notices I'm staring at him. He turns to me, his young charge, his eyes mere slits.

My next hit is easy. "This tastes good," I say, as I hand the pipe back to Jim. He rests it on the table, closes his eyes, and moves his head in time with the music.

I look up at the speakers. They are on shelves I fastened into the uppermost corners of the room above the components.

Jim opens his eyes. "A good way to tell if you're stoned is listening to music. It can be incredible."

"What do you mean?"

"You'll see."

I remember lying on my bed at home in high school, listening to Judy Collins with headphones, eyes closed, in my darkened room. Cream, too, after the experience with my fellow assistant camp counselor. I liked the happy floaty feeling, and I especially treasured the moments when chills would run up and down my spine, my body tingling all over. My father disapproved, though, whenever he found me spacing out that like. Maybe he was jealous—I was joined to something pleasurable, rather than him and his angry depressed state.

Everything looks normal. Still, I'm glad there aren't fluorescent fixtures in my room. It would be too bright.

Jim laughs. "You look like you can't tell if you're stoned." He pauses, considers the problem. "Maybe if *I* get more stoned, you'll see what it's like."

He empties the pipe by banging it against the inside of the wastebasket, locates a paper clip on my desk, and scrapes the bowl clean with it. He breaks off another piece of hash, crumbles it, fills the pipe, and hands it to me.

"After you."

I take a very big hit. Jim goes next and drops the still-burning match into the wastebasket. He lets out a short laugh. "I hope that doesn't start a fire." He peers into the round metal can and sighs in feigned relief when he sees the dead match. "Maybe I don't need any more. But, here. You have another hit. We want to get you stoned."

After taking another big toke, I stare at the speakers, barely aware of Jim, who has quietly taken back the pipe. My resident advisor settles himself against the back of the chair, a look of satisfaction on his face.

I'm smiling a smile, one that is, for the first time in my life, free of conflict or irony. It fills the bottom half of my face, stretching my skin almost uncomfortably.

I hear Jim ask, "Are you feeling anything?"

"This is weird."

Jim's expression, as it were, is expectant.

I explain. "I'm happy."

Jim nods. "I'm glad."

"No." It's more than nod-worthy. "I'm *really* happy."

Jim nods again.

Everything is happy—my mind, my body, and my feelings. Everything is harmonized in happiness. I relax.

I close my eyes—as everyone else does when listening to music stoned—and focus on the sound coming out of the speakers. I am aware of something new.

It's space—the space separating the notes. The sounds the instruments make are separated by space. They exist in space, and I perceive that space. The notes are held and suspended in auditory space, and I am aware, auditorily, of the absence of sound within that space. The space itself is soundless. Just like physical objects in empty space, the individual notes as objects also possess auditory edges and boundaries that limit them, keep them from overlapping. The qualities of the sounds differ—qualities that exist in space. And as the music progresses, I hear minute subtle pauses between every consecutive note.

Musical sound is pure in this novel dimension, the dimension of auditory space. Nothing else mingles with it. It is separate from any other dimension. There is silence and there is music. The silence is an empty expanse, the location of temporary musical sounds. I am rapt, my discovery astonishes me. I had no idea.

I notice something else: empty space within my mind. The monologue ceases. I'm not thinking. There's nothing mixed with the music, distracting me from it, nothing else but hearing it. Just hearing. No anxious daydreams, complaints, plans, hopes, fears, second-guesses, and self-criticism. Free—for the first time in my life—of the all-pervasive anxiety, something I assumed would always be part of my life. I've never been more relaxed, at ease. Or happy.

The music ends and the turntable arm quietly swings back to its cradle.

Jim sighs deeply, shakes his head side to side, eyes closed. "Wow."

He's in his own world. This reassures me—there's nothing to worry about, nothing out of the ordinary.

This is being stoned.

I turn the album over and press "Play."

The sounds caress my outer ears. Without thoughts, I examine more carefully the silence in which the sounds exist. It is black and vast, unending darkness.

A new dimension appears—the relationship between the musicians and the sounds they make.

The artists *cause* the music. Not only do they produce it, but they are its source, its origin. Then I become aware of a force outside of the musicians, a force pulling the notes from them. *This* is the music's source, not the musicians. This force transforms the potential into the actual. And the actual is actualized, made audible, by the musicians. The force doesn't play the musicians as such, like each plays his music, but it generates a field *extracting* the music from the band members. They are responding to its influence, reacting instantly.

But not instantly instantly. There is the slightest gap between this outside force and the musicians' playing. It is not simultaneous—there is space here, too, the slightest gap between the force and the sounds. I marvel at their response time—it's astonishingly rapid. I wonder if the band, only human, can keep up with the demands of the force. Their letting up, however, is out of the question. The bond is too strong.

I am relating to the music, and it is relating to me. I've never experienced an interaction so abstract and yet so intimate and responsive. I am just as much a channel for the music as those who are making it.

What is this? I ask. *What just happened?*

This is a miracle.

Never before so at ease, I'm also dropping my guard, my wariness, the barrier between me and everything else. This is a barrier that fends off not simply specific things, but all that is "not me." I like how this feels, too. But if I let too much drop away, the sheer intensity of feelings nearly overwhelms me. At the same time, the less I resist, the less I'm overwhelmed. How much can I give up, and how much must I hold on to? Rather than resolve this, I instead suspend myself in the music.

I close my eyes and bask. Cloudlike formations of color coalesce behind my eyelids.

Jim's voice breaks in.

"Looks like you're there."

I stand up, walk over to the row of electronics, and sit in front of the amplifier. I fiddle with the nobs, experimenting. The extra dimension of sound-space appears only at a certain volume. As with the mysterious force that both generates and extracts from the musicians the sounds I hear, the volume doesn't cause what I'm perceiving. Instead, the volume controls a process, the process that affects my relationship with the music. There is not a shadow of a doubt about the existence of this relationship. Likewise, this discovery sends waves of pleasure and chills through me.

I return to my chair, sit down, and look up at the speakers. The purple scintillating air in front of them morphs into clouds that billow out from their cloth grilles. The clouds condense into colored fog that expands outward. Green and red join the purple in rapid-fire shiny bursts. The colors are the brightest and most saturated about eighteen inches in front of the speakers and fade away at six or seven feet. I focus on the brightest densest colors because that's where I feel most intensely the altered state—the sound, colors, and ecstasy.

I let out a sigh that seems to never end.

Reflections

LISTENING TO CANNABIS

Where to start? Let's begin with the notion of starting. That is, this experience initiated what eventually led to my studies of psychedelic drugs. One minute I was my normal high-strung self, critical and impatient with my circumstances and ability to deal with them; ten minutes later, I enter a world of wonder—bursting with indescribable peace and joy, and wave after wave of perceptual revelations. How could this happen?

Chemistry. It was chemistry.

The chemistry that so fascinated me when mixing together and igniting fireworks and bombs was the same science that underlay my inner fireworks that evening. There were chemical changes in my brain that the hashish produced that wrought the extraordinary subjective effects: emotional, sensory, and cognitive. I had to know more. I had to experience more. The events of that evening forever changed my life and set my path. It's a perfect example of "research is me-search."

This episode again highlights the essential role of set and setting. I trusted Jim. He was older, mature, responsible, and took a friendly, humorously solemn paternal approach to introducing me to cannabis. He took his role seriously but not too seriously. He knew what he was talking about as well, and he joined me in an act of stoned camaraderie. He established an atmosphere of safety and respect for the effects of the drug. He also let me have my own trip—an approach that I have always brought to bear in supervising anyone's drug experiences. He didn't impose any expectations or goals, and simply pointed me in the direction of my experience. "Listen to the music" was as structured as he got. And once my intoxication was safely underway, he left me alone while keeping a watchful eye and enjoying his own trip.

His choice of hashish was wise, too. Hashish is a general term for the compressed resin of the cannabis plant. It contains a higher percentage of THC* and other psychoactive cannabinoids and terpenes than marijuana leaves or flowers. This was especially true in the late 1960s and early 1970s, when most marijuana contained about 5 percent THC. This, compared to 60–70 percent THC in high-quality hashish. Jim alluded to how first-time marijuana smokers may not realize they are stoned. "Having to learn to be stoned" was much less likely with such a high-potency preparation.

Typical symptoms of a positive cannabis experience include euphoria, increased aesthetic sensitivity, less restrained modes of thinking and feeling, relaxation, and greater awareness of ongoing experience. This latter effect may relate to decreased short-term memory, as a result of which we find ourselves more aware of "now," instead of experiencing the present as part of a longer-term temporal continuity. We can't recall the past and can't hold the future long enough in our mind to consider it.

It's just these effects that produce negative reactions to the substance. That is, one interprets them in a negative light, as something "not quite right," especially in those of a slightly suspicious bent. For example, cannabis-induced loosening of thinking and feeling may magnify a subtle sense that others are judging them. This may lead to feeling mocked or ridiculed. Such self-conscious anxiety can be intense and is what people mean when they say they "get paranoid" when smoking cannabis.

In contrast to "everyday" cannabis intoxication, my experience that evening was psychedelic, like the effects of LSD or psilocybin. High-potency cannabis and cannabis products can produce psychedelic effects, something we now appreciate as the potency of such substances continues to rise.[1] In this account, a striking psychedelic effect was synesthesia, the blending of two sensory modalities. The most common

---

*Tetrahydrocannabinol, the primary psychoactive compound in cannabis.

form of this phenomenon is mixing of auditory and visual perceptions, as in "seeing sounds." While a predilection to synesthesia may be hereditary, psychedelics produce this symptom rather frequently.[2]

That night also marked the start of my nearly continuous use of cannabis. It was love at first sight; or rather, first puff. A perfect match, a hand fitting into a glove. What other choice did I have?

A relationship this long inevitably has its ups and downs, but on balance, it has been a reliable ally. I find it extremely helpful creatively. I have written nearly every first draft of creative writing under its influence: scientific, biblical, and autobiographical. The endless editing process, on the other hand, more often than not requires sobriety.

Cannabis has helped me be less self-conscious and more socially adept. In fact, I find cannabis to be a kind of "reverse truth serum." When I'm uncertain regarding my appraisal of someone, how I feel around them on cannabis—whether or not they are under the influence—clarifies whether we resonate or not. It acts as a reliable interpersonal barometer.

Cannabis usually improves my stammer; however, this is not a guarantee, as unexpected intrusions into the setting can neutralize this benefit. Physical activity is more pleasurable and meaningful: hiking, gardening, yoga, massage, self- or partner-intimacy.

Depending on my intent, I may smoke before meditating. On one hand, I want to be clearheaded when undertaking simultaneously narrowing and expanding my awareness. On the other hand, if I am seeking relaxation more than clarity, marijuana can magnify these effects. The Tibetan Buddhist teacher Chögyam Trungpa—whose predilection for alcohol resulted in an early death from liver cirrhosis—was on record as advising against marijuana. However, I recall reading a comment he once made that the effects of marijuana were "almost like meditation," and this is why he eschewed it. It was ersatz meditation, a facsimile. I believe he was referring to a meditation practice where one directs awareness to ongoing experience—"being in the moment." One *is* in the moment stoned, but it's because that's all one can hold on to, rather than a deliberate result of effortful practice.

There are drawbacks to regular cannabis use. For example, more people do not use it than do, and it has reduced the pool from which to draw my closest friends. And while there is no association between smoking cannabis alone and an increased risk of lung cancer, the combination of tobacco and cannabis smoking raises the risk to a greater degree than with tobacco alone. "Heavy regular" smoking of solely cannabis, on the other hand, may lead to nonmalignant respiratory ailments such as bronchitis.

The primary negative, however, was a stunting of my emotional growth that began with the onset of regular use. Rather than directly addressing the effects of my difficult childhood and teen years—from which I was just emerging—I found cannabis to be an easier path to address my inner and outer conflicts. I could ignore or forget about them, telling myself "they don't matter."

Drawing on my own experience with cannabis when I reviewed a book for the American Journal of Psychiatry—*Living High* by Herbert Hendin—I suggested that regular marijuana use in Hendin's subjects seemed a compromise between the angst of daily life and the rigors of psychotherapy.[3] This is a position I maintain. Nevertheless, during my four-year course of psychoanalysis, I continued regular but less frequent use of cannabis and other mind-altering substances.

A friend who took a dim view of marijuana once asked me to consider what I could have accomplished if I never had used it.

I answered immediately, "Without marijuana, I wouldn't have accomplished much."

10

FLYING CARPET

AGAIN, KNOCKING AT THE DOOR, this time sharper and more insistent. The sudden intrusion stirs Jim and me from our reveries. I turn down the music, get up, and open the door. Tom, Stu, and Ambrose stand in and around the entrance. Ambrose is in front while the others peer over his shoulders. Suddenly, I can relate to the stoned grin, loose posture, and red puffy eyes. I must look the same.

Ambrose—the resident blue-blood Boston drug Brahmin— wears his Friday night best. Baggy white slightly ripped corduroy pants cinched with a rope belt, cream-colored wrinkled blousy linen shirt—the top two buttons unfastened, and the sleeves frumpily rolled up to his elbows. His wrists sport single thin leather bracelets tied in that special knot, exotic items he picked up during his most recent trek through Nepal. Toes poke through holes in his dirty sneakers.

He grins at me wolfishly. "Hey, man."

"Hey, Ambrose."

"We heard the music and decided to check it out."

He whiffs the air and chuckles quietly and knowingly. After picking up the scent, he breaths in deeply through his nose.

"Wow, man. That smells like hash."

Everyone pours into the room.

"Hey!" Tom booms as he enters.

Stu adds, "You're getting stoned?! Finally, man! Congratulations!"

Ambrose directs a knowing smile toward me, nods a knowing nod, and softly cackles a knowing cackle.

I return to my chair. Tom sits down on the Persian prayer rug lying on the floor nearby. Stu and Ambrose sit on the bed, directly below the speakers, resting their backs against the wall. Jim, the senior resident advisor, takes it all in with a bemused sense of accomplishment. He's confident in and proud of his brood.

Everyone settles in and Jim says, "Gentlemen. I am happy to announce that I have initiated your friend Rick Strassman into the delights of the blonde Lebanese. Do any of you wish to also partake and help him celebrate?"

The light in everyone's puffy eyes reflects the joy we feel for one another. Without saying a word, they welcome me—their inexplicably anxious friend—into this new world. I have never felt so much affection and acceptance, nor so safe. I raise the volume of Santana back to its sweet spot. The air in front of the speakers shimmers purple, full of sound, meaning, and ecstasy.

Stu and Ambrose finish what remains in Jim's pipe. They raise their hands in a mock surrender when he offers to refill it.

Ambrose mumbles, "We smoked two joints right before we got here. I am loaded to the max, man."

Jim, pipe in hand, turns to Tom, "How about you?"

Tom ate dinner at one of the women's dormitories and hasn't smoked tonight. He gets up and approaches Jim, who refills the pipe. Still standing, Tom takes several large lungfuls in quick succession and hands the pipe back.

The fragrant smoke dissipates. Stu and Ambrose slouch on the bed. Jim rests comfortably in his white plastic chair by the desk. Tom returns to sitting cross-legged on the prayer rug. I gaze at and appreciate even more the carpet's beautiful intricacy.

My father travels widely for his job in the defense industry. On a trip to the Middle East, he bought this beautiful piece that decorates my room—thick warm wool, six by eight feet, teeming with intricate pink and gray designs, bounded by a filigreed black border.

I want to hear about Tom's dinner. I climb down from my chair, so I don't have to talk down to him. It's also easier to work the stereo from floor level.

Tom is my best friend at The College. Well over six feet, lanky, with bushy mutton chops and mustache—to cover what he calls his "chipmunk cheeks." He's dramatic, speaks in a loud voice, gestures expressively, and his easy broad smile reveals large white teeth. In spite of, or because of, Tom's larger-than-life figure, I enjoy his company. I don't have to work very hard when he's around. I am having trouble relating to my new college friends, and as a sidekick, I can recede into the background.

Tom also gets my dry sarcastic wit, something he's familiar with growing up near where I did in Southern California, and I appreciate the audience. He's majoring in philosophy, and we enjoy frequent psychological and philosophical conversations. For both of us, there's always more than meets the eye.

Tom has a large penis, of which he is especially proud. He loves it and so do the women, at least the ones I hear about. I listen to his tales of sexual encounters with a mixture of fascination, jealousy, and repugnance. I'm a virgin, and the recent breakup with Dulce only reinforces my feeling like a second-class male.

At the same time, Tom is not as self-confident as he portrays. He rarely boasts of his penis and sex life with our other friends when we're together. Maybe he fears competition with them, or that they'll make fun of his dramatics. With me, there's nothing to worry about.

Tom and I sit side by side on the rug. I stare wide-eyed at the floor as it gradually loses its solidity, becomes opaque, and finally disappears under us. Tom, also gazing down, notices the same thing,

"Do you see that?" I ask, astonished and a little afraid. "It looks like the floor is giving way."

"I know. What the . . . ?" He also sounds alarmed.

The floor vanishes but we remain seated on the carpet. It floats slowly, silently, and smoothly one hundred feet above the ground. And it's daytime, not night.

Tom's eyes widen and take in the view. "Do you see what I'm seeing?"

"Those telephone poles down there?"

"Yeah. And the baseball diamond over to the left?"

We're sharing a hallucination.

We look up at each other, confused, and again look down. We're transfixed by the scene.

Jim stirs and opens his eyes. He sees his two freshmen gesturing toward the floor excitedly. Ambrose and Stu remain immobile and silent, eyes closed, slumped on the bed.

"What are you guys doing?" the resident advisor asks.

I wish to maintain the spell and keep my eyes on the scenery while answering, "Flying over outside somewhere."

"Well, don't fall off. Ha ha."

I nod distractedly, as does Tom. Whatever is going on, our safety is most important. We must stay firmly planted on the rug and not get too close to the edge.

Sometimes I pilot our movement through the air: directing the rug, controlling its speed. Then Tom takes over.

"Hey! Watch out for that building!"

"Oops. Sorry, man."

"Do you see the beach down there?"

"Look at all those umbrellas."

"Lots of families."

"Let's go down and check it out."

We descend, now to about fifty feet high, and make out greater detail—sandals, coolers, picnic baskets, and blankets. We suddenly drop precipitously.

"Oh, shit! We're getting too low."

"Right. Up we go!"

The carpet quickly rises to a safer altitude.

Over woods, mountains, crowds, cars, buildings, we share and confirm myriad details. Another sharp turn and I almost fall off.

"Man, I'm getting tired. This is a lot of work."

The linoleum tile reappears and solidifies under us. We lurch to a stop, making a minor commotion while trying to stay upright.

Ambrose and Stu stir from their torpor. It's getting late and time to go.

Ambrose groans as he stretches his arms and legs out in front of him. Stu shakes his long hair loose and bends his neck from side to side producing audible pops. Jim gets up, arches his back, and leans forward, touching his fingertips to the floor.

He says, "Well, gentlemen. This has been an honor and a pleasure."

He dusts off the front of his jeans, lifts the pipe from my desk, and drops it into his shirt pocket. He repackages the hash in its aluminum foil and carefully stuffs it into one of his pants pockets. He makes his way to the door, opens it, and takes a step into the hall. Turning back toward the room, Jim holds the door open to let my three friends out.

Ambrose and Stu encounter trouble maneuvering past Jim. He's too close to the door. They form a congealed bunch and block the exit. Tom moves toward the doorway but stops abruptly before reaching it, as if he has hit a barrier.

Standing in the middle of the room, I watch my magic carpet mate begin to shrink. His face is panic-stricken, eyes wide, pupils dilated, mouth partly open, unable to speak. A black hole opens under his feet, and he sinks into it.

"Help me!" he finally ekes out.

I look at Ambrose and Stu and say, "Help me, you guys." They grab Tom's left arm while I take hold of his right. They're pulling him up and out, but his right side is too heavy for me alone.

Jim moves in. "What are you guys doing now?"

He looks over at Tom, shrinking and falling into a bottomless pit, and bursts out, "Shit!"

I say to Jim, "Here. Give me a hand."

Finally, the four of us extricate our traumatized fellow.

Tom unsteadily walks to my desk chair, sits, and catches his breath.

"What was that?" someone asks.

"Scared this shit of out of me," Tom answers. "I don't know."

Jim says, "Whatever it was, it's time to clear out." The room quickly empties.

The following morning—Saturday—Tom and Stu decide to pick up albums from Stu's house about an hour away. They ask me to come along and, most important, to drive. Tom and Stu are hung over. I don't think I am, but I'm wrong. We loiter around our group's vehicle—a massive tan-bronze Impala wagon resting alongside the curb in front of the dorm. Ambrose's parents gave the car to him as a going-away present. He drove the beast across the country, filled with furniture, albums, clothes, books, drugs, stereo components, and art.

Ambrose hesitates before giving me the keys, recalling how stoned I was last night. "Hey, man. You ever driven one of these?"

"A station wagon? Yeah." My parents' Chevy Nova wagon all through high school. But this wagon is much bigger.

Ambrose's expression is serious. "The steering is a little loose. And I need new tires."

We walk over to the dirty auto. The tires are nearly bald.

"It'll be fine," I venture uneasily.

We get on to I-10 heading west. A light rain begins to fall, the first precipitation in Southern California in almost six months.

I move over to the far-left lane and reach cruising speed.

"Shit," I mutter. "I can't feel the road under me." I visualize the smooth tires floating on top of the slick road. A thin layer of oil, water, and fine dust greases the asphalt. The vehicle can't get traction, and I struggle with the steering wheel.

The rear of the wagon swings left, nearly hitting the highway divider. The front end compensates, sharply turning right. I steer left, worsening the spin. We complete two slow-motion circles, crossing into the adjacent two lanes. All traffic stops behind us. One car flies off onto the shoulder, a VW bug. Tom screams while Stu yells in anger. "Watch it! What are you doing?!"

The car ends up in its own lane, facing forward. I see traffic stopped behind us and slowly drive over to the shoulder in front of the VW. A police cruiser parks in front of us. The officer steps out, grinning.

"Wow. That was something. Glad there weren't any collisions." He shakes his head in amusement.

There are no injuries either, and the policeman makes short order of his stop. No ticket. He pats me on the back, takes the keys from me, and hands them to Stu. The black and white cruiser drives away and traffic resumes. Stu takes the driver's seat while I look for Tom. Where is he?

Behind us, still parked on the shoulder, stand the VW bug and its driver, a pretty blond woman in her twenties. She's sobbing in distress and Tom's left arm drapes over her shoulders, comforting her. They soon begin dating.

Reflections
A SHARED HALLUCINATION

All of us have had the experience of thinking the same thought that someone else is thinking at the same time. This is especially common among people sharing a close connection, such as friends, relatives, and spouses.

References to telepathic communication on psychedelics appear early in the scientific literature. In 1905, chemical analysis of ayahuasca demonstrated high concentrations of harmine,* and scientists called this compound "telepathine." The name alluded to how those under the influence of this psychedelic brew experienced communication without

---

*A beta-carboline that inhibits the breakdown of DMT in the gut. At that time, however, we did not know the chemical synergy between these two compounds in ayahuasca.

speaking. People shared mental contents while tripping. When those shared contents are thoughts, people think the same thing at the same time. When these contents are "hallucinations," we experience the same visions.

In modern terms, these are known as psi, paranormal, or anomalous phenomena. Their occurrence suggests the nonlocality—the diffuse nature—of consciousness. Rigorous, although outside-of-the-laboratory, experiments support its existence.[1] However, objective laboratory-derived data regarding psi are inconsistent. While reports of psi under the influence of psychedelics are common, psychedelics do not enhance remote viewing in the lab.[2]

The term "hallucination" deserves comment, as Tom and I both were convinced of the reality of our flight. Neither of us considered the experience imaginary. Each was fully engaged, body and mind. When the rug's hallucinated movements were too sudden, our bodies reacted accordingly. At the same time, this shared—hallucinated—reality *coexisted* with this world. It did not replace it.

Tom and I also shared the hallucination of his shrinking and falling into a black pit. However, the others may simply have been pulling him up from the floor after he lost strength in his legs and sat down awkwardly. In either case, Tom's unconscious insecurities, despite his size and prowess, bubbled up in his vulnerable altered state.

Several months later, I witnessed another episode of Tom sinking into the ground. We attended a Rod Stewart concert, with ten thousand others, at the Forum in Inglewood, California. Someone passed us a marijuana cigarette containing PCP—phencyclidine—a ketamine-like drug that causes profound changes in body awareness, even an out-of-body experience. I took a tiny puff and passed it to Tom, who took a much larger inhalation. Within seconds, he began shrinking and descending into the cement floor, and once again required help. This time, familiar with the experience, his request was less terror-stricken and drew little attention as we pulled him out of the hole.

11

RUM AND COKE

MY SOCIAL LIFE IS GOING NOWHERE. After our tepid soiree at the keg party, Terry and my paths rarely cross. She's taken up with the upperclassman she met moments after walking out of my room that evening. He is smug, and she's smitten. There's not much to talk about. Exchanges are brief, shared "Hi, how's it going?"

I struggle with Dulce's absence. It pains my heart. I miss her and it's not fair. If we could only get together and talk. I would prove my superiority over her new boyfriend, an East Indian podiatry student, prized son of her parents' best friends.

That's as far as I can take it. It's what I see, not what's true. What's true is that I don't prioritize her or anyone over attending the best possible college and never living at home again. My views on what she values—kids, marriage, buying a house—are uniformly negative.

The forty miles between The College and her parents' house—where she still lives—become further every week. Our phone conversations are brief and frustrating, with frequent silences. What is there to say? Dulce states clearly enough one day, "We're not dating."

I ask, "Why not?"

*

It's Friday night, and one of the women's dorms is throwing a party. Tom and I walk down to the south end of campus where the low-slung, sprawling building sits. This is the first party I have attended since my beer poisoning at the mountain cabin.

I mutter to myself, as if in prayer, "Be careful with the beer."

As we step into the brightly lit and noisy lobby, I say to Tom, "Man, I am not drinking beer. Don't let me near one."

He chuckles, shakes his head.

No one tells me to avoid the rum and Coke.

I hear the term "mixed drinks." That sounds interesting. I might try one of those.

My parents preferred mixed drinks over beer. Martinis, gin and tonics, margaritas, old-fashioneds. When living at home as a teenager, I enjoyed opening one liquor bottle after the other and breathing in their exotic scents. My parents forbade my drinking, however, and I also had no desire. The rare sips I did take under their watchful eyes were unpleasant, biting my tongue and burning my throat.

Tom offers me a glass filled with what looks like a cola drink.

"What's this?"

"Rum and Coke."

"Yeah. But what is it? Is it like beer?"

Tom grins widely. "Be careful with these. It's easy to overdo it."

I sip from the cup. It's cold and sweeter than anything I have ever tasted. I take a full mouthful and swallow.

"Wow! Is that good!"

I love cola drinks: RC Cola, Dr Pepper, and especially Coke. Not so much Pepsi. I can easily finish off a six-pack at one sitting. I like the taste. And while I don't recognize caffeine's effects—I have yet to drink a cup of coffee—how could I not enjoy all that stimulation? I especially like cola with ice. This rum and Coke, it has ice.

I gulp down the rest of the drink. No problem. It tastes better than beer, that's for sure. I drink two more. I feel good and reassure myself that I won't get sick because it's not a gallon of beer. I can't drink a gallon of these! I become more confident and outgoing, once more enjoying the initial stages of alcohol intoxication.

I see Terry. *There's Terry!* I think drunkenly. I sidle up to her and make small talk. I'll show her how I'm growing up and more together. Casual, sophisticated, soulful. I look deep into her eyes and don't remember anything I say.

I lose track of how many drinks I've had. It *is* alcohol intoxication, but amplified and supercharged. I like it more than beer's watery, boggy, bloated drunkenness. Distilled alcohol—more spirit, less matter.

I think of Dulce. It's not fair.

I set myself down on an overstuffed chair at the end of one of the hallways. Looking around, then down at the ground, I begin to cry.

Where's Dulce? I want to talk to Dulce! Where's Tom? I'll ask Tom to make that happen!

I push myself up from the chair, wander the halls, and find my friend talking with one of the prettiest girls in the dorm. I lay my hand on his shoulder. He turns and sees my puffy tear-streaked face.

He says to the girl, "Just a second, Missy."

He then looks at me, concern on his face.

I say, "Call Dulce for me. I have to talk to her."

He looks more closely, and his closer look is skeptical.

"You're too drunk. You don't want to talk to her now. Like this."

"No," I reply. "I feel great. I know I'm the guy for her. It's clear to me now. I just needed time away from her to decide."

I'm unsteady and lean against the wall. My speech is slurred, and I can't feel my mouth too well.

"Um," Tom hesitates.

"It's Friday night! Dulce and I ought to be together. At the movies! Then pie and milk afterward!" Or, a burger at Hamburger Hamlet.

It makes perfect sense to demand to speak with her. I love her. Doesn't our being voted the cutest couple in our graduating class count for anything?

Tom asks, "Are you sure?"

"Damn straight!" I say. This is an expression I've learned recently, and never felt its truth more than I do at this moment.

Tom's drunk, too. We—two drunk adolescents—stagger to a payphone down the hall. Two chairs, one on either side, are empty. No one's on the girls' dorm phone tonight. We sit and empty our pockets of change, laying a pile of coins on a low-lying table below the phone.

I make a rough calculation. "There's enough for at least a half-hour."

I stand up to engage the phone and make the call, but the swaying floor forces me back down. I land on the chair with a thud.

Despite all this, I feel imperious, almost royal in my authority. I've decided it's below me to make the call myself. I feel a confident power over Tom and will soon exert it over Dulce. No longer am I Tom's self-effacing sidekick. Nor someone for Dulce to kick around.

I say, "She's my woman. Not some Indian podiatry student's."

I tear off a corner of a page from the nearby phonebook, write her number on it, and hand it to Tom.

"Call her and tell her I want to talk with her."

Tom has a way with women; he'll convince her as he convinces other women, applying that skill on my behalf. And my authority over my friend will prevent Dulce from falling for him while they speak. After all, he's just my helper, *my* sidekick.

"I want to talk to her!" I repeat, this time stronger.

Tom fumbles with the phone.

Dulce's mother answers. Tom mumbles and stammers his way through a brief explanation. He puts his hand over the mouthpiece, turns away from the payphone, and looks at me.

In a loud whisper, "It's her mother. She says Dulce's isn't home."

I moan, "She *HAS* to be home! It's me calling! Rick! Why isn't she home?"

Is she really on a date with that other guy? How could that be?

I slide off the chair in slow motion and land gently on the floor, sitting at an angle, lopsided. Tom removes his hand from the mouthpiece and resumes speaking, but I can't make out his words.

He looks down at me splayed on the floor. "Her mother says you shouldn't be calling."

"Does she know it's me? Rick?"

I struggle to my feet, wobble to the phone, and grab the handset. I look at it uncertainly—angry, afraid, sad, defeated.

I slur into the phone, "What do you mean, 'I shouldn't be calling'? Is she out with Rahul? Tell me!"

Dulce's mother's voice is a million miles away. In a cave. Underwater. On the other side of the planet. From a painful incomprehensibly distant past.

"Have you been drinking? You shouldn't be calling if you've been drinking."

"Damn straight I've been drinking. Where's Dulce? Is she out with Rahul? Why is she doing this to me?!"

She hangs up.

I look at the phone, then at Tom. "She hung up! The cunt!" That's another word that I had heard but rarely used in high school. Now that I'm a college man, I can say it whenever I want.

"Try again!" I cry.

"Are you sure?"

Tom makes two more attempts. The first ends after his short plea on my behalf. The second ends as soon as he identifies himself.

I need fresh air. Holding tightly onto the banister, I carefully pick my way down the stairs to the lobby, push open the dormitory doors, walk across the lawn, and halt on the sidewalk. Head bowed, leaning over, hands on knees.

I'm not feeling well. At all.

More precisely, I've lost, failed. Dulce is no longer my girlfriend.

I stagger across the thin strip of grass between the sidewalk and the curb. I sit on the curb, my feet in the gutter, little puddles on either side of me. It's a cool damp autumn night.

I have always liked gutters, feeling a rare affinity with them. As a child on the infrequent rainy days in Los Angeles, I liked to put on my galoshes, take a large broom, and step into the gutter. Once positioned, I ran while pushing the broom in front of me. This cleared away any obstructions slowing the flow of water—collections of dirt, gravel, leaves, and branches—toward the storm drain. From there, the water poured into a massive cement-lined wash behind our house. It was fun and I felt helpful, assisting in the water's cleaning action. Storms were brief, and I applied myself hurriedly to the big job. When it was all over, the gutter in front of my and my neighbor's house was so clean! In fact, one day, Mr. Herz came out during the rain and said to me, "Good job, Rick!"

Sitting with my feet in the gutter this evening, I realize they are practical and essential. As I look at this particular gutter more carefully, a new insight comes to me, deep with portent: gutters provide a distinct line of separation, a demarcation, between what's above the curb and what's below it.

I lean over, sit down in the gutter, and settle into its puddles. Then, I wonder if I will be more comfortable lying down. Prone I go. It's dark, quiet, wet, and secluded. I'm by myself, alone, safe. Things are contained and manageable. I'm far from phone calls, Dulce, her mother, and the new boyfriend. All are in that big bright noisy building across the lawn. All that is there. And I'm here. I sigh in contentment. The gutter's cement unstintingly supports me.

I feel something grab my right shoulder.

Tom slurs, "What are you doing, man? Are you lying in the gutter? Get up and get out of there. You'll get sick."

He awkwardly helps me to my feet, brushes off twigs and leaves stuck to the front and side of my shirt and pants. My clothes are wet and muddy, as is the side of my face.

I grab Tom by the arms, look at him uncertainly, and say, "I need to talk to Dulce. Call her for me!"

"We tried, man. Her mom's not going to let you talk to her, even if she's there. And it doesn't sound like she is. We need to get you back to your room."

Reflections

ALCOHOL'S MAUDLIN SIDE

Repeated rapid drinking of alcohol maintains its stimulant-like effects. In "Kittens," I describe using this confidence-enhancing property of the drug to prove my masculine qua masculine credentials among my new peers. I was one of the guys and could hold my own. However, the more you drink, the more toxicity accumulates. That toxicity forced an end to my beer chugging at the cabin party and led to the nightmarish postscript in bed with the cats.

In this chapter, I describe a more variable and labile course of alcohol intoxication from rapid intake in the setting of breaking up with my first true love. The evening began with increased confidence interacting with Terry—a girl in whose presence I felt markedly inept. Then came deep sadness reflecting upon my loss of Dulce. Taking the exaggeratedly dominant role with Tom did not have the desired effect, and my altered state devolved into one of profound resignation. Now, stuporous, I nostalgically reminisced about happier times playing in the gutter as a young child. The symbolic meaning of the curb as a demarcation extended beyond simply separating the noisy commotion of the dormitory party and the quiet street. It also represented the painful, undeniable boundary between life with and without Dulce, between my past and my present.

This lability of the alcohol-induced altered state is one of its most consistent features. When training residents and medical students, I used to make a point of demonstrating this symptom in drunk emergency room patients who were as impaired as I was in this chapter. When interviewing someone in such a condition, powerful emotions erupt in them with minimal prompting, emotions that the clinician can steer surprisingly easily between extremes. At the same time, intoxicated people don't realize how radically different are their rapidly shifting mood states. Talk about happy things, and they will smile and laugh in an animated manner. Quickly shift to sad ones, and quickly the tears began to flow. It is best to avoid topics that will anger such people, as they may become violent just as suddenly. This loss of short-term memory combined with hyperemotionality and diminished self-control is something one also sees in dementias like Alzheimer's disease.

12

LSD CHICKEN

Tom and I make our way to Ambrose and Stu's room, readying for a party at Melanie's across campus.

Before meeting Ambrose, I did not know about trust funds. I soon learn that his keeps him well-stocked with beer, marijuana, psychedelics, and amphetamines for him and his friends, as well as gas for his car. Sales of shares from one particular company maintain his assets' health. It's a business founded by one of his ancestors, a signatory of the Declaration of Independence. Ambrose checks the corporation's stock price daily in the *Wall Street Journal*, a newspaper that arrives every morning in front of his door, and whose print communicating share values is amazingly small. Share prices determine his mood for the day.

Ambrose's stereo is also in a class by itself, producing an otherworldly quality of sound. Full, rich, never-distorted bass from the midsize maximum-sound AR-3A speakers. And the high notes are strangely perfect, an effect Ambrose masters through an exotic combination of treble and midrange adjustments on a massive tube amplifier. Stu and he are roommates by luck of the draw—one played basketball in a nearby high school, the Bostonian played lacrosse. Their two-compartment room quickly becomes our clique's hub of music, drugs, and beer.

Ambrose and I grow to like each other, as we share a far-ranging curiosity about the exotic nature of the world, one that books help

113

sate. I love looking through his library: Hermann Hesse, Jack Kerouac, Henry David Thoreau, Gandhi, coffee table books full of religious art. Ambrose knows about Asia, stirring within me an almost instinctual interest in the East. The summer before college, he trekked through the Himalayas, while studying its Buddhism and Indigenous music. His album collection's range is astonishingly vast: Bach, British blues, African folk, rock and roll, Ravi Shankar. Conversant in socialism, communism, world banking, and New England politics, he shares his knowledge sparingly, in small portions. It's delivered with a conspiratorial, world-weary, cynical sense of irony.

Ambrose's chronically tousled medium length blonde hair is barely distinguishable from his pale skin. He is constantly stoned, and no one knows what he's doing in school—what classes he's taking, who his teachers are, or his academic interests. Women usually don't notice him, but he's quick to remind us that his New England girlfriend is joining him next year and they will live together off-campus.

However, I learn that our friendship goes only so far. There's an unspoken unbridgeable gap separating us. Maybe it is Ambrose's wealth, or my Jewishness. I know I can only ask so many questions before it feels like intruding, stepping over an invisible line. We will never tread on the same ground. I feel like the help, a taint of isolation and aridity constraining and contaminating our relationship.

One afternoon, I move the knobs of Ambrose's amp to see what happens. His temper flares.

"Get your hands off the amp!" he barks and busies himself with reestablishing the perfect combination of settings.

It's the only time I ever see Ambrose angry.

Ambrose's East Coast sweetheart had introduced him to her friends attending one of the two girls' schools within walking distance of The College. They are fun, smart, and attractive. There's a party tonight at one of the girls' dorms. Melanie.

I look forward to the event, but my enthusiasm comes up against feeling as if I don't really fit in. I am less socially adept, with a less refined pedigree. A different social stratum. Again, I wonder if it's because no one in our group besides me is Jewish. I am the token *yid*.

The last to arrive at our pre-party party is Woody, with whom I had earlier engaged in the beer-chugging contest I describe in "Kittens." He bounds in excitedly.

Woody is a strapping loose-jointed kid from Washington, D.C. He looks and sounds like a hayseed, but is as intelligent as any of our friends, majoring in and relishing philosophy. He's well over six feet, and also, like Tom and Stu, is on the basketball team. He loves the railroad, rarely appearing anywhere not wearing his engineer overalls and cap. His career in trains is already set, having worked for them the previous summer, and with a guaranteed job after graduating. He's on his way to a lifelong relationship with the railroad.

Too worked up to sit down, he bursts out, "Hey! You know what?"

"No. What?"

"Guess!"

Someone says in mock hopefulness, "You're pregnant?"

"Fuck you!"

We return to our stoned conversation, listening to music and getting high, and lose interest in our deceptively competent colleague. Fleetwood Mac's *Then Play On*—their most psychedelic album—steers everyone's experience. The river of sound quietly pours into the room. I feel the bass notes, even at low volume.

Woody pretends we've hurt his feelings. "Well, then, I'm not sharing any of the acid I just got."

The four of us do a double take, and Woody grins more broadly.

Acid? Does he mean LSD?

Ambrose, our drug maven, doesn't miss a beat. He asks, "What kind, man?"

Satisfied he's getting the attention he deserves, Woody answers, "Windowpane, man."*

---

*A thin sheet of nearly transparent gelatin impregnated with LSD and cut into small squares.

Ambrose nods approvingly, his eyes sparkle, a wide wolfish smile spreads over his face. His teeth really are perfect. He closes his eyes, leans and bends his head forward, and plays the air drums rapidly, keeping pace with Mick Fleetwood's pounding rhythms. This usually means he's *very* happy. He opens his eyes and looks up at Woody.

"Maaaaaan," he whispers in loud hushed tones. "Windowpane."

Woody beams. "I knew you'd be jazzed."

"I haven't seen any of that since I trekked through Afghanistan." Nostalgia and anticipation seep into Ambrose's voice.

"What's windowpane, oh Ambrose, mighty guru?" Stu asks in feigned awe.

"Man. It is the purest."*

He points to a wall hanging of intricate design, fine brushwork, and startling imagery of a seated Buddha figure surrounded by flames.

"I bought that thangka† in Afghanistan after staring all day at the Himalayas on windowpane." His voice drifts off mysteriously. I try conjuring the vision but can't.

Tom says, "Hey, man. I've never seen the Himalayas."

Ambrose's mind returns to the room. "The heavens split open. You'll see God."

He laughs, adding, "But you'll find out there is no God." More laughing.

Woody reasserts himself. "Shit, man. Cut the crap." He's still standing. "This just came in the mail. My friends say it's clean, pure, and strong, really a great trip. No cramping, and you can still fuck on it!"

An approving murmur passes through the group. My own brow furrows. Mixing LSD with losing my virginity is a heady mix.

Ambrose says slowly, drawing out every word, "This . . . is . . . the . . . best . . . LSD."

---

*Not necessarily. Purity refers to LSD alone being the active ingredient. A "carrier," in the case of "pure LSD," is an inert substance such as gelatin or milk powder that contains the LSD. An "adulterant" is an added substance without subjective effects—such as food coloring—or with psychoactive properties, like amphetamine or PCP.
†A wall hanging or painting of Buddhist iconography.

I reflect: Jim got me high on blonde Lebanese hash. That was the best, too. Maybe The College is working out after all, but not how I expected.

"I've never taken LSD," I volunteer. I don't want to add I've never had sex. "No Himalayas, either."

Ambrose grins and reassures me, "This is *the* best LSD to start with."

Woody sits on a chair next to the bed where Stu and I are sitting while drinking Coors. He carefully pulls individual doses out of a little envelope.

"Shit, man. I needed to find an X-Acto knife to divide up these babies. They are really small."

He hands each of us a tiny quarter-inch gelatin square.

I look down at the shiny glistening flake. Despite the heavy black curtains in Ambrose and Stu's cave, a few errant photons sneak in and reflect on the tiny objects beautifully, like mica. I stare in puzzled wonder.

Tom, noticing my expression, offers, "You'll be among friends. And I will keep an eye on you."

It's true. He is the only person I feel I can rely on. He proved that after recently pulling me out of the gutter when I was drunk, bewailing the end of my relationship with Dulce, which I describe in "Rum and Coke." If I need support on LSD, I'll turn to Tom. Feeling reassured, I gaze at the dose of LSD on my palm.

No one other than Ambrose is familiar with this form of acid, but his mystical endorsement and Woody's enthusiasm are enough. Each of us carefully places his dose of windowpane onto his tongue.

I feel it on the middle of my tongue, its weight almost imperceptible. Tom lifts up his can of Coors, "Down the hatch!"

"L'chaim!"* Ambrose declaims, eyes twinkling in my direction. I wonder if he's positively acknowledging my Jewishness.

We wash down the already dissolving LSD with our beer in a communal gulp.

Stu says, "I don't taste anything. Are you supposed to?"

---

*"To life!" A traditional Jewish toast.

Ambrose says, "No, man. Odorless, tasteless, colorless. Pure LSD." He lets out a long, satisfied sigh.

We walk downstairs and mill around in front of The Dorm, get our bearings, and set out on the twenty-minute walk to the girls' college. A cloud of Tom's Old Spice trails us for the first several dozen yards. He nearly pours it onto his face and neck before meeting any women. Thankfully, it soon dissipates.

I'm not feeling anything as we meander through a maze of college buildings en route. It's unusually cold and cloudy, with snow expected in the mountains. The previous day had been a jewel, the winds having cleared the air pollution that regularly hangs over our urban valley. In a rare display, the nearby peaks, some over ten thousand feet tall, were visible. Today, heavy leaden clouds hide them.

Suddenly, we arrive at the girls' dorm and bumble our way up a flight of stairs to their suite. The girls meet the boys at the door and let us in.

"Hey. Hey. You're here!" Melanie greets everyone warmly, sweetly, seductively, and cheerily. I recognize Donna her roommate, but not the others. They too are cute, giggle readily, and each is drinking a beer—Michelob. One step up from our Coors.

Melanie is the daughter of an inordinately wealthy cold cuts magnate from the Midwest. Everything about Melanie is the finest. I sense it without knowing it. Without pretense, she takes the opportunity to show us some of her objects in the common room.

"This is the table from France we brought back from one of our trips when I was kid. It used to be next to my bed. It's where I kept all my photos and mementos growing up. I had to have it here!"

I lower myself onto a chair next to the little side table. It glows in the dim light. I compare it to my parents' furniture, which had always seemed special, but Melanie's is a privileged piece. It's an encounter with a new category of thing. Rare, valuable, old. I wonder if this is an antique and assay its solidity with a gentle nudge.

Melanie laughs at my gesture, recognizing the high rank such a piece bestows on her, as well as my ignorance about such things' quality. Its excellence isn't garish, though; you need to examine it closely.

Melanie knows she's wealthy and pampered. It makes her happy. She loves her life, no one begrudges her, and she lords it over no one.

I feel dimmed in her presence. Her wealth, status, and embeddedness in the upper class are alien. I'm jealous, but that is only part of it. There's also insecurity. Below that, something deeper: fear. Her last name, Gunther—German if there ever were one. A tingle of Nazi horror buzzes nearly imperceptibly. At best, I'm an outsider—even a lamb not so long ago ready for slaughter—standing behind an invisible barbed-wire fence.

We walk into Melanie's bedroom—a cleaner, better-lit, and tidier version of Ambrose's. A Jimi Hendrix poster on one wall, Jim Morrison and The Doors on another. A lava lamp burbling happily in the corner next to a stick of burning incense. The tie-dye draperies are open and the last rays of light stream in. The Beatles play on her stereo—more than competent equipment, but nothing like Ambrose's.

I draw near the overhead bookshelves to examine what's resting on them. Textbooks: English, American history, sociology, college algebra. Nothing that serious, at least to my eye. What's more striking are the shiny softcover catalogs from her father's cold cut company. At least a dozen.

I say, "Man, that's a lot of catalogs." Not, "That's a lot of cold cuts." I must be careful not to mock Ms. Gunther and her status.

Melanie stands next to me and says, "I know. I'm going to inherit the business when my dad retires. I ought to learn what they sell." She laughs.

Donna the roommate, another East Coast teenager, joins us. I smile at her and she returns a warm one.

Donna says, "She'll be one of the richest women in America. Isn't that right, Melanie?"

Melanie smiles slightly sheepishly and doesn't deny it. I look around, searching for something or somewhere allowing me to withdraw.

The smell of food wafts in through another door. I follow the scent into a small room, beyond which I see Donna's bedroom.

Against one wall is a picnic table overflowing with tonight's meal. The most prominent item, fried chicken, sits in a mammoth pile on a serving platter. "Mt. Chicken," I whisper to myself. Surrounding the mound are side dish foothills of coleslaw, potato salad, Jell-O, bread rolls, and salad. A beer- and soda-filled cooler packed with ice rests comfortably under the table.

Mt. Chicken?

Maybe I am feeling the LSD.

I peer into Donna's room and see no one there. Suddenly I hear her voice behind me as she enters. I quickly turn away from her and rejoin the crowd in the common area.

I ask Tom, "Are you feeling anything?"

A big grin, not a smile, spreads over the lower half of my friend's face. His pupils are big and very black. I don't remember that being part of the hashish high.

Tom straightens his right arm in front of him and extends his wrist, fingers facing upward and spread, as if he's signaling "stop." He examines the back of his hand, bringing it close to his face.

"Look at your hands," he instructs. "Look at your hands." Fascination and amused delight in his voice.

I look at the back of my left hand.

Its skin is mottled. Pulsating colored blotches move along its wrinkled, aged surface. The strange shiny and bruised shapes blend, shift, and morph in slow motion, reminding me of oil on water in sunlight. The tendons squirm wormlike when I extend my fingers. Glowing fleshy worms, made of animated light. I laugh. It's comical, beautiful, and slightly horrifying.

Tom says, "Weird, huh?" He starts laughing. His eyes shoot sparks.

I laugh, too. Not as much because of how my hand looks, but because Tom laughs. And laughing itself is funny, a funny thing that makes me laugh.

Woody comes up to us. "Are you guys looking at your hands?" He pauses for effect. "Or what?"

We look at him but say nothing. He laughs. "You must be on acid. Ha ha."

I ask him, "Do your hands look weird?"

"Shit, yeah, man," he laughs.

I wonder if Woody is laughing at his hands because of how they look. Or is it because he's looking at his hands, which itself is funny?

My laughter bubbles up from inside of me, deep in my abdomen. I am amazed at its effortlessness. I've never laughed like this before. But what is that deep abdominal feeling, what is its source?

It's a tense pressure head driving the laughter upward and outward. An accelerating tension, a force moving rapidly within me. Or, is it moving toward me? It's physical, strong, and exciting, an enormous sense of anticipation, an anticipation that expands in all directions. A premonition of . . . what? Of *everything*: things I am about to see, hear, feel, think, and do. But *what* specifically am I anticipating? Something's about to happen. Or, it already is. It's unrelated to anything objective— simply the feeling of excited expectation. I can't find its object, its target; there's nothing to direct my attention toward, certainly nothing that merits such a strong drive.

I'm familiar with excited anticipation and the tension it creates: Before a test, meeting someone important, the starter's gun readying for the 100-yard dash. But now, the feeling's strength and diffuse nature threatens to overwhelm me. Laughing releases the pressure. And the enormity of the pressure is itself somehow hilarious, and feeds back on my laughing. Hilarity pushes out from inside me everywhere I turn.

Laughing is a compromise. Whatever is about to happen could be good, in which case it would be the best. Or bad, in which case it would be the worst. It feels like both. Ecstasy just slightly outweighs terror, but only slightly.

Stepping back from my reverie, I am startled to see Woody, Tom, and Ambrose looking at me with humorous curiosity.

Ambrose is leering wolflike. He looks like a wolf. A long mane of pale hair, sharp features, long nose. A mouth full of straight white shiny sharp teeth. I laugh. Ambrose's face is mottled just like my hands, but even more striking because his white skin accentuates the swirling, deeply saturated colors. His face begins growing blonde hair. I blink to clear my vision, suddenly unsure whether I'm wearing my contact lenses. Are my eyes dry or tearing?

Mesmerized, I say, "Man, have you seen your skin? It's really weird. Your face."

Ambrose chuckles. "I know. Do you see a wolf?"

Eyes wide, pupils even wider, I ask, "How did you know?"

"That's the acid, man."

I look around for something to drink. Or eat. Should I smoke marijuana? Or sit down? Or be by myself? Or talk to somebody? I can't decide.

Here are the chatting girls. I enjoy looking at them. I'm intrigued by the sound of their voices; sounds I feel entering my ears. However, their speech is unintelligible, gibberish. Whatever they're saying, I know their happiness relates to the words they share. Or maybe because of something else.

Realizing the possibility that they are happy for no reason leads me to wonder if they have no brains. The giggling girls sound like chickens. Chickens have no brains, or barely any. And there's chicken to eat, piles of it, in the other room. I laugh.

The other young men come up to the young women. They all engage in conversation. Is this some kind of mating ritual? I wonder. It could be. I laugh at the idea, or at its reality playing out in front of me.

My social skills among my new group of peers, even when straight, feel marginal. I've never had sex and all of my friends here have. I'm out of everyone's league. One day. But now, I don't know the rules, can't rely on experience, and there's no one to teach me at this moment. I realize my laughing at everything I see or think might distance me even further. It's a simple decision to slip into the middle room, alone with the food and beer. I sit on the couch that doubles as a bed pressed against the near wall. I look over at the table. And laugh. The girls in Melanie's room are chickens. And we are eating chicken.

One of the girls, Frieda, enters. She's a dancer. Beautiful, muscular, and looking for food. I look over at her from my perch on the couch, and then at the table.

Noticing me, she smiles warmly—or, is it oddly?—and asks, "Hey, Rick. How's it going?"

I start laughing, first in response to her question, and then in response to my laughing.

I wonder, What's so funny? I've got no explanation. Except that the LSD is responsible. Somehow. The battle between ecstasy and terror resolves, for now, in everything being funny. My entire being, body and mind, under the influence of something new, or something newly discovered. I am simply laughter and can only laugh.

This paroxysm of hilarity passes, and I ask, "Are you going to eat chicken?" I start laughing again.

"Yeah. It looks good. I'm really hungry, too!"

I'm incredulous. "You're going to *eat* that chicken?"

Frieda looks at me more closely, first puzzled, then, recognizing the signs, more knowingly. She returns to the table, picks up a paper plate, and grabs a breast and other chicken parts.

"You know, don't you, that that's chicken?" I burst out laughing again. "You do realize that, don't you?"

Undeterred, digging through the piles of fried meat, Frieda murmurs distractedly, "Right, Rick. Chicken. What's so funny about chicken?"

I laugh so hard I lose some urine. I start sliding off the couch and catch myself, just barely.

I reply, loudly, "'What's so funny about chicken?'! Is that what you said?!" Now, everything is laughing—my toes, knees, belly, chest, head, especially my face. Tears run down my cheeks. I can't stop smiling. It almost hurts. It reminds me of the night smoking hash, wondering if my face could contain the entirety of the smile, employing muscles I'd never used before.

She says, "Yes. I like chicken." She finishes gathering her food, looks over her left shoulder at me as she makes her way back into Melanie's room. She's relieved that I don't fall off the bed and gives me a good-natured wave.

Catching my breath, I think: Now, that was odd. What *is* so funny about chicken?

I'm alone again and look around the room. I know the walls are white, but rainbow hues pulsate from them, keeping time with the music next door. I notice something about the sound. There's a background noise almost as loud as the music. It's not a ringing in my ears; rather, there's a warping, a distortion of auditory space.

At that moment, I understand. The distortion reflects the laws of nature regulating and controlling sound, allowing it to manifest, to become audible. Underlying or within the notes, that background noise is the sound of those laws in action. The laws of nature, the laws of sound formation, have their own sound—a sound I simultaneously perceive just as clearly as the music itself.

Woody comes in and smiles broadly at me. I look at him and laugh. In normal reality, Woody is as tall as Tom, and thinner. Now he looks like a stick figure, even taller and skinnier, and so gangly and loose-jointed that simply standing upright seems to require effort. And his ears. They stick out hilariously from his head. I can't laugh at Woody; I know that much. I quiet myself. But the urge to laugh, the feeling of unbearable pressure, requires release, a subjective experience. Suppressing it, the balance tips in the direction of fear.

Who *is* this person Woody? And more pressing, is he mocking me? Is my alienness—my lack of fitting in, the absence of a common bond or shared nature—that obvious? I feel unsafe and my body becomes lighter. I want to flee. But I can barely move.

I wonder, Am I going to explode? I lean back against the wall, desperate for support. It's hard to breathe, and I must make a conscious effort. If I forget, will I stop breathing?

Without waiting to find out, Woody's voice booms. "Pretty great acid, huh?"

At first, I can't answer. My lips are numb. Then, I feel my mouth move and speech comes out. "I don't know. I've never taken acid before."

"Oh, right," Woody says. "What do you think?"

I start breathing normally again.

"I like it. I'm laughing a lot."

"Cool, man. Cool. That's great. I'm happy for you."

I relax. Woody goes over to the food table. I watch with awe as he fills his plate with chicken and fixings. Before ducking out of the room, he nods at me sprawled on the bed.

"Have a good trip, man."

Reflections
THE KNIFE-EDGE OF UNBRIDLED HILARITY

LSD, or lysergic acid diethylamide-25, is a psychedelic drug, one of the "classical psychedelics." Other members of this group are (1) DMT, which the mammalian brain produces, occurs in hundreds of plants, and is the visionary ingredient in the Amazonian brew ayahuasca; (2) psilocybin, from "magic mushrooms"; and (3) mescaline, which occurs in the peyote cactus—the Native American Church sacrament—as well as the San Pedro cactus.

Psychedelics differ from other psychoactive substances in their affecting every component of consciousness. This contrasts with other classes of drugs like stimulants and depressants that modify fewer mental functions. For example, amphetamine, a stimulant, increases energy, mood, and attention; while sedative-depressants like benzodiazepine antianxiety/sleeping medications impair concentration and reduce anxiety. Psychedelics, on the other hand, exert effects on all components of subjective experience: mood, thinking, perception, body awareness, sense of self, and willpower. We can also differentiate these drug classes pharmacologically. Psychedelics activate serotonin receptors—specifically the 2A subtype—while stimulants modify dopamine function, and sedative-depressants affect the activity of GABA, or gamma amino butyric acid.

While my experience several months earlier with hashish partook of psychedelic qualities, this first experience with LSD was more compelling, strange, paradoxical, contradictory, fascinating, and complex.

It is no exaggeration when people on a full dose of a psychedelic drug say that they feel like eating, vomiting, shitting, pissing, laughing, and crying all at the same time. One could add more to this list with little effort.

Psychedelics' stimulation of serotonin receptors on individual neurons in the brain initiates a cascade of effects on brain circuitry. These circuits consist of various centers whose functional relationships regulate particular mental functions. We know, for example, that psychedelics decrease functional connectivity within the default mode network (DMN), a collection of neural hubs whose coordinated activity mediates our sense of self. In other words, psychedelics loosen our fixed sense of who we are. At the same time, control by the DMN over "lower brain centers"—such as those subserving emotional, memory, and sensory functions—weakens, and this allows entry of information into consciousness from normally suppressed brain centers.

While these new scientific findings are impressive, they simply confirm what careful introspection reveals when we are under the influence of a psychedelic drug. If the subjective experience were different, we would similarly characterize our experience's biological underpinnings using the same technology.

Psychedelics work on our individual mind, our personal psychology, our unique psyche. We call them "psychedelic" for that reason. They are "mind-manifesting" or "mind-disclosing," nonspecific amplifiers of more or less conscious material already residing in our mind.

My first LSD trip exemplifies these mind-disclosing properties, their magnifying preexisting mental contents. A slightly humorous assessment of the pile of fried chicken—and associating the chicken with the girls' chattering—exploded into volcanic hilarity. The drug caused my mind to convert Ambrose's wolfish features into full-blown facial metamorphosis. My social awkwardness became nearly paralyzing fear alternating with inappropriate laughter around others.

We see again the importance of a supportive environment; that is, a proper setting. The outcome of my experience became increasingly uncertain as it progressed. Would it be a "good trip" or a "bad trip"? Here, Woody's reaction to my state was the crucial turning point. He was warm, supportive, empathic, and encouraging. It was the perfect response that set my mind at ease and allowed the rest of the trip to unfold without incident.

13

SNOW CULVERT

I LIKE HOW I FEEL ON LSD and look forward to taking it again. The wait isn't long. My childhood friend Sam, who recently transferred to one of the other colleges within the multi-college complex, calls on a Friday afternoon, only weeks after my first acid trip at Melanie's party.

There's excitement in his voice as he says, "Let's go hiking tomorrow in the foothills. I've got some Orange Barrel LSD."*

"What's that?"

"Tiny Day-Glo orange tablets. I guess that's where it gets its name. Really small. Spencer and Rusty tried it. They loved it."

"What's it like?"

"Strong. Visual."

"When do you want to come by?"

"How's 8:00 a.m.? It's supposed to snow tomorrow up there. Let's get an early start."

I hang up, pad down the hall, and knock on Ambrose and Stu's door.

Ambrose answers, stoned, eyes barely visible. Stu's sitting on the bed, listing, just as stoned, drinking a Coors.

---

*Most likely Orange Sunshine. Northern California chemists made tens of millions of doses of this LSD in the late 1960s. Doses were high, 300–800 micrograms, compared to 75–100 micrograms in a typical present-day dose.

Letting myself in, I ask Ambrose, "Have you heard of Orange Barrel LSD?"

Ambrose's eyes widen but remain slits.

"Do you have Orange Barrels?"

"My friend does. We're going to take it tomorrow and hike."

"Your friend has Orange Barrels?" Ambrose repeats. He becomes slightly more animated. What *doesn't* Ambrose know about drugs?

"See if you can get me some. I love Orange Barrels. It's really visual."

"That's what I hear. "

Knowingly cackling, eyes squinting, wolfish, quietly but intensely nodding his head up and down. He says, "See you later . . . Maybe at dinner. Ha ha."

Saturday morning at The College is cold and cloudy, and it smells like rain. Sam drives Spencer's pickup to The Dorm. I toss my duffel bag into the truck's bed, open the passenger side door, and climb in. Sam's bag sits up against his right leg on the seat.

He says, "Bring your bag inside. It's going to get wet."

I comply and reenter the cab, which is packed but comfortable.

We sit quietly while the engine idles. The heater, running at low speed, keeps us warm. We've each got a change of clothes, water, and sandwiches. We are at ease: healthy, happy, and young. Ready for adventure.

Sam says, "It's about a half-hour to where we're going—a wide open wash, dry riverbed, down from the road." He adds, "The snow may get heavy."

This should be fun, I think—snow on LSD.

"If we take the acid now, we'll be coming on just as we start walking."

He digs into his shirt pocket and draws out a tiny silver pill case. Flipping open the lid reveals two tiny Day-Glo orange barrel-shaped tablets. They take up almost no space, about three millimeters in both diameter and height.

"Wow, those are small," I say. The windowpane tabs of LSD the other day were tiny, but I've never seen pills this size.

Sam opens his mouth and places one of the Orange Barrels on the middle of his tongue. He turns and looks at me, mouth open, tongue extended, showing how it's done. He pulls a canteen from his bag.

"Down the hatch," he says with a laugh. He washes it down.

He hands me the other tablet and the canteen. I deposit the minuscule orange pill on my tongue and feel its edges. It has neither weight nor taste. I swallow mine with a gulp of water.

The drive is uneventful, as the two-lane state highway is nearly deserted. A light snow is falling as Sam slows the truck, makes a careful U-turn, and parks on a solid wide dirt pullout, facing downhill. We each check our watches. It's 9:00 a.m.

Sam says, "How about we return to the truck by three thirty or four? We'll be back on campus by four or four thirty."

"Great." I will arrive just before dinner starts.

It's snowing harder as we don our bulky down jackets. I shiver—from the cold or the first intimations of the acid, I'm not sure. The leading edge of the storm passes over, and we take in the sunrays cutting through the lowering clouds. Bright light briefly illuminates the damp high desert. The smell of sage wafts around us in the briskly swirling breezes.

My legs are rubbery as we head out from the truck. We drop down the highway embarkment onto a wide level plain, rocky and punctuated by sparse twiggy brush. Further ahead, a jeep road parallels the wash, a dry creek bed. We walk along the primitive road, glancing down at the arroyo's floor, about ten feet below, watching for water.

"We don't want to be swept away by a flash flood," Sam chuckles.

"Me, neither," I agree, although I've never seen one. I laugh, too, and remember how much I laughed on my first LSD trip. It is a strange bubbling laughter.

I hope I can keep walking and not laugh so hard. I don't want to lose control. This is different than lying on a bed, watching my friends eat chicken. A similar brush with catatonia out here would be dangerous. This is a different environment, more physical than mental.

As if reading my mind, Sam says, "Try this. Think about walking while you're walking. Nothing else."

I do so and slow to a halt. Sam laughs.

"See?"

We aren't sure what we see, but both of us see it. And it's funny.

Once I begin moving, I grit my teeth and push my body harder. I feel stronger. I'm not thinking *about* how I feel; rather, it is *that* I feel myself moving through space. Thinking about it withdraws energy from attending to it.

Sam has never been a robust hiker, having dedicated his childhood and adolescence to competitive swimming. But today there is a spring in his step. It looks as if he is gliding an inch or two off the ground, and it's work to keep up with him. I soon shake off the chill, despite the wind growing steadier and stronger.

Mud hills appear to our right. I slow my pace and gaze intently at their complex surfaces. Wind and running water have shaped ornate, intricate multicolored formations. Clefts within clefts, holes within holes, outcroppings on outcroppings. Pebbles, stones, rocks, bits of wood and leaf, wet spots and dry, everything in bold relief. Multicolored, flashing, and sparkling. It's difficult to distinguish between background and foreground.

I take a deep breath and look around. Where's Sam?

"Rick!" Sam yells from the wash, below and to my left.

"Where are you?"

I approach the edge of the wash and look down, but still can't see him.

He emerges out of a four-foot-diameter metal culvert set under the jeep road.

"Come on down here. It's incredible."

I half-slide, half-walk down the loose dirt and rocks. Again on level ground, I stand next to the opening of the large drainage pipe.

"You should see it in there. The colors, the crystals, the light. It's unreal."

I rest my hands on my knees and peer into the tunnel. There's light at the other end, thirty feet away. The middle is impenetrably dark. A thin layer of snow dusts the culvert's opening. Its inside is damp, but I see no puddles.

Sam leans over and crawls in, and I follow. We're able to sit cross-legged, hunched over, and settle into a spot near the entrance. We have good light and are far enough back for protection from the snow. Sam brings out and opens his short-blade camping knife and pokes at clumps of minerals attached to the corroding inner metal wall.

"Check this out," Sam whispers, eyes wide, pupils dilated. "Look at this!"

The crystalline growths coalesce into glowing lumps. One in particular draws our attention: blue with irregular edges, two inches wide, three inches long, and an inch thick. A collection of excrescences, like tumors, linked to each other by thinner bridges of the same material. Blue, but not only a visual blue—that is, a color—rather, it's the essence of blue. The crystals themselves aren't blue; instead, blue light comes out of them. And it's not even blue light that I perceive. I am *experiencing* blue, as if it registers directly into my brain, bypassing my eyes. I wonder if it's just as blue with eyes closed. I shut them and my mind fills with blue crystalline light. A veil pulls back from a familiar perception and reveals its underlying nature.

I turn to Sam and feel tears in my eyes. I'm not sad, am I?

It smells blue, and it sounds blue as a light breeze passes over it.

I say, "Man, that's really blue."

He says, "But check this out. It doesn't taste blue." He scrapes and chips at the surprisingly hard clumps, catches a few shards with his other hand, wets his index finger with his tongue, and dips his finger into the little pile. Returning his finger to his mouth, he makes an unpleasant face.

I taste a little. It's salty and acidic.

Millions of years before we sat down in this rusty culvert, a vast inland sea containing all manner of minerals covered this land. Rising mountains eventually block the rain and the area dries out, leaving behind deposits of zinc, tin, copper, lead, iron, cobalt, and boron that now pigment the dry hills. Rain dissolves the salts, which when running through the tunnel, corrode it. Copper and/or cobalt predominate in our azure crystal.

"Look down here," Sam says as he crawls and slides deeper into the culvert. "Here's a nice one. Red! And over there. An unreal green!"

The light is dimmer, and as I reach to touch the crystal-studded metal, an afterimage trailing behind my hand startles me. A trail of rainbow colors in the shape of my moving hand. The colors are denser close to my real hand and fade at about eighteen inches out from it.

I laugh. "What is this?"

I wave my right hand in front of my long-time friend's face, generating a shimmering swirl of afterimages.

"Do you mean this?" Sam laughs as he lifts up his hand and sweeps it through various arcs. The movements leave behind a wake of patterns amplifying, intersecting, and interfering with each other.

"Yeah. That."

"They're trails. Afterimages.* Unreal, isn't it?"

It *is* unreal. Something else acid does.

I love LSD. Or rather, I love LSD's effects. On it, I'm happy, strong, genius, focused, and luminous. I also fear it, afraid of the immense power pushing for release. Can I continue channeling it in an ecstatic direction without veering off into similarly extreme dark states: sad, weak, scared, helpless, and confused?

I am getting cramped and groan as I straighten my neck and lengthen my back.

"Man, I'm stiff. And cold. And my butt's wet. Let's get out of here."

We awkwardly unpack ourselves and stand in front of the tunnel's entrance. There's a break in the weather. We stretch mightily, arching backs, arms reaching for the sky. Joints pop and we laugh. The sun comes out and the snow melts quickly under its rays.

Sam moves away several yards and lies face upward on a clearing of

---

*A common visual phenomenon resulting from LSD and other psychedelics. They usually resolve with the acute effects of the drug, but rarely persist and may even cause significant distress in cases of post-hallucinogen perceptual disorder.

sand. I wander off a few steps and examine the rocks—smooth pebbles, larger stones, and boulders. Scrubby plants struggle for stability in the loose dirt. I empathize with their effort.

Sam sighs and settles comfortably deeper into the ground, flat on his back. I feel a moment of estrangement, a disconnect, and a tremor of panicked abandonment. We have different plans, are attending to different things at this hyper-real moment.

I wish to reestablish contact. "Okay if I sit down, too?"

He says nothing, and his eyes remain closed, an enormous smile covers his face. I find a soft-looking spot on the ground a long stone's throw away, giving Sam space, but close enough for easy voice and visual contact.

Sam wears reflective aviator sunglasses and sports a day's worth of beard. He's pulled his black ski hat down over his forehead, and it almost touches the top of his sunglasses. I am learning to recognize the look: someone on acid. He's making strange sounds that become increasingly high-pitched and mechanical, moving his head from side to side as if following something. I can't tell if his eyes are open. I look around and see a kaleidoscopic, arabesque, baroque geometric visual overlay. Swirling, buzzing, shining with its own light. I wonder if Sam is seeing more than this. He seems to be.

"You all right?" I ask.

"Yeah. Yeaaah . . ."

After a long pause, he adds, "Unreal."

That's good enough for me.

I lower myself down onto the ground, face up, and close my eyes. Colors, unimaginably brighter than with eyes open. And a simultaneous flood of ecstasy. I wonder: Is this joy the cause of the lights, or are the lights causing the joy?

My body feels cool, light, and airy. Fascinated, I explore sensing my limbs, chest, head, face, and mouth. If I withdraw my attention from them, they drop away. They're not numb; they're simply absent, no longer there. It's empty space. I relax more deeply—letting go of all tension. More of my body drops off. Then it is gone.

I enter a state of perfect completion, absolute equanimity and equipoise, within and without. A state only possible without an inner and outer, no boundaries between my mind and space. Perfection whose essence is endless possibility. A vast timeless infinite horizon opens up before my mind's eye. Total emptiness, filled to overflowing with *something*, something *potential*. The state of potential. Seared with intensity, pulsing with energy, no longer constrained by matter.

What is this? A premonition? Of what—a miracle? A wish? Is it the drug? If so, how? What *is* LSD? Whatever it is, I love it. More than anything I have ever loved. My mind knows this and my heart sings.

But is it true? I've always wanted to feel free, happy, and beautiful—not constrained, criticized, and defective. Whenever I've considered my existence, nothing makes sense. I envy what I imagine are the lives of my friends at The College—confident, comfortable, moving toward a clear goal. And today in the snow on LSD, I achieve something new and unfamiliar. I now know that it is possible to direct my own fate. Of course it is. Who else is responsible?

Sam laughs loudly, cackles. He sits up and shakes his head, looking baffled but happy. I rouse myself and check my watch: 3:00. Time to start walking back to the truck.

Sam stands and wobbles, and I am only slightly steadier as I arise. The cold dampness of the air and LSD overcome us at the same time, and we both, as if on cue, shiver like dogs shaking off water. We laugh.

I ask, "What were you seeing?"

"I was in a dogfight."

I wonder what he means, but we need to move.

The light's fading, the temperature's dropping, and it's snowing again, harder. We walk quickly and warm up. Halfway back to the truck, we slow down, focusing less on the rocky path underfoot and more on our surroundings. Sam comes to a halt, gaping at the scene around us. I stop a few feet behind him and catch my breath.

"Look!" he exclaims.

We gaze at the broad expanse extending northward. The distant mountains come into focus, covered with forest and snow—melting, pulsating, morphing, and shimmering green streaks and white patches. Gradually we return to our immediate environment.

"Look!" Sam exclaims.

We are standing in a sea of colorful sparkling snowflakes, icy particles that emit a strange hissing sound. I step a ways off the path and into the scrub, facing away from Sam. I see each flake flashing pink, blue, red, purple, and sometimes yellow. More exhilarating is seeing just as clearly the emptiness, the space in which the flakes exist. There's still daylight, but the sparks—the scintillating points of light, the colorful twinkling each snowflake contains—are stars suspended in black space. I'm learning to recognize that underlying stratum—the emptiness in which perceptions occurs. It depends on where I focus, and how, and at what.

I inhale deeply and my entire body expands just beyond its normal boundaries, feeling nearly weightless. The cold wet air blows by my cheeks. I breathe in through my mouth. The sweet dampness pours across my lips, past my teeth, over my tongue. It cools and moistens my throat. Are my eyes open? I check. They are.

I close my eyes, then whisper under my breath: *Remember this. Remember this. Today, you have been shown a new life.*

I open my eyes and see my childhood friend catching snowflakes with his tongue. We look at each other and laugh.

Covering the remaining distance quickly, we are happy to see the truck parked by the side of the road, just where we left it. Two inches of fluffy snow blanket the hood and windshield, and we quickly sweep it off.

As Sam unlocks and opens the doors, my abdomen cramps and I get a chill. We stamp our boots on the ground to shake loose accumulated mud and ice, and brush the snow off each other's jackets. Dry clothes await, ones we change into while the crowded cab rapidly warms.

The exertion in close quarters intensifies the acid's effects. I know Sam is a good driver, but also that he's inexperienced with snowy roads. He waits for a plow to drive past us on our left, clearing a path. He pulls out behind it and starts descending the mountain road. The mammoth machine— bright orange, coated with grimy snow—comforts me. It's our protector, our guide, our helper. At a deeper level, it is a miracle. A synchronicity, an event with meaning beyond its simple occurrence. It has to be that way. It's destiny, something that opens the future to every one of us.

The windshield wipers' movement distracts me from my trance, but their rhythmic sound pulls me into another. Up and down, back and forth, they clear the snow from the windshield and leave behind shimmering rainbows. I gawk.

"Sam. How the fuck are you driving?"

I close my eyes and open them again when Sam slows and passes by the snowplow, which has pulled off the highway and onto the shoulder. The road ahead is clear, and we pass our titanic orange, mechanical, angelic protector. I look behind us and see it turn around, now clearing snow in the other direction, climbing back into the mountains, and rapidly diminishing in size.

Within minutes we enter The College's cool leafy campus, a mile lower in elevation than where we had hiked. The deciduous trees lining the streets display only traces of yellow and red. The buildings, many over one hundred years old, are immaculate, scrubbed clean. I sense an imposing medieval, powerful, ambiguous energy—expansive yet constraining. Sam parks along the curb, facing the wrong way, near the walkway that leads to the common area to our left. The cafeteria sits at the far end of that large plaza.

I turn to my friend and say, "Man. That was great. Incredible. What a fun day! Thanks for the acid. And driving."

Sam's face is lumpish, puffy, bruised, blotchy, with necrotic colors. His right eye bulges. It's fascinatingly morbidly misshapen.

"You look weird, man."

He laughs, "You're not looking so great either."

I grab my duffel bag and open the passenger door, checking for oncoming cars before letting myself out. I carefully step around the front of the truck, and stand on the curb, facing Sam's door. He rolls down his window.

I ask, "What were you doing lying on your back out there?"

I peer carefully at Sam's eyes as he's speaking. I can't see his irises.

"Oh. I was in a dogfight."

"Right. That's what you said."

"We were flying at each other and flying away from each other. It was unreal. We were high above the sky. Incredible speeds and near misses."

He pauses, that faraway look, and repeats. "It was unreal."

We exchange one final look and smile crookedly at each other.

"Have a good dinner, man," Sam says cheerily and laughs.

"You, too," I laugh.

He drives away.

Reflections
BODHICITTA AWAKENING

In this narrative I describe an experience similar to what also occurred in "Cloud Speakers" and "LSD Chicken." These are "aesthetic insights" concerning a sensory modality; in the case of the two earlier chapters, that modality is sound. In "Cloud Speakers," I gained an appreciation of the space in which sound occurs, and in "LSD Chicken," the operation of the natural laws responsible for sound. The aesthetic insight I describe in the present chapter relates to light—emanating from mineral deposits inside a metal culvert, and within and around falling snowflakes. In addition, I had my first encounter with visual trails.

This account also describes what I later understood as the experience of *bodhicitta*, the first and therefore most important step in Buddhist training. Bodhicitta is one's earliest intimation of enlightenment, the knowledge that enlightenment exists. Without bodhicitta, one will never practice Buddhism. He or she will see no need to seek out and engage with a system of belief and behavior that focuses solely on expanding, deepening, and integrating into one's life that initial "flash."*

---

*A term to which the 14th Dalai Lama refers in the title of his book on bodhicitta, *A Flash of Lightning in the Dark of Night.*

On that precious day with my closest childhood friend, bodhicitta awakened in me, providing a preview of a categorically novel manner of seeing and relating to the inner and outer worlds. Sam's suggestion to "think" only of walking while walking led to a most unexpected effect: realizing how connected—or rather, disconnected—were my body and mind. Later, I saw the means of correcting this through Zen Buddhism's teaching of "harmonizing body and mind." When pulling weeds, just pull weeds; when walking, just walk.

In addition, later that stormy day, I experienced the "dropping off" of my body, which then provided access to a realm of overflowing emptiness. This emptiness, called *sunyata* in Buddhism, is an emptiness of infinite potential out of which all existence emerges. With respect to subjective experience, it precedes, so to speak, the big bang. Because of its relationship to enlightenment, and its essential role in Buddhist philosophy, sunyata is a critically important topic in the religion.

In that brief encounter with the infinite potential of sunyata, I sensed a new relationship with my own life, one of expansion rather than burdensome stasis. The LSD catalyzed seismic inspirations. However, as Thomas Edison said, "Genius [i.e., true creativity] is 1 percent inspiration and 99 percent perspiration." Without working on such inspiration, these experiences would remain only pleasant memories and gradually fade away.

14

STEAK ON ACID

SAM DRIVES AWAY TO THE EAST, heading back to his dormitory. After losing sight of the truck, I reorient and recognize where this is. The Dorm across the street is in its usual location, the stop signs are also where I remember them. The air is damp and smells of smoke. A handful of lucky seniors live in rooms with fireplaces, and this is an ideal night for using them.

Carefully climbing the short flight of steps leading up to the plaza, I walk the fifty yards to the dining hall, barely feeling my feet. I finally arrive and make my way one cement step at a time up to the landing in front of the cafeteria. Perplexed and awed, I stare helplessly at the massive brown wooden double doors. They look immovable.

Stu appears suddenly, smirks and laughs—at, rather than with, me—and effortlessly pulls open the doors. Almost friendly, he asks, "Man, you look fucked up. Are you on acid?"

Stu's face strikes me more than his manner. His chin is impossibly small and his mustache improbably thin. But his hair is beautiful, pulled back in a perfect ponytail. His chestnut locks glow in the light beaming down from fixtures hanging from the high arched ceiling. His ponytail leaves sparks in its wake.

"Yeah," I mutter.

I follow Stu through the doors, forcing myself to maintain a casual air. However, the din, brightness, and busyness of the hall create an immediate obstacle, stopping me in my tracks. It's sensory overload. Oh, to be back in the snowy sparkling pristine mountains with Sam.

"You okay, man?" Stu asks as he takes me by the arm.

We step into the line snaking through the serving area.

Saturday night, I realize. That means steak.

Servers cheerfully labor behind the counter under the banks of fluorescent lights. I squint against the glare. The workers' faces are lumpy and misshapen, their skin splotchy and bruised. They're not aware of their morbid appearance, and of course no one else is. I sigh. A large Mexican server, a big deformed smile on her face, grabs a flaccid steak with her tongs. She holds it up a few inches above the tray full of other steaks, awaiting my approval. Somehow, I manage to nod, and my selection thuds onto a dirty white plate. The server next to her sets a baked potato on one side of the plate and a large serving spoon full of moldy corn, streaked with gray and green, next to it. She hands me the loaded plate over the abdomen-high glass barrier that separates us.

Emerging from the serving area, I blink and look around. Where will I sit? Stu is busy at the soda dispenser, a mechanical entity that now looks hopelessly complex. I don't want to embarrass myself, fumbling clumsily for my usual Dr Pepper. I notice pitchers of water and glasses at each dining table. Good news—I'll drink water. Then, I spy Tom and Ambrose sitting at a table in the middle of the hall. This is my opportunity to lose Stu and spare myself from contending with his edge.

I take a seat across from my two friends.

"Heyyyyyy, man," Ambrose says. A smile breaks out in the lower half of his face. His eyes keenly take in my every move. He lowers his head, looking sideways at me, and whispers conspiratorially, "How was the Orange Barrel, man?"

I look over at Tom. We smile a greeting and I turn back to Ambrose.

"Wow!" I say. "Fucking unreal." Miming Sam's recurring refrain from just a few hours ago.

Ambrose laughs. "'Fucking unreal'? What the fuck is that, man? What the fuck is 'unreal'?"

Overcome by laughter, Tom nearly chokes on his water, and it flies out of his mouth.

Undeterred, Ambrose continues, now more warmly, "You look beautiful, man. Congratulations."

He reaches over the table and we shake hands.

The chaos of reentering the world of The College lessens slightly. I relax and look down at my steak. And gasp. It's *alive*.

Holding my breath, I examine the undead slice of beef muscle, tendon, and fat. An aura of black light surrounds the object, outlining it. The effect creates an even more striking contrast with the whitish plate and the pale, vague potato and corn side dishes. The vegetables look flat, as if they have lost a dimension. Or perhaps it's the steak that has gained another one.

Finally, I begin breathing—but shallowly—and continue to stare. The meat pulsates. Well, maybe gently writhes. There's some kind of movement, rhythmic and regular. I feel curious horror. Lifting my fork, I gingerly poke the steak. The meat instantly recoils. It's not simply yielding to the fork's pressure; rather, it reacts to the jab and withdraws, protecting itself, trying to move away.

Ambrose and Tom watch my growing horror with increasing amusement.

Ambrose says knowingly, "Yeaahh, man."

I say, "Man, that steak is really fucked up."

"Yeah, man. It's the acid. Steak looks really bad on acid."

"I can't eat this."

I rotate the plate, bringing near the languid corn and potato. I'll eat these instead.

But I can't pull my gaze away from the miserable flesh. It radiates injury, an animal indignation.

I think: It's just a steak. I've eaten lots of them. I'll just cut into it with my knife. See what happens.

Rotating the plate again, I bring the steak close, slice a two-inch slit down the middle, and separate the edges. The pulsating instantly becomes a beating, an incessant beating, directing all of its energy toward survival.

"Steak looking weird, Rick?" Tom manages to get out between gasps of laughter.

"Man, you're tripping," Ambrose adds.

"Yeah. Whatever. I'm not going to eat this. It's still alive. I may never eat a steak again."

Five years pass before I again eat red meat.

—≺—

Reflections
HOW I BECAME A VEGETARIAN

Did the LSD that day convert me to vegetarianism? This is not a trivial question, as much of the lore surrounding psychedelic drugs suggests that they possess inherent invariant properties. For example, they make you more politically liberal, environmentally oriented, open and compassionate, antiwar, and lead to awareness of the consciousness of nonhuman life-forms—the list goes on. However, this notion minimizes, if not ignores, the two other legs of the psychedelic tripod: set and setting.

We simply need to look at how Charles Manson used LSD in his followers to promote malignant beliefs and actions,[1] as well as the role LSD played in the sarin attack on the Japanese subway system by a Japanese religious cult—the Aum Shinrikyo—in the 1990s.[2] These examples reflect the more realistic notion that psychedelics amplify and lend more credence to preexisting mental contents. What else can psychedelics be acting upon than who we are? These contents may not be fully conscious; nevertheless, they reside in our minds—our set. And our set is heavily influenced by myriad long- and short-term interactions with others—our setting.

I was not thinking about giving up meat that evening as I entered the cafeteria still mightily tripping on LSD. However, both positive and negative experiences had been accumulating that encouraged a vegetarian diet, and the LSD catalyzed that change-in-waiting.

The College's dining hall fare emphasized meat, including pork chops and ham. While my family did not keep a strictly Jewish kosher diet, I had never eaten undisguised pig meat before leaving home. Nevertheless, we did enjoy sausage at our Sunday morning pancake breakfasts, and I loved the bacon and eggs my mother often cooked for breakfast on school days. Somehow, we overlooked these tasty items' porcine source. At The College, I initially enjoyed the taste of the ham, ribs, and pork, as well as the sense of breaking free from my family ties. Thus, there existed a semiconscious cultural, religious, and familial backdrop for rejecting at least this form of flesh. Also, I was gaining weight eating so much meat, increasingly uncomfortable with how I felt. Finally, the visual properties of the LSD amplified the steak's unappealing appearance.

Adducing more positive motivations, my nascent yet powerful attraction to Eastern religions—which Ambrose's library and Asian art had kindled—introduced me to the beneficial aspects of vegetarianism. While eschewing meat epitomized nonviolence, ascetic Asian religious traditions also added a spiritual dimension to the truism that we are what we eat. In that context, a meat-free diet benefited one's spiritual development; assuming, that is, the desire to be less animallike.

15

BASKETBALL GAY PANIC

IT'S FRIDAY AFTER DINNER and time for a crucial basketball game. The winner of tonight's matchup between The College and our cross-campus rival, The Men's College (TMC), advances to the conference title game. A lot is at stake. The venue is The College's gymnasium, less than a block from The Dorm. I have never been on LSD while attending a sporting event. Tonight, I will be.

"I wish I could, too," Tom says as our group gathers for the traditional pregame ritual in Ambrose and Stu's room. He adds, "But I'm afraid to. What if I lose it?"

Three of my friends are on the team: Tom is tall and strong, Stu is quick with lightning reflexes, and Woody is a dependable defender and team player. The tallest player is Reginald, the center. Black with a huge Afro, Tom and he clash frequently, on and off the court. Two alpha males. Reginald rarely attends pregame parties.

Tom gets worked up in preparation for games. He asks Ambrose to play loud, fast, pulsating, primal rock and roll on his mythic stereo. Waves of Old Spice evaporate from his freshly shaven face as he pounds his fists on his knees, stamps his feet on the floor, closes his eyes, and moves his head back and forth to the music. He nearly vibrates off his chair.

The College lost the first match against its rival several months earlier. Everyone wrathfully blames one particular player on the opponent's team: Zebulun Cohen. He's a fierce competitor who usually scores more points and makes more rebounds than anyone on either team.

We have our opinions about Cohen, opinions focusing on his appearance. His most striking feature, so striking that one might even consider it a disability, is his hairiness. A thick mat of black hair covers his arms, back, neck, and legs down to his ankles. The topic, or the fact, of his hairiness agitates us as we pass along a joint.

"Yeah," drawls Woody. "He's a fucking hairy ape."

Tom joins in. "Ah, come on guys. He can't help it. His mother's a gorilla. And his father a chimpanzee."

Ambrose shakes his head, his eyes barely visible, his grin crooked. "His mother's a gorilla . . ." I can't tell if he's questioning Tom's insult or confirming it.

Yeah, I think. He's a fucking hairy ape.

The physicality of basketball and that of sex merge at these times for Tom. He similarly prepares for a date. That is, before a basketball game, he grinds his pelvis to and fro, flicks his tongue in and out, squeals in a mimicry of the woman upon whom he is performing oral sex. In either case, if he were feeling especially optimistic, he might take out his penis and swing it.

I have nothing to add when my friends talk about sex. And the conversation before a game usually flows from sports to sex and back again. Everyone is more well-endowed and experienced than I am. Discussions of blood-tinged sheets are both alarming and baffling. Even the mostly alien Ambrose joins in the sexual banter, which confirms my outsider status.

Ambrose and I take a square of Woody's windowpane acid. The Boston Brahmin has a Buddhist negative attitude toward sports. Too aggressive. What does it matter? Vanity. So, as is his custom, he begs off attending the game. As I stand by the door zipping my coat against the late winter chill, I notice the telltale onset of the drug: physical excitement, nervousness, and anticipation. We pile out of the room. The hall and stairs look splotchy, smudged, casting shadows where there had been none before. Pale spots everywhere—in the air and on the surfaces of objects.

I arrive at the arena and look for a good seat, while my friends march into the dressing room. I find a perfect spot, just to the right of midcourt, halfway up the rows of bleachers. I notice two pretty girls twenty feet to my left.

The teams assume their positions. Facing each other midcourt, The College on the right and TMC on the left. Cohen, as usual, stands out, even more so in my acid-modified consciousness. His hairy mantle glows, pulsates, and shines under the gymnasium lights. His name is Jewish, and his looks also strongly suggest membership in my tribe. I consider his Jewishness, which we share. Yes, of course, I conclude. That being so, he's the only apparently Jewish player on the court. I shake my head. A hairy fucking *Jewish* ape. But I'm Jewish. I might have gotten angry at my Jewish high school friends, but I never hated them. Besides, I've never met Cohen—my reaction to him has no basis in reality.

I look around surreptitiously, wondering if others are similarly staring at the hirsute player. The coeds to my left are shooting *me* furtive glances. They turn to each other and giggle. I hadn't planned on meeting anyone this evening. Besides, I'm on acid, have never had sex, and my prowess cannot compare with my friends'.

A loud awful searing buzzer announces that the game has begun.

Instantly, it is too much. My nervous system pegs to overload. The thud-thud-thud, like a booming bass drum, of the dribbled basketball. The hoofbeats of stampeding players running from one end of the court to the other. Reflections from the overwaxed parquet floor are pools of swirling and morphing light. The announcer's voice over the public address system is a shrill staccato cacophony. The crowd is modest but loud, especially a pocket of TMC supporters close to the court. They excitedly encourage Cohen, vigorously celebrating every time he handles the ball.

A sweaty gleam appears on the players' bodies. Reginald's shimmering black skin is especially mesmerizing. I've never seen a Black basketball player perform in front of me—his tall muscular lithe body, his awe-inspiring Afro shining in the light, and LSD-induced trails following him. I feel a stirring in my pants.

I focus on my other friends' bodies as they move through space. Not really who *they* are, but what their shining damp over-breathing bodies are. Running, jumping, throwing, shouting, and barking. They

whistle to each other encouragement, reproach, and strategy. Their athletic shirts cling to their bodies, and everyone's tight-fitting nylon shorts
are filled to bursting with massive penises. My head swims.

I hear one of the girls nearby speak—the dark-haired one. Is she
calling my name—*Rick, Rick*? How could she? I don't know who she
is. She whispers something to her blonde friend, looks back at me, a big
grin on her face, she waves, and they both giggle. How can I hear them
laughing over the din?

I think: Oh, shit. Am I busted? Do they know I am in a dick-filled
acid black hole? Is the brunette mocking me?

They aren't moving toward me, and that's a relief. I'll ignore them
by turning away, which I do, looking back toward the basketball court.
The College is closing in on the lead. The tempo heats up, more sweat,
more yelling, and I can't take my eyes off my friends' crotches.

The question appears in my mind like a rifle shot: Am I gay?

I see the individual penis outlines under the players' shorts. Stu's:
broad at the base and small at the head, just like his face. Tom's is long
and snaking, thick throughout. Woody's is less clear, although he's
bragged about his "thigh holster" holding his large member; the penis-
shaped faded blue of his jeans in the right area supports his claim.

I want a giant penis for myself. Does that mean I want my penis to
be like one of those giant ones on the basketball court? Or is it because
I am gay and want to have sex with my friends with big penises? I don't
know what I would do if my own penis were that big, because big and
sexually experienced go hand in hand. These are big, *experienced* penises,
and I have never had sex. Thus, how could my own be big? Maybe I *am*
gay, and that's why I haven't succeeded with members of the opposite sex.

I try distracting myself by looking away from the game. Involuntarily,
I turn toward the two girls.

I wonder: These girls. Do they want sex? How often must I be
reminded that I don't know anything about it? They scare me. And my
friends on the court have turned me on, but I don't know why.

I look at the back of my hands to determine how stoned I am. My
fingers have become little penises. I bend and straighten them. The

same color and consistency of a penis, with penis heads replacing my nails. My lips are dry, and I rub them. Horrified, I know this is what a penis feels like against my mouth.

Desperate, I must break this malignant spell. Staring at flesh, flesh everywhere, I am going mad. A furious standoff between fantasized sexual pleasure and terror.

I get up and stretch my LSD-chilled bones in the overheated atmosphere. Cohen is having an especially successful night, and the rival team increases its lead. The tragedy of my team losing cuts into my heart.

Still standing, I cup my hands around my mouth, look at Cohen, and I scream. As loud as I can.

"Fuck you, Cohen! You hairy ape!!"

I regain my equilibrium briefly. Giant dicks on the court and pretty girls in the stands disappear.

"Fuck you to fucking hell!!"

The shaggy ballplayer looks up toward the stands and peers in my direction. He looks puzzled and a little hurt. But not mad. He is, in reality, a nice guy.

What have I done? I have just screamed an obscenity at a complete stranger at a public event. I sit down, look at my feet, then back to the court, and down again. I am ashamed, but shame is easier to bear than a mesmerizing fascination with my friends' penises.

The girls' giggling explodes into a peal of laughter at my outburst. They must think I am a fool. They probably know I'm on acid, too. They know I'm a fool on acid. Will they report me?

I have to get out of here.

Without looking at the girls, but with a parting glance at the game's intolerable intensity, I start descending the far end of the bleachers. I am visually assaulted, not by what I see, but by the mere sensation of vision, immersion in this overwhelming visual environment. The light beats down on my body. Just as painful is being an object for others to see—others who are scrutinizing, judging, and condemning me. I pick my way carefully down the rickety stairs. The crowd's roar and announcer's voice press around me, and my depth perception flattens. I don't want to fall. Finally touching down on the wooden floor near an exit, I am out of the building with a few long strides.

It's dark, and the air is chilly and damp. The streetlights illuminate the uneven sidewalk outlined by masses of something black, shimmering, and menacing. Moss? The crowd's tumult fades rapidly behind me.

I need a shower, I decide as I close the dorm room door behind me. Tom and I are roommates this year, and his clothes are strewn about our common room. The smell of Old Spice, though less than before the game, permeates the air. I pick up his clothes and toss them onto the bed in his side room; I return to mine, strip down, and look in the mirror.

My face is discolored, lumpy, and misshapen. My glasses are too thick and my eyes too small. It's hard to focus, and drawing nearer, I peer into my black massively dilated pupils. My long hair has never felt good on my head—too wavy and greasy. Now it's hopelessly matted. A sickly halo surrounds my face. I pull back and appraise the rest of my body.

Cadaverous, listing at a strange angle. I can barely locate my penis, shrunk as it is from the acid and my distorted visual sense. I feel more than asexual. Or more precisely, the inverse of sexual—negatively sexual, like a negative number. I look nearly dead, neutered.

I put on my bathrobe, grab a clean towel, and walk down the hall to the communal bathroom. I set my glasses on the four-sinked countertop, hang the towel on a hook attached to one of the two stall showers. My body is indescribably uncomfortable, but the hot water soothes my left hand with which I assess the temperature. The water *looks* good, too. Even in the dim gray light of the bathroom, the sparkling cascading stream is beautiful, and the mist shimmers with bright iridescent rainbows. Pretty. Unlike my body.

I step into the square thin metal enclosure and pull the curtain closed. Soaked, my hair extends halfway down to my shoulders, and shampooing it is laborious. Nor do I like contending with it on a daily basis. The waves are embarrassing, like hairy wings emerging from either side of my head. However, if I comb my hair forward after shampooing, the wings don't appear. My father's gay hairdresser—who also cuts my hair—taught me that trick. My acquiescence to the homosexual stylist's advice adds another layer of uncertainty to my crisis of sexual orientation.

I pour Day-Glo blue creamy fragrant Head & Shoulders shampoo into the palm of my left hand and spread it out with my right. Lifting both hands to my head, I apply the shampoo and begin massaging it in.

I feel clumps of hair falling out from my scalp. I lower my hands, take a look, and can't tell what it is I see. Looking more closely, there are one or two strands on my palms. Out of the corner of my eyes, though, I see large wads of hair in my hands.

Is my hair falling out? It doesn't seem possible, yet appears to be the case. I hope not. Does LSD cause hair loss? I know that cancer patients lose clumps of hair.* Is this the first symptom of cancer? No matter what it is—cancer or LSD—something is off. I feel for bald spots but don't know if I'm touching skin or hair.

I focus on my normal shampooing routine. Shampoo, rinse, repeat. Every time I run my fingers through my hair, more appears to fall out. I devise an experiment. I tap my forehead and assess the resulting sound. Then I tap the top of my head. Without hair, the sound should be the same; with hair, it should be muffled. When I try this, there is no difference.

I turn off the water, climb out of the stall, and dry myself off. Instead of briskly rubbing my hair with the towel, I gently pat the top of my head. I take a deep breath, wipe away the fog on the mirror, and even with my acid-drenched vision, I see that my hair is fine. After more thoroughly drying off, I put on my robe and walk back to our room.

I decide to check in with Ambrose. I knock on their door, and when he opens it, I ask, "Do you have a beer?"

"Yeah, man. Come on in."

I sit in a chair, staring at nothing.

He asks, "How was the game, man?"

"Intense." My mind is empty.

We sit quietly in the dim dorm room, and the familiar audio atmosphere surrounds and comforts me. I drink the Coors in quick gulps, wish Ambrose good night, return to my room, and go to bed.

---

*Actually from chemotherapy, not cancer.

Reflections
WHO AM I?

In addition to fears of permanent insanity (see "Permanent Insanity"), "homosexual panic" during psychedelic drug intoxication is not rare. In this narrative, attraction to my male friends playing basketball developed into intense anxiety and confusion around my sexual orientation. Was I gay?

Despite its notoriety within the psychedelic world, the literature on this phenomenon is meager. All the foundational papers are psychoanalytic and rely upon Freudian concepts: the unconscious, the defenses of denial and projection, and the function of the ego.[1]

According to this model, there are two types of homosexual panic. In one, the scenario plays out in this manner:

The catalyst for the episode is when someone, say Person A, propositions someone of the same sex, say Person B. Person B is a "latent" homosexual in whom same-sex "cravings" are unconscious. The intensity of the anxiety Person B feels reflects the strength of the denial of one's "true" homosexuality. Faced with the fear and shame accompanying such a threat to one's identity, the ego projects that fear onto Person A, rather than becoming conscious of one's own homosexual drives. Person B now sees Person A as life-threateningly dangerous. Person B attacks (and may even kill) Person A in "self-defense" while "temporarily insane."

This understanding of homosexual panic is the basis of the legal homosexual panic defense. Defense attorneys argue that their client committed the offense while psychotic. While still in use in many states, the legal and clinical bases of this defense are weak, and there is a concerted effort to ban it.[2]

The other use of the term is more relevant to my case. This is the eruption into consciousness of homosexual feelings and its attendant anxiety, shame, and confusion regarding one's identity. I did not project these impulses onto my friends. To the extent that projection did occur, however, the visual illusions of giant penises magnified the erotic element rather than converted those feelings into fear of harm.

My feelings of heterosexual inadequacy were pervasive at that time, and the two pretty girls flirting with me amplified that sense. The idea bubbled up from my unconscious: "You can't make it with the opposite sex because you're really craving the same sex. You're gay."

Not entirely discordant with the first definition of homosexual panic, I diffused my anxiety aggressively; that is, by screaming obscenities at a player on the opposing team. Paradoxically, instead of him being a sexual persecutor, he was more related to me than anyone else on the court. Here, my sense of alien Jewishness—and wish to disavow it—added another coal to the fire. I loved my male gentile "friends" and hated my Jewish "enemy."

Finally, my hair falling out in the shower. The association of hair with masculinity and physical prowess is perennial and universal. For example, it appears in the account of Samson and Delilah in chapter 16 of the Book of Judges in the Hebrew Bible. Delilah was a Philistine woman with whom Samson, a mighty Hebrew warrior, had an affair. Samson was wreaking havoc among the Philistine occupiers of the land at the time, and Delilah's compatriots implored her to determine the source of his strength. He relented after her unceasing demands by informing her of his Nazirite status—a razor had never passed over his head. In other words, his hair provided his physical strength. Delilah cut his hair while he slept one night and informed the Philistine military, who captured, bound, and tortured him. Miraculously, he regained his strength for one last act of vengeful destruction, bringing down the arena in which thousands of Philistines were celebrating his degradation.

I knew of this legend both from Hebrew School and Bible-themed movies popular when I was a child. It's not difficult to make the connection, then, between my fear of being gay—that is, losing my identity as a potent heterosexual male—and my hair/masculinity/prowess falling away/off. In fact, the psychoanalytic study of patients with homosexual panic also revealed the presence of "castration anxiety." In the first type of homosexual panic, the persecutor will castrate his target. In the second, the one from which I suffered, being gay means being less than a man, someone who has been castrated, and who now has no penis.

16

DEATH VALLEY

LATE ONE AFTERNOON between Christmas and New Year's, Spencer and I begin our descent into Death Valley National Monument.* A wide swath of the 140-mile-long valley comes into view as we round a turn midway along its western flank via Wildrose Canyon. What I see is astonishing.

The six-thousand-foot-high Black Mountains, which form the eastern wall of the valley, stand in striking display twenty-five miles ahead. The sun's last rays illuminate their upper third, glare glistens off the peaks' dark earth, and the shadows are deep blue, almost purple. The valley floor, much of which is below sea level, shines snowy white from salt and other minerals. Those areas still in sunlight almost blind us, while the clouds cast rapidly moving brownish-gray blobs of shadow hundreds of feet across. Spencer is behind the wheel of his pickup, and five miles of steep descent remain before we reach the bottom of the valley.

It's dark by the time we arrive at the campground. The week after Christmas is always popular, but we locate an isolated corner behind a patch of creosote bushes. Lying in my sleeping bag on the sand and dirt, I feel the ground calming and energizing me at the same time—a strange sensation. We fall asleep quickly, drink our morning coffee as the sun rises, pack up, and head out to Cottonwood Canyon. We drive

*Now Death Valley National Park.

south, skirting the edge of the Panamint Mountains, rising over eleven thousand feet, that form the western wall of the valley.

Spencer has brought along several doses of Purple Barrel LSD. They are even smaller than the Orange Barrels.

He laughs when my eyes widen at their tiny size. "I think these are even stronger than the orange ones."

We drop down onto the sandy mouth of the canyon and stop. Each washes down his acid with a little water. Not that it's necessary, but it's become a ritual.

I'm secure driving with Spencer, even in this alien terrain. He's rebuilt his old Ford pickup, and everything works. We get out and he lets some air out of the tires. This provides more surface area and lessens our chances of getting stuck in the sand. We lock the hubs that engage the front wheels, and now we are in four-wheel-drive. After an uneventful half-hour crawling over sand and loose rock, we're back on smoother solid ground and park. One hundred yards ahead, we see our destination—a grove of cottonwood trees. Cottonwood Creek, sparkling and diminutive, flows out of the little forest.

Spencer looks up at me as he reinflates the tires. "What do you think of them girls?"

"What girls?"

"Those cottonwoods!" He guffaws. "Don't they look like girls to you? So pretty, coquettish, showing off their leaves."

The combination of early morning sun and LSD elicit a most powerful rush. As we approach the trees, we see that their pale gray limbs—most of which are thick with corrugated, almost corduroy, ridges of bark—are nearly bare. What leaves do remain are crispy dry, waiting for a good wind to knock them down. Yet, a rare firmly attached greenish-yellow specimen appears among these stragglers.

As the valley floor heats up, it sends warm air upward, and the cold air flowing down from the nearby snowcapped peaks reverses course. The breeze moves through the limbs of dozens of cottonwood trees, creating a tremor in the leaves, and the grove begins to sing. It's a gentle melodic rustling, rising and falling, falling and rising, higher pitched, lower pitched. The slow-moving stream, one-to-two feet wide at most, no more than two-to-three inches deep, provides a steady background babble. When the breeze strengthens and lifts the grove's voice, we no longer hear the creek. It's more than an oasis. I've stumbled into a paradise, and a great love of the place swells my heart.

The canyon walls rise thirty to forty feet on either side of us—brown and gray dirt, gently sloping upward. Innumerable furrows cut through the surface, evidence of rare torrential rains that pour down to the flats. Between the trees and the canyon walls, low desert surrounds us, just steps away. Silent blazing light, earth barren and exposed, the occasional cactus and creosote cling to the loose dirt. Two different realities side by side—one of magnificent lushness, one of awful death.

The grove pulls me toward it. I enter and arrive in beauty. Preternatural color, sound, smell, the patches of sky a shade and intensity of blue I have never before seen. My body feels light, joyful, and as I close my eyes, I visualize jumping into the air and flying above the trees. Then, floating at tree level, hovering and gliding among the trunks and limbs.

"Wow, Spencer. Unbelievable. What are we going to do?"

He's been here before and knows the area.

"The ground here is too rocky to lie down on. Let's walk through the grove to the other side, where it's sandy and more comfortable. The stream runs partly underground so there are fewer trees and it's more open."

Spencer takes a closer look at me, and I at him. A big grin fills his face, pupils dilated and glowing, his face a radiant red.

He chortles. "Are you pretty high?"

Reflexively, I extend my left arm, flex my hand, spread my fingers, looking for the telltale signs of mottled, distorted, squirming skin. I draw my hand closer.

"Yes."

"Ha, ha. Me, too."

He adds, "Let's get water and fruit from the truck and start moving. Pretty soon, we won't be able to walk."

Inside the grove it's both sensory overload and an isolation chamber. We are entombed by sound and color, shimmering leaves, gurgling brook, smell of the composting leaves below us, the ever-shifting light sparkles everywhere. Six-to-eight-inch rocks, mostly volcanic and moss-covered, slow our advance as we clamber our way over and through.

We exit the grove and now the stream appears only in short stretches. Trees here are farther apart and larger, having prevailed in the battle for scarcer water. Our gaze follows the path of the stream up the wash for several miles. Then, it enters a shadowy steep tree-lined canyon that disappears behind a small ridge. Beyond, the snow-covered Panamint Mountains tower thousands of feet above us.

Almost to myself, I say, "I wonder if we could walk up that canyon." However, I'm having trouble keeping my balance, and sit down on the ground near a narrow section of the stream. The distant canyon beckons.

Spencer guffaws. "Right! It would take a day to walk up there, and it looks oh so cold." He adds, "And you don't look like you're going anywhere anytime soon."

A gnarly ancient cottonwood stands near the rivulet and draws me close. After clearing an area of small rocks and twigs, I lie on my back. The tree's branches extend directly above me. Its lower limbs spread in all directions and provide abundant shade.

"Mmm hmm," I manage to mutter.

Spencer removes his day pack carrying our water and snacks. "Now that's a great idea."

He retraces our steps several yards toward the upper end of the grove. Finding a comfortable spot, he sits down, rests his back against a two-feet-diameter cottonwood log, and pulls the brim of his straw hat over his forehead. He lets out a huge sigh, extends his legs in front of him, wiggles his feet, and giggles.

The vast and silent desert surrounds us—an auditory vacuum that I hear beginning only yards from our oasis. The tiny trickle of the creek generates a soft bulwark, an aural cocoon, tenacious and cheerful. The wind rattles the dry leaves and sways the smaller branches.

I look over at Spencer, who isn't moving.

"Spencer."

He turns toward me, his hat obscuring his face.

"What?"

Did he say that? Or did I? I can't tell. It doesn't matter. Spencer is in his own world. Eyes opened or closed, that's where he is.

He laughs. I'm sure of that. He then loudly whispers, "The colors. The colors."

I return to my reverie. Here I am in Death Valley. Surrounded by two-billion-year-old rocks. On LSD. The babbling stream and nearby silence alternate one with the other; at other times, they blend together.

I listen to the softly insistent tiny rivulet. Water produces noise as it moves. I open my eyes and watch the clear iridescent sparkling liquid flow by my feet, a foot away. It gives life to dozens of trees, trees that live through 130-degree summers every year. I struggle painfully to accept this fact. I close my eyes and the sound of the stream produces spectacular fireworks. They fill my body with ecstasy, moving from head to toe and toe to head. Up and down.

The all-encompassing deafening silence opens my mind to the vastness of time. The absence of sound means the absence of time. It goes on forever, never changing. Everything that existed before has led to this moment—but everything is forgotten, forgotten, forgotten over billions of years.

Unexpectedly, a tremendous sadness emerges. Its poignancy tears at me, and tears run down my face. This is the world, this is how it works, I exist in time, surrounded by silence and infinity, a speck of dust, momentarily existing. No different than the stream and trees. Then I will no longer exist. My existence and nonexistence meet in this moment. Is this death—the most difficult thing to comprehend? I bridge the past and the present. I straddle the here and the there. I don't know how I possibly exist, yet my existence has great meaning. I am significant because I realize this, and am insignificant because, well, because I will be long gone soon enough. I will never penetrate the vastness, the emptiness that fills me to bursting. But I have contacted it. I now know it exists and how it feels.

Reflections

DISCOVERING MY POWER SPOT

People usually look at me in disbelief when I tell them that Death Valley is my favorite place on Earth. This chapter recounts the first of many peak experiences there, ones that could not have taken place anywhere else. How could I not love such a place? And how could I not fear it, too? It's where I learned to "love and fear" at the same time. Its unending horizons of time, space, and silence free the mind to roam without constraints. There's nothing to rein you in and everything to draw you out.

You've never *met* a Steel Seraph? He must be behind you, or in
front of the sea-encrusted rock. Kristian's goodness — it lingers,
kindly and unfailing.

17

BEETLE

IN THE SIERRA NEVADA MOUNTAINS one perfect summer day, Spencer and I split off from the group and lie by a creek that rushes through a high mountain meadow. The sky entrances us. We watch fluffy clouds form and dissipate as they make their gray and white way across the vast expanse of the blue heavens above. Sparkling gems of the LSD kaleidoscope fill the air around us. I float in and out of my body, ecstatic.

As if on cue, we sit up at the same time and reach for our water bottles.

I spot a massive beetle, more than two inches long, plodding across the blades of grass at the edge of the cheerful brook. Reflexively, I move away from the shiny black, iridescent creature as it relentlessly lumbers on multiply jointed, hairy, bristling, monstrous legs. Its huge bulbous abdomen ends in a menacing point. A dangerous evil creature, ready to inflict a poisonous painful bite—or sting.

"Yuck," I utter.

"Yuck?" Spencer teasingly-mockingly repeats. "What's the matter? You've never petted a beetle before?" He lowers his hand, palm up, in front of the terrifying object, which dutifully climbs onto it. He gazes fondly down at the bug.

"You are sick," I say.

"Naaw. Come on. They're cute!" He draws his index finger along the back of the insect, lightly stroking it. "See? He likes it." The beetle shambles around Spencer's palm, oblivious to the attention, seeking lower ground.

He adds, "You try."

I gingerly poke it. The creature possesses some heft, while also being extraordinarily light, like a tiny piece of cardboard. I wonder if it's because of its sticky feet.

Spencer says, "Don't poke it. That's no way to treat a beautiful insect. Pet it. Like this." He demonstrates again.

I try a gentler touch. It's not so bad. Now the beetle is harmless, a small mindless animal.

Spencer laughs. "See?"

"It seems kind of stupid."

"It's not stupid, it's just not human. It's a beetle. Isn't it beautiful?" He brings it up to his face almost touching his nose.

I grudgingly admit it. My friend transfers the insect onto my own hand. Those monstrous legs appear mechanical rather than nightmarish. How can it possibly walk on those things? I feel pity and love. Compassion. What a terrible fate. And what a determined and hopeful attitude. Now on my hand, I pet it again. The bug turns to me, curiously waving its antennae.

Reflections

ABANDONING OLD REACTIONS

Psychedelics increase suggestibility. That is, under their influence we are more likely to do, think, feel, or perceive something after receiving a suggestion by someone in authority (the "expert") in an altered state of consciousness (the "trance"). These suggestions may take any form, for better or for worse. This is the essence of hypnosis, a greater susceptibility to suggestion.

In addition, psychedelics and MDMA inhibit fear responses. This contributes to their beneficial effects as psychotherapeutic or wellness tools. These effects on fear occur through modifying the activity of an area of the brain called the amygdala. Oxytocin, a prosocial hormone, may also play a role in reducing our negative reactions to previously fearful stimuli. Finally, psychedelics' lessening of functional connectivity within the default mode network—the brain circuitry responsible for "who I am," "my likes and dislikes," and other relatively fixed aspects of my identity—make it easier to modify one's habitual reactions and opinions. In my case, I did not have to react negatively to the insect—I had other options.

When this episode occurred, I was not phobic about bugs; that is, they did not arouse crippling anxiety. I liked butterflies and moths, and I avoided ants, bees, and hornets. I regarded black shiny beetles more ambiguously. They were bizarre little tank-like things, and I was never quite sure what to make of them.

That day's LSD amplified my positive emotions—happiness, relaxation, and expansiveness—but also led to exaggeratedly negative feelings about the beetle. Spencer had been teaching me how to be in the wilderness, and I trusted his judgment in these matters, so I was receptive to his suggestions. The combination of drug, set, and setting made it easy to reexamine—actually, reverse—my habitual aversive response to this type of insect. Interestingly, ever since that encounter, I have remained much more equanimous about bugs—both harmful and harmless.

18

BIRD HEADS

SCHOOL'S OUT FOR A WEEK and Sam's parents are on vacation. So, Sam, Spencer, and I meet at his house one afternoon to take LSD. My family lives just down the street, but I don't let them know I am in the neighborhood. Inviting a glowering father, an unhappy clinging mother, and a needy resentful sister into my mind before tripping on acid seems unwise. I'm hiding from my family and feel a thrill in doing so. I *can* control how much and in what circumstances I'm around them. The day will be challenging enough. I've never been on LSD in someone's house before and am nervous.

Even the smell of Sam's house differs so much from mine. My parents smoke cigarettes and drink tap water, whereas Sam's father smokes cigars and everyone drinks Sparkletts bottled water from a cooler in the kitchen. Walking through his front door never fails to infuse me with a relaxed, happy, safe, and energized feeling.

Like Sam and I, Spencer King is a native of the San Fernando Valley. He also ran sprints for his high school track team. These factors probably contribute to a slight but unmistakable rivalry between us. That is, who is the faster runner? Who would win a race? It's also impossible to ignore his last name. There is something imperious and entitled about his carriage. Finally, even though I've known Sam my whole life, Spencer and I subtly vie for his attention. In spite of, or because of, these subterranean conflicts, we like each other and enjoy each other's company. Most important, we both count Sam as a dear friend.

I especially value Spencer's experience in nature, as I describe in the previous two chapters. Under his tutelage, I've begun backpacking, tramping through the Sierra Nevada mountains, Southern California deserts, the Oregon coast, and Northern California redwood forests. An entire world has opened for me. And, as I noted in the previous chapter, he's helped me develop an entirely new relationship with insects . . . on LSD.

We take our Orange Barrels late in the afternoon, sit around the kitchen table, and play cards. The game is gin because I've never learned, nor cared to have learned, bridge; this, in contrast to Sam's parents and his friends at The Men's College. Within twenty minutes, the drug's effects begin—an expansion of the space between my ears. Another telltale sign—feeling my eyes water when I know they are not. And the familiar inner excitement, lightness, acceleration, inner pressure, and anticipation.

Spencer says, "I'm feeling it."

Sam chuckles, smiling, almost sardonic, shaking his head back and forth, looking down, as if he's keeping time to music.

"I don't know what I have in my hand," I say, examining my cards.

"Let's go into the living room," Sam suggests.

I detour to the bathroom to pee and laugh when I see beautiful sparkling colors in my flowing urine. I laugh again when I observe my reflection in the mirror.

"Ridiculous," I say and rinse my face with cold water. After briskly drying myself off with a rough towel, my skin looks redder than before. I decide it's the acid. Rubbing my face wouldn't change the color that much.

I return to the living room where Sam is putting a record on his parents' stereo, another reason I like his house. I recognize Miles Davis, whose music Ambrose from The College introduced me to not long ago. It's *Bitches Brew*, the first popular album featuring jazz-rock fusion. Saxophone, electric organ, trumpet, drums, electric guitar, bass, all flowing together in jazz time signatures.

Spencer wraps a blanket around his shoulders and sits on the couch to my right. After a few minutes of mutely staring straight ahead, he lies down. Sam takes his seat in a stuffed chair directly across from me, while I settle into the recliner near the coffee table between us.

The music is exhilarating. Its heavenly, otherworldly notes and melodies weave in and out of the LSD visuals. With eyes closed, I marvel at endless waves of fantastic euphoric colors appearing and disappearing, moving in and out, intersecting and interacting, blending and separating. With eyes open, there are hues, contours, and hidden recesses everywhere in a house I've been in thousands of times. The environment emits weighty importance, power, and significance. This is Sam's house, my childhood haven, without which God only knows how my life would have turned out. I look at my feet resting on the glass-topped coffee table and move them back and forth, flexing and extending, loosening the tightness in my ankles. Tension in them melts away to the accompaniment of intense pleasure.

I notice Spencer curled up on his left side, facing the back of the couch, hugging a pillow against his chest, a blanket over his head.

"What are you doing?" I manage to ask.

He rotates along his long axis, curls up again, lifts his head out of the pillow's recesses, and looks at me.

"The bird heads. I can't look." His eyes are wild. Dilated pupils. Thick oily black eyebrows covering a thick bony brow. A fearful smile on his face, nearly trismic.

Sam laughs, "You're stoned, man. There are no bird heads." He laughs again, then closes his eyes and resumes his meditation on Miles.

Curious, I follow up. "What bird heads?"

"They're coming out of the wall."

I look up and see dozens of bird heads emerging from the wallpaper. It's a single species, dark-colored, a cross between a crow and jay, narrow-headed, with long beaks. Their eyes are open and watchful, moving in their sockets, but their heads are fixed. The birds' eyes glisten, as do their neck and head feathers, black and malevolent.

"You see them, don't you?" Spencer asks feverishly.

"Yeah." They are unpleasant, unsettling. "Just ignore them."

Spencer sputters. "Ignore them? With those eyes??"

Sam looks up.

Spencer turns around again and faces the back of the couch, clutching his pillow and covering his head.

His voice emerges from the pile. "I don't know how you can do it. I can't look at them. I'm staying in here, it's safe."

The music ends but continues reverberating in the living room. It's weird and magical—a residual waxing and waning of what we had just heard—an aftereffect, not an echo.

I say to Sam, "Isn't it interesting what the music does after it's over? It must have something to do with our brains."

"Right. You would know."

He stands and walks over to the bar. It's much smaller than the one at my house, more like a built-in bookshelf behind a counter. But it has a sink, unlike my parents'.

He asks, "Cognac, anyone?" His father's favorite drink.

I again notice the bird heads behind Sam's. They're watching, all of them in unison. If I keep my eyes on my safe childhood friend, I know nothing untoward will befall me.

"Perfect," I reply.

Spencer emits a pale and thin chuckle and says, "Don't forget about me."

Sam and I turn in the direction of the croaking cracking voice. There's Spencer, lying on the couch, facing away from us, pressed ever more tightly against its back, covered in blankets.

Reflections

A FRIGHTENING SHARED HALLUCINATION

In "Flying Carpet," I describe and discuss a shared hallucination that Tom and I experienced. In this chapter, a less pleasant—and for Spencer, a terrifying—one likewise takes center stage.

A psychiatrist, say me in ten years, might find Spencer's LSD reaction ironic. Well, not exactly ironic, but revealing underlying insecurities. As with Tom, the ostensible bravado and overestimation of one's prowess crumbled when unconscious doubts erupted unexpectedly under the influence of the drug. In Tom's case, he shrank and fell into a black hole. Here, Spencer who pets big black beetles in the wilderness, now in a comfortable house, is assaulted by hallucinated bird heads. His casual comfort and familiarity with the natural world masks deeper fears, fears of animals attacking him.

Spencer's anxiety-provoking visions may have come about from his uncertainty about where he ranked in his relationship among the three of us. With Tom, there was a clear-cut hierarchy—he was the macho womanizer, and I was the trusty sidekick. With Spencer, more ambiguity existed, and, in fact, he may have felt threatened and abandoned in the context of Sam and my long-standing friendship. The physical setting, too, was more supportive for me than Spencer. This was one of his first times in Sam's home, whereas for nearly ten years it had served as my childhood refuge.

19

TEUFEL

IT'S A SUNNY EARLY SPRING SATURDAY during my sophomore year at The College. I'm about to borrow Stu's Honda-90 dirt bike, which I plan to drive around the mountains all day after I take LSD.

Ostensibly good-natured, Stu displays an irritable, aggressive edge that comes out in subtle bullying. He delivers his hurtful criticism with a wide smile. While not as magnetic to the women as Tom, he makes up for it with his outgoing, edgy, ambivalently friendly energy. His girlfriend is a wholesome Minnesota lass from across campus whom he is happily debasing. More than once, I see her leave his room crying. He chuckles while showing us dried blood and other secretions on his bedsheets.

When Stu and I get together, neither seems especially interested in the other. More to the point, we subtly resent each other, as we share the undignified role of sidekicks—I'm Tom's and Stu is Ambrose's. Our primary friendships are with someone who isn't around at the time, and we know it.

Midway through the school year, Stu buys his little trail bike. It quickly becomes the go-to vehicle for short around-campus trips—the library, other nearby colleges, and the small town that The College calls home.

Stu agrees to lend me his bike whenever I wish, but it feels like he's doing me a favor, more so than with anyone else. I believe that if it weren't for the group's peer pressure, he would refuse, or threaten to refuse, to let me drive his bike. It would be an act of spite, lording over his rival #2.

Earlier in the week, he returned from test driving it in the mountains behind campus.

"It struggles, but it got me there." He bounces up and down hyperactively on the narrow black seat, swings his ponytail from side to side, and grins a toothy grin.

This gives me the idea of returning to where Sam and I had tripped in the snow earlier that winter.

After breakfast this morning, Stu hands me the keys. I make my way out of the campus and swallow the tiny Orange Barrel.

I happily motor my way up the winding canyon road. The red motorbike—and especially the metal gas tank between my legs—gleams with the sun's reflection. I gaze upward at the increasingly deep blue sky and watch misty clouds form and dissipate, dissipate and form, and marvel at the acid's effects on my vision. I glance down, watching the asphalt pavement pass beneath me. The juxtaposition of the red and blue—which normally produces a vibrating effect—set against the black is intensely pleasurable and possesses great portent. It's almost too perfect.

I arrive at the pullout next to the flats leading to the arroyo with the psychedelic culvert and turn off the motor.

"Unreal!" I laugh aloud, remembering Sam's favorite expression that day. My words form Day-Glo colored waves in front of me. As an added treat, I pass my hands in front of my face, delighting in the trails.

I wonder if I can manage riding off the highway. I contemplate the "90" embossed on the gas tank. The engine's displacement of 90 cc is almost half of what powers a standard walk-behind lawnmower. I'll try it but will stay on gravel spur roads. I don't want to risk damaging Stu's bike on the open flats that are full of cactus, rocks, and other hazards.

Having decided on a course of action, it's time to begin exploring. The engine is hot, and I must bow my legs slightly to keep them from touching it below the tank. The first kickstart attempt fails, and painful panic wells up. It passes. I've got a task at hand. Quickly, I hit upon just the right combination of kick pressure and feeding gas. I rev the engine to clean out the exhaust and settle back onto the seat.

For the next few hours, there are scenes: bright sunlight, dark shadows, blue sky, green trees, rocky gray and brown dirt, red motorcycle. I carefully explore several canyons. Climbing beyond a certain elevation makes the little vehicle sputter and that's as high as I go. I'm focused on this machine, and the motorcycle knows it, albeit dumbly, like an obedient beast of burden with which I enter a dynamic relationship. It's an especially novel sensation, since I've never ridden a horse. I wish the bike to speed up, slow down, turn in a particular direction, and it does so with little effort on my part. More than the bike's speed thrills me—it's the machine's wiry tenacity and responsiveness, its refusal to give up. I let the bike's straining vibration fill my body and resonate with its high-pitched power.

The air begins to chill as shadows lengthen. Patches of snow still cling to the sides of not-too-distant mountains. I turn around and begin a leisurely ride down the main highway. The Honda-90 breathes easier with more plentiful oxygen.

I drive onto campus and see a group of friends congregating in the street in front of The Dorm. There's no traffic and I roll up to them in neutral. Seeing Stu, I turn off the engine and hand him the keys, still straddling the little shiny red motorcycle.

"Thanks, man." I genuinely mean it. "What a great day!"

I notice Teufel in the group, an unusual occurrence.

Teufel plays football for The College. He's a defensive lineman, someone who shoves the faces of the opposing team's offensive linemen—who protect the quarterback or make openings for the running backs—into the ground. He's a mean, slow-witted Aryan, well over six feet and 220 pounds, with a thick skull, pale skin, piglike blue eyes, and a shock of blonde hair. I remember the adage: You look like what you eat. I conclude Teufel eats a lot of pork.

People recognize him as a dangerous fool, and he likewise recognizes whenever someone treats him that way—which is most of the time. Both his Aryan appearance and character frighten me, and I avoid him whenever possible. Now, his normally pale white cheeks glow red, and his perpetual smirk is more pronounced. I wonder if he's drunk.

He emerges from the group and approaches me, malevolently leering.

"Wow! What a macho motorcycle!" His face, never pleasant, is even more lumpy on LSD—misshapen and sporting a multitude of discolored bumps. His uniquely battered look must be from all the hits he's taken on the football field.

He continues, snarling, "Does that mean that you're macho, too? You don't look macho. You're just a skinny little guy."

His eyes flash angrily, a haughty cruel smile curls his lips. I look around nervously. All of a sudden, this is not going well.

"It's just Stu's bike." The air around me takes on a malevolent sheen.

"You stole Stu's bike?!" He chortles and looks around the group for approval. No one is encouraging him. But some are smiling.

I look away and down at the ground and say, "No. I didn't."

Stu interjects, "No, he didn't, Teufel."

The lineman ignores him.

"Did you have a fun time up there, Strassman? Wait! Look at your eyes! Are you fucked up? Did you take acid?"

He looks at Stu and adds, "Hey, Stu. Did you know Rick drove your bike around high?"

I'm not especially high, but I'm not normal, and my dilated pupils evince a lingering intoxication. The last few hours on LSD require a calm atmosphere. You're neither fully in one world nor the other. It's a fraught transition. I want more than anything to be alone—skip dinner, take a long hot shower, and lie on my bed.

I try placating him. "It's okay, Teufel."

He brings his thuggish face within inches of mine, his breath hot as he hisses, "It's okay? What do you mean, 'It's okay'? You think you're so much smarter than I am?" I do, of course, but this isn't the time to remind him.

My sudden nemesis's eyes take on a diabolic menace.

Uh-oh.

No one in the group is smiling now, and it's unclear where this is heading.

Without warning, the massive football player thrusts both his arms forward and outward against my chest, using all his strength. Somehow,

I avoid smashing to the ground, lying under a several-hundred-pound motorcycle. But there is an explosion of pain in my left ankle as I break my fall, and I cry out.

The burning in Teufel's eyes fades. He's momentarily surprised and afraid. Then a look of sheepish guilt. Then he regains his bravado and appears pleased with himself. He looks around the group, snuffling, then returns his attention to me, glaring.

"Macho guy, macho bike. See how smart he is?" He adds for good measure, gritting through his teeth, "You pussy!"

Woody steps forward out of the circle of young men now surrounding this volatile unfolding scene. While not so sturdily built, he's a few inches taller than Teufel and gets between us.

"Hey, Teufel. Back off, would you?"

Still combative, he says, "It's okay. Rick even said so. Didn't you?"

Woody says, "Fuck off, Teufel. You're a fucking idiot."

The others join in. "Yeah, you're a fucking idiot, Teufel."

The young psychopath considers the situation. With a crafty expression, he mimes surrender.

"Sure. No problem. But just you wait, Strassman. I'll be coming for you. When you least expect it." He spits at my feet.

Woody gives me a hand and turns to the demented giant. "That's enough, Teufel. Lay off."

I appreciate the support but it's too late, both for my ankle and my sense of security at The College.

Leaning on Woody the entire way, I limp back to The Dorm and up the stairs to my room. The next morning my ankle is swollen, painful, and nearly immobile. Tom helps me to the student health center, where Dr. Chapman applies a cast and provides me crutches. I use them for the next ten days. Healing is quick and without incident. Within a month, I'm pain-free and back to my normal activities.

Teufel keeps his word, however, and begins harassing me, with or without others around. Walking back from class one day, I see my tormentor walking toward me on the sidewalk. I cross the street to avoid him, but he runs across, too, responding to my maneuver. He charges toward me, a fleshy locomotive, and halts abruptly, a stride short of mowing me down.

"You pussy, Strassman! What are you afraid of? Huh?"

In a group setting, it's more subdued, but the message is the same. "You're a pussy, Strassman, and I'm going to get you. *A fucking pussy.*"

The confrontations wear on me. The protofascist now occupies a dreadful place in my mind. When are his classes? Where does he hang out? Who are his friends? I brace myself whenever I leave The Dorm. My sophomore year is over in a couple of months. I ponder, Is this how the next two years are going to be?

———

Reflections
BULLYING MEETS PAST ABUSE

While the highlight of this narrative is not the subjective effects of LSD that day, it nevertheless describes a particular type of encounter under its influence. That encounter may not have taken the turn it did if I weren't tripping. And, as a corollary, the outcome of the confrontation with the bully might have been different. That is, my response could have modified Teufel's subsequent behavior. It's impossible to know.

Bullying and abuse share many features. Abusers and bullies may perceive their victim as a threat to their self-esteem or competition for attention. With bullies, that threat also includes the victim's "otherness"—racial, religious, physical, or intellectual. Both abusers and bullies suffer offense easily and seek to shame and dominate their target. Both also exploit preexisting power imbalances in strength, age, and social status. In the latter case, Teufel was a social pariah, in contrast to many bullies who are popular in their peer group.

Add to this toxic mix the dynamic between Jews and Germans, one that stretches back centuries. Here, historical and religious factors magnify these bullying dynamics. For example, the victim's pleading submissiveness and their inability or unwillingness to defend themselves further inflames the perpetrator's fervor. In the same vein, both abusers and bullies blame their victims.

In this narrative, my altered state—dilated pupils, unusually relaxed and happy demeanor—may have alerted Teufel to a vulnerability in someone he already disliked. My LSD-catalyzed hypersensitivity exaggerated my normal responses, especially fear, which my nemesis may have even smelled. And if the scent of fear didn't biochemically play a role, any number of abuse-related ingrained behaviors and speech patterns— like averting my eyes and a placating tone of voice—afforded Teufel the taste of blood. Especially salient was my reaction to his staring at me malignantly. This interpersonal posture, reminiscent of my father's angry stare portending a beating, was profoundly anxiety-provoking.

The abuser and bully wish to create the illusion of support by others, the "bystanders." These third parties in any bullying/abuse dynamic play a vital role. The aggressor often seeks an audience for approval, and that audience may overtly encourage or passively acquiesce to the attack. While I was not paying attention to Stu at that moment, his subtle but pervasive snideness toward me also may have encouraged Teufel's behavior.

Bystanders who identify with the victim may freeze in fear, empathizing with the attacker's target. However, for fear of becoming another victim, they do not intervene. On the other hand, helpful bystanders may show what Freud called "moral courage," as when Woody stepped in to interrupt the assault, albeit only after Teufel injured me.

The psychological origins of bullying-abusing are complex and interwoven. One may have experienced bullying and/or abuse as a child. They then learned to imitate the abuser in hopes of establishing a common bond. Freud's daughter Anna, the first child psychoanalyst, called this coping strategy "identification with the aggressor." Or, the future bully may decide that the only way not to be bullied is to bully. Sadism—experiencing pleasure by inflicting pain on another—certainly plays a role. However, sadism is not always the primary motivation in those with a conscience or sense of remorse. These emotions briefly appeared on Teufel's face after injuring me, but they seemed to play no moderating role in his continuing to torment me.

20

REDWOODS MAILBOX

WE'RE EMBARKING ON A WEEK of camping and taking acid in the Northern California redwoods during spring break.

For this expedition, Rachel and Stella join us.

Jewish, from Chicago, Rachel often joins us on our psychedelic outings. The daughter of a Seattle banker, she's The Acid Queen. She also is Spencer's girlfriend and is a regular visitor to the complex of buildings where Sam, Peter, Bruce, and Spencer live. Dark-haired, dark-eyed, undeniably Jewish features and personality—edgy, smart, funny, and self-effacing—she and I possess a natural affinity. On drugs and/or marijuana—the only times we're together—we effortlessly engage in discussions that Spencer can't keep up with. His jealousy is obvious, which adds to my feeling a certain protectiveness about her.

When tripping on LSD, Rachel keeps a white plastic spoon in her mouth. One day on acid, I ask her, "Why do you keep a white plastic spoon in your mouth while you trip?"

Her answer with the spoon in her mouth is unintelligible. She removes it and tries again, "I like having something to chew on. And it keeps my mouth wet."

"It's kind of ridiculous."

"That's another reason," she laughs.

Stella is more of an enigma, and I've never taken acid with her. Likewise Jewish and hailing from a wealthy family, she keeps her distance. Sam and she date intermittently, but dance around commitment.

The first time we meet, I recognize her.

I ask, "Weren't you sitting near me at a basketball game between The College and The Men's College?"

Her dark eyes darken. "I don't think so."

"I started screaming at Zebulun Cohen and had to leave. You and your friend were laughing at me. Or with me."

She laughs. "Oh, right. You."

I can't resist. "You were flirting with me."

She laughs even louder. "No, I wasn't!"

"Well, I was on acid. But I could swear."

"Dream on."

Losing interest, she makes her way into Sam's room to study.

Spring weather in the redwoods is dramatic: rain, sun, wind, all rapidly mixing with and replacing one another. The forest bursts with life. We establish a base camp and a routine. Breakfast in the morning. LSD after. A hike for the rest of the day if the acid isn't too strong. If it is, we lie on the ground and watch the sky, listen to the wind blow through the massive trees, and check in while smoking joints. Heavy downpours force us back into our tents until they pass. Then dinner and copious marijuana. Jack Daniels before bed.

Bruce used to camp in this park with his family as a child and is the designated trip master for our week's adventures. The next day, his high school girlfriend Molly will be driving up from the Bay Area to join us. Molly knows none of us and upon arrival is uncomfortable around this odd lot: grubby, hairy young men and grubby yet refined and wealthy Rachel and Stella. Adding to her outsider status, she has no experience with psychedelics. Everyone tries engaging her in conversation, but it's more than she can manage, too much out of her comfort zone. Neither does there appear to be much affection between Bruce and her.

Toward the end of the week, after Molly's arrival, we need supplies. Four of us—Bruce, Rachel, Rusty, and I—take only a half-dose of LSD after breakfast. Molly takes none. We head into town, Bruce behind the wheel of his truck, a large Ford with a simple camper shell covering the bed. Molly sits next to him, Rachel next to her, and I'm pressed against the passenger door.

Rusty is happy to climb into the back of the truck, where he sprawls among the pile of blankets Bruce keeps there for emergencies.

As Bruce closes up the tailgate and camper shell door, he takes a closer look at Rusty and laughs, "Man, you look like a firework. Or some kind of red-orange alien."

Rusty appears more disabled than any of us. When we point this out, he admits to taking a full dose of LSD.

Evidence supporting Rusty's nickname isn't hard to come by—a full head of orange hair extending below his shoulders and a full orange beard. Today, he wears a fire-engine red bandanna, aviator reflective sunglasses, and a red plaid tartan flannel-lined shirt. Even without the LSD, the orange-red energy pouring out of him vibrates at high frequency.

"I feel the acid, man," the mumbled words tumble out of his red face, red everywhere. "I need to keep my sunglasses on." In the dark recesses of the truck bed.

The trip into town is uneventful, at least from our perspective, making sure to minimize our contact with the locals. We're all familiar enough with the effects of LSD to maintain an air of normality despite the malformed, misshapen, bizarre, tragic, and hilarious appearance and behavior of those around us. Those not under the influence of the drug often look stranger than those who are.

Grocery store: check. Outdoor equipment store for stove fuel: check. Well, not entirely.

Striking up a conversation with the clerk about the weather, we hear him say, "Only fools and strangers predict the weather out here, fellas." We all laugh sagely and resume our errands.

The truck needs gas, and we find a service station. Molly ducks into the bathroom as the rest of us load up on gum, chips, and soda. Bruce pumps gas. After paying the attendant, we check in with Rusty.

Opening the shell, we find him wedged into the far-left corner of the bed, directly behind the driver's seat, blankets covering all but his face.

I say, "Hey. How's it going?" in his direction.

Our increasingly Day-Glo tangerine hair-colored friend moves his head around, somewhere between a shake and a nod. The shadows and sunglasses hide his eyes.

No answer is forthcoming. I follow up. "Well, you know how to get in touch. We'll be up front." No answer.

Bruce, Rachel, and I amble unsteadily to the cab and climb in. We're waiting for Molly. Or at least Rachel and I are.

Rachel notes, "Rusty looks pretty wasted. I hope he's okay. He wasn't saying anything or moving. He just had that stupid smile on his face." She adds, "Like a Cheshire cat."

We set out on the highway in the direction of our campsite. Rachel and I exchange a glance, as if to say "Uh-oh. Molly's still at the gas station." Neither of us mention the fact, waiting for Bruce to realize she is not with us. We drive for five minutes, then ten. Rachel and I can no longer contain ourselves.

She says, "I sure like having the extra room up here."

I reply, "Yeah. There sure is a lot more room up here."

The music is loud, Bruce is puffing away on his marijuana-packed elkhorn pipe, in his own world.

Finally, I lean over Rachel toward Bruce and say, "I think you forgot Molly."

Horror-stricken, Bruce slaps his forehead with his right hand, his left continuing to hold the pipe and steering wheel. He looks around the cab; in particular, where Molly had been, should be, and now is not.

Returning his gaze to the road, his predicament sinks in. He groans, "Oh, shit."

He adds, "Would you guys mind going back with me instead of my dropping you off first? Otherwise, she is really going to let me have it. If you're around, she will have to behave, and it will help her cool off."

"Okay."

Bruce pulls off the road onto the shoulder and brings the truck to a stop. He makes a careful U-turn, pauses on the opposite side's shoulder, and makes certain it's safe before merging with traffic. Back at the gas station, Molly is stamping her feet in front of the convenience store door. She's cold. Or enraged. Or both. The heightened emotions suddenly amplify the LSD's effects, and waves of intensity wash over all of us. Storm clouds of angry light envelop us. Tension in the chest, bitterness in the mouth, and cold hands. Sound takes on ominous overtones and distortions.

Bruce jumps out of the truck, puts his arm around his angry girlfriend. I get out, and she climbs in, squeezing next to Rachel, and I return to my spot, next to her. Molly fumes, says nothing.

Bruce tries to sound cheery, but it comes off strained. "I know a really pretty drive we can take around here before returning to the camp. It goes by the water, along some cliffs." Anything to delay the moment of reckoning.

It is a pretty drive, but the tension in the cab grows even thicker. And we still haven't heard a peep from Rusty.

I raise the latter issue. "I hope Rusty is okay back there. We ought to have told him we were taking a detour before returning."

Chewing a fresh white plastic spoon, Rachel says, "He'll be fine. He always is. That Rusty."

She rummages through the valise of cassette tapes and puts on *Eric Clapton's Rainbow Concert*.

The road narrows to barely the width of the truck, as low hanging trees nearly envelop us.

Bruce says, "We need to turn around. It's too thick."

He stops the Ford in the middle of the road on a long straightaway, thus visible to vehicles coming from either direction. He looks around to get his bearings.

He turns the steering wheel as far left as possible, moving the seemingly ever-larger truck slowly forward. The front wheels barely remain on the edge of the road. He begins backing up while turning the steering wheel as far right as he can, looking carefully at both side view mirrors, as the camper shell obstructs his rear-view mirror. We hear a loud crack.

Bruce slams on the brakes, puts the vehicle into park, and turns off the engine. He and I get out of the truck and walk back to see what we've done. We stare in surprised dismay at a wooden post, topped by a mailbox, nearly snapped in two at truck bumper height. Looking around, we see a house twenty yards down a gravel driveway. There's no sign of the owner.

We also need to check on Rusty. Bruce pulls up the camper shell door and lowers the tailgate. Rusty is there all right, leaning against the back wall of the truck. He's closer to its center, most likely to better appreciate the stereo effect from the shell's two little upper corner speakers. Eric Clapton is playing, but it sounds like a loop, repeating over and over. Pathetically tinny psychedelically distorted "Layla."

Rusty is not only tilting, he's melting into his surroundings. His outline merges imperceptibly with the mounds of blankets around him. Not moving, his face is impassive. Everything oozes with radioactive oranges and reds—his hair, skin, flannel shirt, and bandanna. He's still wearing his sunglasses, and it's impossible to know where he's looking, or even if his eyes are open. He tilts his head, however, in the direction of the owner of the little house whose noisy footsteps announce his arrival at the top of the driveway. He's in his mid-fifties and looks angry. We turn around to face him.

"What's going on here . . ." he begins, before noticing Rusty in the back of the truck. He stops mid-sentence.

We join him in peering at Rusty's immobile listing figure. Clapton continues playing the same riff, the music tinkling unpleasantly. Mr. Homeowner's expression changes from anger to fear. I wonder if he sees the glow. I hope not.

Bruce steps up skillfully. "Man, I'm really sorry. It's totally my fault. I'll give you my name and phone number, and I'll help take care of replacing it."

The homeowner raises both of his hands in front of him. It's a gesture of surrender, retreat, and a wish for mercy. He looks furtively and uncertainly between us and our catatonic friend.

The increasingly anxious stranger nearly supplicates, "No. No. Don't worry about it. It's just a piece of wood. I've got more. No problem. It's fine. Don't worry." He shakes his head, looking slightly downward, trying not to see any more of us than absolutely necessary.

Eric Clapton continues playing the Layla solo.

I turn aside to Bruce and whisper, "Do you have auto-repeat on?"

He shakes his head and returns to the problem at hand.

"Are you sure?" Bruce asks.

"Yeah. No problem."

Our nervous new acquaintance walks down the drive to his cabin, stands in front of his door, and watches us. He doesn't want to lose sight until we are gone.

Bruce and I consider Rusty's state before closing up the shell. We've seen him almost this bad before, and aren't especially worried, but one never knows. Besides, we'll be back at the camp soon and will check on him there.

The sun is setting by the time we return.

Rusty climbs out of the back of the truck, stretches, yawns, and looks contented. "Now *that* was *amazing*," he says.

I'm also reassured that his orange glow is fading. Whether this is due to me or him doesn't matter.

Stella comes up to Rachel and me, looks over at Rusty, and says, "You've been gone a long time. What happened?"

Molly takes Bruce by the hand and leads him to their tent. Her raised angry voice broadcasts throughout our site. More difficult to hear are his intermittent soft apologies.

Reflections
ADVERSE EFFECTS OF PSYCHEDELICS IN THOSE WHO DON'T TAKE THEM

There are several ways that people in an altered state—regardless of its cause—may affect others. In the case of drugs, psychedelics occupy a unique position because they modify every component of human consciousness, not just one or two as with sedatives or stimulants. Therefore, we would expect a correspondingly greater range and/or intensity of both positive and negative interpersonal effects of psyche-delic intoxication. In this chapter we see how the person in the altered state's behavior has a direct, negative impact on another—leading to adverse consequences for the person *not* under the influence. In this case, it was Bruce abandoning Molly at the gas station.

A psychoanalytic approach understands Bruce to be acting out—via his behavior—his unconscious, unacceptable negative feelings toward Molly. We know from both brain imaging and introspection that LSD imbues more salience to usually unconscious memories and emotions. As a result, this content now attempts to enter awareness. "Acting out" refers to substituting maladaptive behavior for experiencing painful or anxiety-provoking mental contents. Bruce could not admit his lack of love for Molly, but he nevertheless demonstrated it by his actions. When sober, he may have been able to keep his unconscious attitude under greater control; however, he was unable to in the LSD-modified state. Molly was aware of this subliminal message, as we see by her anger rather than her forgiveness.

In addition, a person in an altered state may indirectly affect others' consciousness. If someone is emoting under the influence of alcohol—maudlin or garrulous—those around that person may find themselves feeling similarly. However, psychedelic effects are more variable than those of other drugs, and if those around a psychedelicized person are not familiar with the state, they may have difficulty tracking him or her, which can be decidedly unpleasant. The chapter "Ubehebe" describes an example of this type of "contact low."

Another closely related phenomenon occurs in this chapter. That is, being in an altered state may frighten others simply because of how one looks or acts. The wide range of psychedelic effects again plays a role. Bruce and I did not look as if we were simply drunk or on mari-juana. Rather, we presented with a complex picture: dilated pupils, silly smiles, uncertain shuffling gait, clipped telegraphic speech, and staccato giggles. If the homeowner had never seen people on LSD, he would be alarmed. He also would likely be alarmed if he recognized the state.

An interesting element of this episode is Bruce's being able to carry on a normal conversation with the homeowner when the situation required it. Forcing oneself "down" by an act of will is a rarely discussed but well-known property of the psychedelic state. This phenomenon underscores the essential role of one's own psychic/mental apparatus—the set—in determining the nature of any individual psychedelic experience. It is possible to modify the intensity of pharmacological effects, at times radically, through a conscious decision.

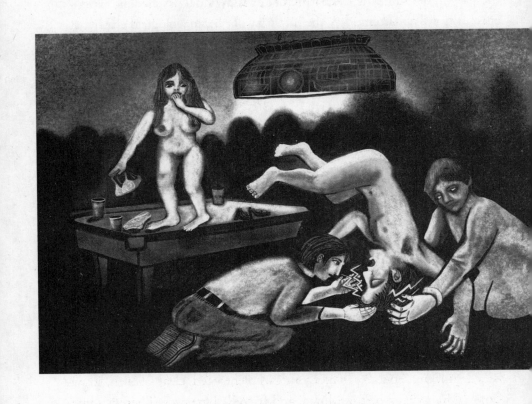

21

STRIPPER

SOPHOMORE SPRING AT THE COLLEGE means rush time, when fraternities seek new members to join their ranks as juniors in the upcoming fall. Fraternities are novel for me, and I haven't decided if I'm interested. Hints and intimations I overheard during my parents' cocktail parties linked fraternities with "country clubs." This then led to conversations about "quotas" and "anti-Semites." Thus, I'm uncertain whether they are good for the Jews; that is, good for me as a Jew. Further, fraternities are not especially popular now in the setting of antiwar and antiestablishment protests and heavy drug—not alcohol—use.

So, I react cautiously when Nils, the captain of the football team, comes up to me one day in late March and asks, "Rick. How are you?"

Nils is the archetypal all-American; in his case, by way of Swedish stock. Sincere, reputable, wholesome, wholehearted, clean-shaven, straw-colored hair that won't lay down, and friendly blue eyes. There is something odd about him physically, though: very short legs and a very long torso. His fiancée Chelsea is the daughter of the owner of one of the world's largest shipping companies.

I've heard that The Fraternity is the best at The College. Nicest guys, best parties, sweetest girlfriends. Pledging is easy, too—no humiliating, exhausting, or potentially dangerous orientation after joining. It's more of a beer culture, guys and their girlfriends, a steady ship. Less pot and LSD. Nils is secretary-treasurer and his current task: inviting potential brothers to this year's rush party. He's making the rounds.

He presents the invitation. "A number of the brothers know and like you, so we thought we'd reach out."

I thank him and ask, "What goes on there?"

An impish grin forms on Nils's face. "We'll have kegs, pool tables, plenty of food. We'll try to get everyone to say hello to you during the party."

"Oh, and also . . ." Nils's grin becomes even more impish. "We'll have a stripper."

Sidestepping the implications of this news for the moment, I ask, "Did you invite anyone else from The Dorm?"

"Stu and Tom. Ambrose doesn't seem like the fraternity type."

I first consider why not to go.

Limitless beer is one reason. After my early misadventures with alcohol, I've limited my drinking to one can of Coors every evening, along with a shared joint, at Stu and Ambrose's before dinner. Being immersed in the realm of cavorting (anti-Semitic?) Gentiles is another. Finally, it's a test where my friends are my competitors. What if they like Tom more because of his romantic prowess? Or Stu, because he's brasher? And I decided against joining the track team, so I no longer belong to the athletic corps as they still do.

Finally, a stripper? I've never seen one. Will she take off *all* her clothes? Will she have sex with people there? I worry I will have to perform something sexual about which I have no experience or knowledge.

"Okay," I finally answer. "I'll see you there. Thanks for the invitation."

The Lodge is tucked away in an obscure cranny of a medieval cement complex of residences built in the 1940s. It's only a few steps from the dining hall, but the narrow walkway leading to its small common area is easy to miss. This is the first time I learn of its existence.

The evening begins quietly. Small collections of young men playing pool, good-natured conversation wafting in and out of a steady stream of music. I stand by a keg, chatting with several brothers whom I know, but not well, and become more congenial and outgoing after two or three beers. The gathering quickly expands in number and activity. It is the most new people I've been around since the first couple of weeks of freshman year.

The stripper, whose name is Dolly, appears as if out of thin air. Everyone turns to look at her, cheer, and shout. Two burly members of the football team lift her up onto the pool table in the middle of the room. She is Mexican, older than anyone at the party, early thirties. Fleshy, pretty, dark, heavily perfumed. Her makeup gives her a youthful blush. She looks over the crowd from her elevated perch, smiles wickedly and charmingly. The crowd approves.

As the loud, lascivious music builds, so do the drunk young men's hollers, handclapping, and foot stamping. Dolly adjusts her black top hat, shimmering silver silk pants, and green silk blouse. She bends forward toward the crowd and adjusts the buckles on her black shiny patent leather shoes, showing off her breasts. Then she turns away, leans forward again, and her pants slide down to expose the top of her buttocks.

I down another beer, embarrassed by the display, and look around to see if anyone else is. There doesn't seem to be. At the same time, I'm happy. Happy because I'm having fun.

Dolly somehow makes direct eye contact with each member of the crowd. She strides across the pool table, if that were even possible on such a small surface. Two or three strides at most. Innocent yet naughty. Not spectacularly beautiful, but pretty enough considering the circumstances.

Dolly has a system. She invites one of the young men to dance with her on the pool table, and that fellow helps her remove one item of clothing. She only allows someone to touch her clothes, not her body. The black top hat goes first. She pushes away her undresser's hands when he gets too close. His mock frustration rouses the crowd to greater raucousness. One fellow lowers himself off the table and another jumps up to take his place.

I feel as if I were about to take a test, haven't studied, and don't know the material. I finish another tall red plastic cup of beer.

She recruits Jack, a popular senior classman, to unbutton her blouse. Once undone, Dolly deftly removes the green silk garment. Large soft jiggling breasts in a black push-up bra, lacey, with hearts. Nils is up next, and the gentle giant helps her out of the silver silk pants, revealing her alluring electric-pink thong. The roar is deafening.

Tom sidles up to me, his eyes glistening with animal hunger, a drunk grin, flicking his tongue in and out between his lips.

"Man! I could eat her out!!" he hollers.

By now, I've learned that this refers to oral sex that a guy performs on a girl. Yet, it is just an idea to me, still a virgin. Tom, on the other hand, is a connoisseur and ready to go.

He adds, "I can't wait for her to start grinding." He thrusts his pelvis back, forth, and around to demonstrate. Now that he mentions it, I look up and notice that Dolly *is* grinding. I hadn't previously equated "grinding" with the rhythmic pelvic movements that she now performs.

Stu leaps onto the pool table. They are dancing together, not touching, each grinds their pelvis mere inches from the other. After a few minutes, she seems to tire, and a fresh round of yells, hoots, and hollers revitalizes her. She gently and titillatingly pushes Stu away from her. This is his cue to climb down.

I have another beer. I sense I am due up any minute. Jesus.

Soon, after two or three others make their way onto and off of the pool table, she's free of her bra and panties. She spins around, seductively drawing each in, coquettishly pushing him away, all in playful fun, it seems. There are no hard feelings, anger, or aggression. It's a ritual that everyone seems familiar and comfortable with.

As the heat and fervor in the room rise, those dancing with Dolly begin removing their own clothes. Stu jumps up again, strips down to his boxer shorts and athletic socks—the barest anyone has gotten yet. The crowd goes insane.

Someone turns to me and yells over the din, "Your turn, Rick! Go on up and dance with her!!"

Tom looks down at me, canine leer filling his face, and says, "Go at her, killer! Eat her out!!"

I want to. I finish my beer and look around for how to climb up onto the pool table. Strong hands on each side lift me up.

Unsteady yet light on my feet, Dolly and I appraise each other across the green felt expanse. The Lodge's stereo system blasts a new song, a thumping, driving Creedence Clearwater Cajun-rock classic; in this case, the extended version. Dancing has never been my strength, but at this moment, my body is loose, limber, responding to the music intuitively, almost magically.

We dance, approach each other from opposite ends of the table's long axis. I reach out to touch her shiny flowing hair. She gently pushes away my hand. As a consolation, she begins unbuttoning my shirt, effecting another wave of shouts and roars. I help her and once done, fling my shirt down below to the eager crowd. I point to my belt, an invitation to unbuckle it. She hesitates briefly before complying. I quickly remove my blue jeans, stumbling slightly as I stand on one leg at a time. I am further ennobled by that act, and someone hands both Dolly and me a full cup of beer. She takes a sip of hers and puts it down. I drink mine in one draw, to more approving shouts.

She helps me take off my T-shirt.

I think: Here I am, Rick Strassman, dancing on top of a pool table with a beautiful naked Mexican stripper, in just my boxer shorts and socks.

"Take it off! Take it off!" the crowd yells. Dolly is stark naked, so the only thing this could mean is a call to remove my boxer shorts. Which I do. The woman looks alarmed briefly, but quickly regains her composure, keeping her eyes on mine.

The pace and volume of the Cajun rock song increases. I close my eyes to focus on the music, feeling even more the sound vibrating and moving my body. I spin around on the table once. Twice. Opening my eyes, I see Dolly is concerned. I shut my eyes again and begin to beat imaginary drums.

Ambrose often does this while we listen to music in his room. Eyes closed, pounding imaginary drums, legs bouncing up and down unimaginably fast, shaking his head back and forth, transfixed by a particularly driving beat from his awesome speakers. I've always wondered about this because I can't identify with his excitement. Is he faking feelings, feelings that nevertheless drive his ecstatic-looking behavior? Pretending somehow?

Now, I am in that place. Eyes shut, head bobbing up and down, maniacally drumming the thin air in front of me. I begin spinning again, around and around. In a frenzy, uninhibited, released from the bonds of gravity. Released from the bonds of my virginity, my Jewishness, my non-belonging.

I lean over and topple off the pool table, headfirst. I land on my head, though not with full force. Two fraternity members, doing security duty and thus sober, catch me just as my head hits the ground. Now laying face up, I turn over onto my right side. Nils kneels next to me, and he places his left hand under my head.

With worry in his eyes, he says, "I think you've had enough, Rick. Let's get you dressed and back to your room."

They lift me by my shoulders, one on either side. I vomit on my new cowboy boots, purchased that day for the party, as we three make our way toward The Lodge exit.

I'm alone, standing in front of my dorm room. I vomit again on my new boots. I fumble with the key, unable to insert it. The third try succeeds. Before crossing the threshold, I look down at my boots.

I say through the open doorway, "I can't walk into my room wearing these."

Sitting down, I remove my boots and set them by the door outside the room. I fall onto my bed. Before losing consciousness, my hand moves up toward an egg growing on my scalp.

I arise at eleven the next morning. The egg is larger and throbs painfully—dull and sharp at the same time. My entire head hurts. Sick.

I grab my soap and face towel, open the door, and see Ernesto, The Dorm's Mexican janitor. He is an extraordinarily kindly man whom we all like and trust. He is always looking over his brood from the shadows and behind the scenes. He's mopping the floor in front of my door. He shakes his head when he sees me.

Laughing, he says, "Barf boots! Ha ha. Boots have barf on them! Ha ha."

I emit an inarticulate groan and my head spins.

"No worry. I clean them off for you. Too much drinking? Get sick?"

He tsk-tsks while smiling sadly, shaking his head good-naturedly but attentively. He has seen a lot of sick college students and knows what to look for.

"Yeah. I drank too much last night. I fell on my head from on top of the pool table."

Ernesto stops cleaning and leans on his mop. He looks more closely at me. He thought he had heard it all.

"Fell off pool table? Onto head?!"

"Right."

Suddenly, I become frightened. How close a call was it? What if no one had broken my fall? I have never had such a large bump on my head, nor one as painful.

"I was dancing with a stripper. It was great. I fell off, though. Lucky someone caught me."

The arc of Ernesto's headshaking becomes greater, and he tries but cannot stifle a laugh.

"Dancing with stripper? Fell off pool table onto head? My, my, my."

It's too much, even for him.

"I know." I notice my washed-off boots at the door.

I need food, coffee, water. Fresh air.

"Thanks, Ernesto. Thanks for cleaning my boots."

"Ha ha. Not just boots. All in front of door, too."

"Oh, I guess so. I was throwing up a lot. Thanks for that, too."

My attempt at a wan smile sends shooting pain across my skull.

The hot water and soap wash away a layer of grime and discomfort.

Ernesto remains nearby, mopping. I return to my room, dress, and step out again. I am careful to look straight down the stairs before beginning my descent. My head hurts too much to turn around and say goodbye to Ernesto.

Lunch has begun. I spy Tom and sit next to him after gathering fruit salad, coffee, and two glasses of water. Nothing heavy to eat today.

I say to him, "Man, that was crazy shit last night."

"How are you doing, man?"

"My head really hurts. I puked all over my boots and the floor in front of the door. Ernesto gave me shit."

"I saw him this morning and told him what happened. Good thing those guys caught you."

"Good thing."

Tom leans in closer, wearing a conspiratorial look. "You know the worst part of last night for you?"

"Um, that I fell off a pool table and landed on my head?"

"No, man. It was that your dick looked so small."

Later that day I walk over to the student health center and ask if Dr. Chapman has any openings. He does, and after being led into the examining room, I ask the kindly doctor to examine my penis.

"Is it small? Or average? Or what?" I ask.

An understanding warmth exudes from the white-coated middle-aged physician.

"Sure, I'll take a look. Are you worried about it?"

"Sometimes."

Compassionate Dr. Chapman nods agreeably and asks me to pull down my jeans and boxer shorts. I look down, feeling small.

He squats in front of me and takes a careful look. From the front, both sides, lifting it up to examine its underside.

"Everything looks fine to me. I would say your penis is average size."

"Are you sure?"

"Yes, I'm sure. Nothing to worry about. It looks completely normal."

Just like that, I no longer feel small.

Dr. Chapman straightens up and says, "I see you have a lump on your head. What's that from?"

"I got drunk last night and fell on my head."

"Let me take a look at that."

I wince and pull away from the gentle probing touch.

"Did you lose consciousness?"

"I don't think so. It sure hurts, though."

He looks at my eyes, asks me to follow the motion of his finger from side to side, up and down. He flashes a light into my pupils, evaluates my reflexes with a little hammer. The same friendly noncommittal approach.

"You're lucky. Everything looks okay. But come by if you start getting drowsy, your vision deteriorates, it's hard to walk or talk, you vomit again.* Anything like that."

"OK. Thank you, Dr. Chapman."

I want to be like Dr. Chapman one day.

And I don't want brain damage.

Walking back to The Dorm, I feel relieved but not released. My thoughts turn to my application to transfer to Stanford in the fall. I wonder when I will hear from them. It's where I've always wanted to be, not The College, with its too freely flowing LSD, alcohol, marijuana, and unrelenting sexual one-upmanship. Not only do my classmates not support me, they deride me. And the Neanderthal Teufel is a constant threat. In my heartfelt essay accompanying my transfer application, I shared how my time at The College had matured me, and that now I need higher level academics at a larger university.

After a fitful, painful nap and before dinner, I walk over to the mail room. There, waiting in my mailbox, is my acceptance letter from Stanford.

---

*Signs and symptoms of an epidural hematoma, a blood clot that forms between the skull and the dura, a thick lining covering the brain. After head trauma, one may form rapidly, compress the brain, and potentially lead to death.

Reflections

FINAL ALCOHOL FIASCO

With this chapter, my life at The College ends on both ignominious and salvific notes. No new elements appear in this episode; rather, those from previous narratives reach their limit—academically, psychologically, socially, and vis-à-vis altered states of consciousness.

Being invited to a fraternity rush party shone an uncomfortable light on the sense of not belonging that permeated my two years at The College. I again availed myself of the stimulant-like effects of rapid repeated alcohol intake to paper over social and sexual anxieties. *I* would be the most provocative of the young men who took center stage on the pool table with Dolly. And again, overdrinking led to an adverse effect on my health, one that this time might have led to grave injury or even death. One also sees the repetition of a more primitive unconscious pattern laid down in my early development: endangering myself in order to see who might miraculously appear to save me. While the alert fraternity brothers actually saved me this time, I remained unaware of the psychological mechanisms behind this dangerous behavioral pattern.

How does one explain reward after so much duress? To whom or what does one attribute it? The Stanford acceptance letter that came on the heels of the catastrophic rush party was a striking example of such a reversal of fortune. It provided escape from an untenable set of constraints at The College and entry to a new expansive university experience. Was a merciful God overseeing my life and decided that enough was enough? How much was due to the exercise of my own free will? That is, did I actually determine this positive outcome? Or, was it simply one in an infinite number of effects resulting from an infinite number of causes within the karmic matrix?

From the psychospiritual perspective, suffering—whether due to our own or others' actions—may serve a valuable function even without the promise of reward. For example, it may serve as a lesson to others to live a more virtuous life. For a theologically oriented person, suffering leads us to question God's wisdom and love, even the Deity's existence. By attempting to understand God's ways, one draws closer to God. Forbearing suffering, examining its causes, protesting against it—all force us to confront one of life's greatest paradoxes. The paradigmatic Hebrew biblical example of how one deals with unrelenting suffering is the character of Job. While Job receives bounteous material reward after his inexplicable (to him) travail ends, his more enduring recompense is God demonstrating to Job the existence and nature of the Deity's sovereignty over existence.

In Buddhism, suffering—or at least "unsatisfactoriness"—is the first of the Four Noble Truths of the religion. The first item in this declaration of Buddhism's fundamental tenets asserts that for most of us, we do not have what we want and have what we don't. This then leads to the next three of the four Truths; that is, suffering results from desire, abolishing desire abolishes suffering, and the means to do so have been laid out by the Buddha in his Eightfold Path.

22

NUCLEAR REACTOR

IT'S A HOT SUMMER DAY when Tom and I take a trip south to San Onofre beach. We've heard that the surf and sand are ideal and are reassured by reports of the nearby nuclear reactor's safety. The water is warm, discharged back into the sea after cooling the power plant. No radioactivity, they say. Tom has Orange Barrel LSD. We'll take it and have a wonderful day.

I pick my friend up at his house and meet his parents. His father grunts a greeting and quickly disappears.

His mother is kindly but dubious about our plans.

"*Where* are the two of you headed off to?" she asks. She can't hide her skepticism about our swimming in nuclear reactor discharge water.

I reply, "San Onofre. Near that reactor. The water is supposed to be bathtub warm. It should be great."

Two hours later, we park on the highway's shoulder and walk down to the beach. It's a beautiful day and no one else is there.

Tom looks around. "I guess because it's a weekday." True, it's a Monday, but also midsummer and perfect weather.

After laying down our blankets, we each swallow our little orange tablet. Down the hatch and down to the shore.

Even before the acid exerts itself, it's apparent that the water is freakishly tepid. I love it. In all my years of going to the beach, it's the cold water, as much as fatigue from body surfing, that forces me out of the ocean. That won't happen today.

"Man! It's like swimming in piss," laughs Tom.

"Have you ever swum in piss?" I ask.

"Fuck you. I have."

We find ourselves in a cove with little surf. So, instead of body surf-ing, we tread water, float on our backs, splash around, effortlessly hour after hour, oddly buoyant.

I can't tell if there is an orange tinge to the water, to the light, to the sun, or to the color of Tom's and my flesh. I wonder if it's an effect of the Orange Barrel acid. Orange acid—orange light. Maybe it's the radioactivity; conveniently, I conclude that's unlikely. No reason to worry.

The ocean's soft warm pressure soothes, caresses, and laps at my body. Lying on my back, I've never floated more comfortably and easily. The breeze wafting over my exposed skin is a delight. I languidly bob up and down. Sometimes my ears are above the water and sometimes below. The radical shifts in sound are mesmerizing. Open, closed in, open, closed in.

This is a quiet, solitary experience for each of us—a contrast from the busy larger groups in which we had previously taken acid. However, neither of us floats too far away from the other. Intermittently, we check in—examine the water, remark on its amazing buoyancy, keep track of time. Very much at ease together with minimal interaction.

We return to dry land by early afternoon and walk north along the beach. Remarkably, the steady sun has burned neither of us.

I say, "I wonder if the acid is protecting us from the sun."

"Or because of the radioactivity we swam in."

"Or a combination of radioactivity and acid. A new form of sunblock."

After an hour, we're ready to turn back. Looking behind us, we see that the tide has come in, water now covering two hundred yards of beach between us and where we need to be. We have to traverse a steeply angled outcropping of black sandstone that sharply climbs to high cliffs above and ends in the crashing surf below.

"Shit," Tom says.

He adds, "Looks like we just need to go for it."

I protest. "I don't trust my ankle." The ankle I sprained when Teufel pushed me off Stu's motorbike earlier this year.

We look more closely at the black outcropping. There are three-to-four-inch-deep fractures crisscrossing everywhere along its rough surface. Two hundred yards of rough cracked black sandstone at a 30 degree angle? On LSD? Barefoot?

I hesitate. "I don't know if I can do this. My ankle."

Tom beams a big acid-drenched smile toward me. "Don't be a pussy." He laughs.

He adds, "But seriously. The acid will help. Don't think about it. Let your body control your body. Get out of the way. Don't think about it. You'll see."

Tom sets out trotting, nearly running over the black expanse. He looks over his shoulder and calls out, "See? Run across it. It's easier that way. You'll have no time to think about where to put your feet."

I shake off a chill of fear. Then, uncertainly, I set off behind him.

My first steps are tentative, watching where I step. Slow. Tom is twenty yards ahead, then stops and turns around. "Come on. Run. You'll never get across walking that way."

I look up from my feet. The steeply sloping wall of rock extends seemingly in all directions. Far ahead is a sandy beach. Tom starts up again.

A calm enters me. I begin to run. Or rather, my body begins to run. Now there is exhilaration. I no longer see my feet but rather where they need to be. It's one smooth uninterrupted movement forward. I don't land on any one spot as much as briefly alight on it, nearly weightless. I do not lose my balance, feel pain in my ankle, nor tear my feet on the rough stone. I move like the wind. I am more wind than body. I am the wind.

I jump two feet down to the sand where Tom waits for me. "That's the way! Wasn't that easy?"

We return to our beach towels, pack up, and make our way back to my father's Mustang. We brush off our feet and climb into the car.

I love this car. This is the first time Tom has been in it, and he is full of admiration. I drive fast, the stereo is loud, and I feel as if we are once again crossing the black sandstone. I barely feel the road below us, traffic flows smoothly, and we quickly arrive at the McDonald's near my parents' house. We park and enter the restaurant, still tripping on acid but hungry. Each of us orders a Big Mac. Then another, which we barely finish.

My parents are gone for a couple of days, and we have the house to ourselves. After washing off, we open the well-stocked liquor cabinet. It's difficult to decide what to drink, and after my tragic rum and Coke episode, I must be careful. We first smoke a joint and then decide to start with gin. We empty the bottle after each of us drink two large gin and tonics. This is my first time drinking on acid and I don't feel especially drunk. Is the acid counteracting the alcohol? If so, it's not having a similar effect on Tom.

He mutters, "Man. I'm burning up! Aren't you burning up?"

I answer, "No. I wonder if it's the radioactivity. You're having a reaction. Ha ha."

"No, man, I'm serious. I'm burning up."

"Try taking a cold shower."

He brightens a little, "Good idea."

Ten minutes later, he returns to the living room. The smell of his Old Spice is excessive. I wonder if he applied an extra-large helping of cologne, something familiar he can hold on to. Or, is his body in fact overheating, and the cologne is evaporating more rapidly? His face doesn't look red, but I know I can't trust my perceptions.

Tom pulls at the front of the neck of his T-shirt. "I don't know what's the matter. I need fresh air. I'm going out to the front yard. Your lawn looks cool and comfortable."

The backyard also has grass, but it's a small patch, and too close to the swimming pool for my comfort. I don't mention it.

"Okay. I'll go out there with you."

It's dark, and we sit on the front lawn. Crickets chirp and a cool breeze blows up the street.

Tom lies on his back and spreads out his arms and legs. "Oooooh. That's better. It's so nice and cool. Let me just lay here for a little while."

Five minutes, ten minutes, fifteen pass, and I get restless. I look down at my friend and say, "I'm going back into the house. I'll leave the door unlocked. Come on in when you're ready."

Midmorning the next day, I wake up to a ringing doorbell. I get out of bed and open it. It's the neighbor, Mr. Gold, wearing an amused and slightly worried expression. Looking over his shoulder, I see Tom spread out on the grass, face down.

"Do you know this person?" Mr. Gold asks.

We make our way to Tom, and I lean over to shake him by the shoulder. He groans, groans again, opens his eyes and looks up at me and the older stranger.

"Are you okay?"

Tom answers, "Yeah. I guess I fell asleep."

Mr. Gold shakes his head, chuckles, and goes on his way. He crosses the street and sidewalk, walks up his driveway to his front porch, and waves before entering his house.

Reflections

MIRACULOUS PHYSICAL EFFECTS

Neither Tom nor I suffered long-lasting ill effects from our day floating in water that the nearby nuclear reactor had warmed to such pleasant temperatures. One has to assume, then, that its operators' claims of safety were true. Nevertheless, one wonders if the LSD afforded us some protection. Similarly, our lack of suffering sunburn from a sunny day at the beach without sunblock may point to an unexplored potential benefit of psychedelic drugs! Speculation aside, I was unable to find any recent scientific papers describing psychedelics' benefits against either solar or plutonium radiation toxicity. However, there is an older literature, especially from the former Soviet Union, indicating that tryptamines like serotonin (5-OH-tryptamine), 5-methoxy-tryptamine, and alpha-ethyl-tryptamine afford protection from ionizing radiation.[1]

Anecdotal accounts abound, but scientific data are meager, regarding two highlights from this narrative: how psychedelics reduce alcohol's acute effects and how one can perform extraordinary physical feats under psychedelics' influence.

Most lay "drug abuse" literature emphasizes the dangers of combining alcohol and psychedelics but presents no scientific data. Rather, it simply assumes that concurrent drunkenness and tripping produces additive negative effects.

I have found only one published scientific paper addressing acute interactions of psychedelics and alcohol. It is a retrospective study in which self-referred individuals describe experiences with the combination. Subjects' use was "in the field" and not in the laboratory.[2] They reported that LSD nearly totally blocked alcohol effects either before or after drinking. Psilocybin was less consistent—reducing, enhancing, or having no effect on responses to alcohol.

The stimulatory effects of LSD—which appear to be dopamine related—may play a role in its antagonism of the acute effects of alcohol. In support of this idea, we know that dopamine active drugs like cocaine and amphetamine also decrease alcohol's subjective effects. Nevertheless, while psychedelics and stimulants may decrease acute subjective effects of alcohol, they have no effect on its toxicity. That is, fatal doses are still the same. It's unclear why Tom's reaction to alcohol did not change, but other factors may have intervened—overeating, sun exposure, and marijuana.

We all have heard about remarkable physical accomplishments on psychedelics. The most renowned case is that of Dock Ellis, the Pittsburgh Pirates pitcher who threw his only no-hitter on LSD.[3] Closer to home, the quarterback for The College's football team once took LSD before a game and had his best ever performance.

In these cases, we are dealing with a multitude of contributing factors: emotional, perceptual, coordination, pain sensitivity, and balancing intense passivity and activity. My racing along the jagged, angled rockface differs from, but builds upon, my previous experience of "just walking" on LSD that I described in the chapter "Snow Culvert." There, I became fully aware of walking and learned how it felt to simply allow my body to move through space. However, there were no extraordinary physical demands in those circumstances. In this account, I entered into a similar psychedelic zone, balancing on the knife-edge between me moving my body and it moving me. Accomplishing such a feat sober may have been impossible; at the very least, painful and time-consuming.

23

THE MANIFESTO

ONCE AT STANFORD, it is as if I had never attended The College. I make no effort to remain in touch with my old friends—Tom, Ambrose, Stu, and Woody—and no one writes to or calls me. I am glad to be gone and they must realize it. I also acquire new friends at my new school who neither remind me of my sexual naïveté nor denigrate my wishes to academically excel.

The pervasive intellectual enthusiasm of Stanford—where I always dreamed of attending—sweeps me up. I study, think, and write more freely than any time since high school. My College embryology professor encourages me to seek out and work with one of his former colleagues who is doing research at Stanford. After repeated requests, I secure a place in Dr. Wessells's world-class neurobiology lab. It's a position I enjoy for over a year, and my research there results in my first two scientific publications.[1]

I continue smoking cannabis but use it to relax rather than to survive. Psychedelic experiences are now rare, and my LSD use at The College has taught me how to plan them more carefully.

In addition to the world of the intellect, Stanford also exposes me to the world of the spirit in the form of Eastern religious studies and practice. My introduction is Transcendental Meditation, a Hindu method that the Indian yogi Maharishi Mahesh popularized through his relationship with The Beatles' George Harrison. One of my classmates, a psychology major, learns TM, and while he describes no psychedelic effects, it reduces his migraines and "mentally refreshes" him. I feel my brain needs healing after all that LSD at The College and enroll in a course.

The technique is simple. It's relaxing and I enjoy the discipline. However, the follow-up classes—watching Maharishi's videotaped lectures and studying the Bhagavad Gita—fail to inspire me. The yogi's giggle-filled talks ramble, and while the underlying theme of Hinduism's foundational text—nonattachment—resonates, its context of war obscures this fundamental teaching. The story seems garish, too, as do the illustrations in the edition we are reading.

As if in answer to my wish to study an Eastern religious alternative to Hinduism, Stanford hires a Ph.D. in Buddhist studies who just graduated from the University of Wisconsin. Nancy Lethcoe belongs to the first wave of Western doctorates in Buddhism from that era. The origin of this academic discipline as she tells it is fascinating.

Buddhist monks setting themselves on fire in protest of the Vietnam War in the 1960s prompted the U.S. Department of Defense to establish centers of Buddhist study at high-ranking universities. They wanted to know how to deal with this phenomenon: "Who are these monks?" "What is Buddhism?" "Why are they setting themselves on fire?" "How can they do this?" "Should we be worried about Buddhism?" "Is it a threat to national security?"

Professor Lethcoe's interest in Buddhism has less to do with national security concerns than a fervent desire to study and teach the religion. I take and love her class on Indian Buddhism—its original form—and read everything she recommends. We learn about the life of the Buddha, his earliest disciples, and the different branches of Indian philosophy and religion springing from his teachings. Buddhism's essential lessons are profound yet simple; for example, the Four Signs,* the Four Noble Truths,† and the Three Marks of Existence.‡

---

*Prompting the Buddha to leave his life of luxury and become an ascetic: (1) disease, (2) old age, (3) death, and (4) an itinerant monk.

†(1) Life as we live it is unsatisfactory, and (2) this is due to craving. (3) Freedom from suffering comes with the end of craving, (4) which is possible through Buddhist practice—in particular, via the Eightfold Path emphasizing meditation.

‡Impermanence, unsatisfactoriness, and no self.

In Buddhism I find a system that teaches and practices a worldview that I had only glimpsed during my psychedelic experiences. It begins by highlighting the ephemeral and illusory nature of everyday existence, and it describes why and how we fail to make direct contact with reality. It exhaustively and authoritatively lays out a framework to progress from suffering to ultimate enlightenment—nirvana.

D. T. Suzuki's books on Zen and Edward Conze's on Indian Buddhism move me deeply, and I'm especially encouraged by a book attempting an intersection of psychology and Buddhism by the psychoanalyst Erich Fromm, Suzuki, and Richard de Martino: *Zen Buddhism and Psychoanalysis*. The more I read, the more sense Buddhism makes; in fact, it makes more sense than anything I have ever read. For months, I am an insufferable cheerleader for the religion.

I remain at Stanford during the summer between my junior and senior years in order to continue my laboratory research. I rent an inexpensive room in a nearly empty dorm on campus. When not in the lab, I pore over Charles Tart's *Altered States of Consciousness*, which provides a scientific model for studying what I am most interested in. I read Jung, Freud, "transpersonal" psychologist Abraham Maslow, religion scholar Mircea Eliade, American Zen master Philip Kapleau, *Function of the Orgasm* psychoanalyst Wilhelm Reich, comparative religion scholar Frederick Spiegelberg, Hindu teacher Swami Sivananda, the Bible, Carlos Castaneda's books on the Mexican Indigenous shaman Don Juan, Sufi scholar Indries Shah, fourth-century Taoist Chuang Tzu, Prabhupada's version of the Bhagavad Gita, Chilean psychedelic and meditation scholar Claudio Naranjo, consciousness researcher Robert Ornstein, among others. Heady times. I'm feasting—in retrospect, overdosing—on a plethoric smorgasbord of psychological, scientific, and spiritual information.

One of the most compelling books is Ram Dass's recently published *Be Here Now*. Here is a Jewish Harvard psychologist studying psychedelics who turns to the East for the answers to the questions his research raised. The bibliography is a gold mine of additional reading. Gopi Krishna's *Kundalini* is an astonishing work, describing the author's prolonged, fully psychedelic experiences resulting simply from meditation. In it, he makes a convincing case for a biological basis of spiritual experience. Aldous Huxley's *The Perennial Philosophy* ties together this radical reading list. I love his writing style, his organized manner of presenting disparate religious traditions, and tying them together with their common themes. He is an outstanding synthesizer. In fact, during discussions with my roommate that summer, we predict that my work one day will build upon Huxley's—combining neuroscience, Eastern and Western religion, and psychology.

But, as one of my later mentors Daniel X. Freedman liked asking: "If so, so what?" What am I going to do with all of this information? The path forward is frustratingly murky. My classmates are applying to medical school, but I'm too busy developing a vision to consider the prospect of practicing medicine. My aims are loftier. Nevertheless, it's time to decide what comes after college.

I seek counsel at the Student Health Center. They assign me a Black psychiatrist, and I note his resemblance to the Buddha figures from my summer reading. He's rotund, soft-spoken, intelligent, friendly, and interested in my dilemma. Rather than suggesting one career path or another, he recommends I meet Jim Fadiman. Jim recently completed his psychology doctoral training at Stanford studying the effects of psychedelics on scientific creativity. He should have good advice.

I describe this meeting at length in *DMT: The Spirit Molecule*[2] and will not repeat the details here. In brief, Jim suggests I look into the pineal gland as a candidate "spiritual organ," one mediating highly altered states resulting from drugs or other means. He also takes note of my stammer and introduces me to the notion of a "divine impediment." It's a gift, he says, an external indicator of internal imbalance and lack of centeredness, something most people lack. My stammer makes me "lucky," not unfortunate. Our meeting convinces me I'm on the right track, but the specifics of that track elude me.

It's Saturday midafternoon in July. I return from the lab and decide to take a tab of Orange Barrel LSD that Sam has sent me from Southern

California. I assume my prone position on the mattress lying on the floor, turn on the stereo, and within an hour am watching the music emerge from my speakers: classical, Ravi Shankar, rock and roll, and Leo Kottke. The swells of sound and color envelop me all afternoon. The light in the room changes as the day wears on, and it's time to look at the sky. Climbing up from the mattress, I gaze out the window. The sun is setting.

God rays* pour through gaps in massive cumulus clouds. Reds, yellows, oranges, grays, whites, blues. I close my eyes and the colors continue entering into my mind. Suddenly, I see the goal of my studies. The multicolored lights turn into one white whole.

I sit down at my desk, smoke a joint, and begin writing, continuing feverishly for the next three hours. I will become a psychiatrist, a brain chemist, and a Zen monk. I will undergo Freudian psychoanalysis and learn the master's theories and techniques. It will take time, but I will do it. There is no longer any question about my life course. The first step is to become a physician. I finally know what to write for my medical school application essay. The initial draft follows, unedited, but with footnotes clarifying obscure text or references.

I have stuttered all of my life, it is the only constant. It gives pause for constant introspection so as to cause duress or deprecation of the self. It gives an uncanny empathy with a majority of, or a familiarity with, self-deprecation problems that arise. If not the specific, then a familiarity—a firm familiarity, which is normally unavailable due to its questionable content and being socially unapproved of—with the general; to a degree of fusing with that person, maintaining my integrity as an individual (which has been one of the hardest problems to counter) and still being able to drop back into yourself and keep a detached, experimental air of helping solve one (of your fellow) man's problems which for a moment have become yours. As deprecating self is not an unfamiliar circumstance concomitant with

---

*Shafts of sunlight passing through clouds, especially inspiring when on LSD.

a tension-releasing habit so socially unacceptable.* One which I hope I've turned to use empowers (against) me to help me and aid in my understanding others.

I may have this introspective ability to a degree requiring hospital-ization and intensive psychotherapy;† however, I feel I can use it to help other people, as well as learning more about people and myself in the process.

Familiarity with altered states.

This experience, this knowledge, and this feel for altered states of consciousness and my awareness of ego processes and machinations, on the negative side out of necessity, I feel I can offer or be a rare and potentially valuable instrument, member of a society, which lacks both the know-how or material for dealing with such problems of any ego subject to almost terminal strengths of correctness of the ego's func-tions and responses in such a disorienting civilization.‡

This lack or absence of being centered, this unawareness and/or the failure to accept the relativity or the reality of things on the sur-face and intra-psychically, is what obviously, I feel, is the cause of so many disturbed, unhappy, apathetic, paranoid, ignorant, insensitive, stupid people§ and what makes life for them uncomfortable enough in it to watch television. To plot wars, fight for resources of a starving planet.

I feel strongly that this and that will do it, baby, so accept me and give me money.

My academic record shows I am capable and recently motivated to keep on pursuing an academic career in medicine, better—society! And share, use, what I have where I can use fully my emotional, non-logical mind‖ to as great an extent in a universe whose entire surround-ings mystify me.

---

*A stammer.

†An allusion to my fragile self-identity and dim view of psychotherapy.

‡A reference to pathological conservatism.

§Not a rousing endorsement of my fellow man.

‖That is, a feeling, not an idea.

I feel that a medical career (background, school, training) rather than a purely psychological approach to this area would benefit me immensely, as an understanding of all the parts of the whole gives a much more full understanding of the parts contributing to the whole (of the mind). The human body's physical-chemical-biological intricacies are no less fantastic or awe-inspiring or exciting to me as the workings of the mind. It is just in the area of the mind that I have found myself being drawn and where I feel I can best use my capacities of empathy and experience.

The non-logical, non-verbal experiences in meditation, drug-induced experiences, hypnosis, some dreams are intrinsically valuable as a method of communicating with, or utilizing, verbally and logically inaccessible problems based upon nonverbal or preverbal experiences. Since creativity and spontaneous growth are also nonverbal and unconscious in origin,* any method that can more readily make accessible these nonverbal and preverbal states to experimental manipulation is utilizing an extremely potent and potentially fantastically creative and problem-solving force. I feel man has an innate impulse toward creative expression (and a plethora of experimental evidence has been gathered to show that most people can greatly expand their ego's vistas without impairing, indeed with a more genuine contribution) in dealing with conventional reality, and reconciliation with this environment, as well as homeostatic desires† which have run amok in a world or country that today provides most of the necessities of life to all its inhabitants and this homeostatic drive which is no more necessity to exist is being misdirected in the very unnecessary national and corporate homeostasis which is slowly making everyone in this country crazy.

"Regression in the service of the ego."‡ Depth of feeling of

---

*Only partly true. Those states and feelings can only enhance more or less conscious material. For example, Francis Crick could not have visualized the double helix of DNA on LSD without being Francis Crick.

†Survival and other basic instincts—food, clothing, shelter, companionship.

‡A psychoanalytic concept. Reversion to more primitive levels of thinking and feeling may be beneficial with the proper set and setting. I discuss this notion in more detail in the chapter "Tense Infant Analytic Session."

the profundity of an altered state experience may be a delusion;* *however, this profound reality orientation provides the motivation to effect profound behavioral changes towards the insightful paradigm realized in this more altered state.*

A final note: Increased knowledge causes an increase of scientific facilities of [facility in] studying altered states of consciousness which then causes a decrease of black market of material and dangerous self experimentation, and some of these areas, especially in the case of drugs.

Many, if not all, great steps forward in philosophy, psychology, science, religion have come mainly by nonverbal intuitive means,§ as well as our own great steps forward in self actualizing growth. What a tremendous possibility for mankind in general to be able to call into action the states where our intuition, rather than our misdirected homeostatic impulse, can have full sway in finding solutions and providing inspiration for everyday existence! How much more fulfilling and meaningful could life become if we could begin to harness this vast source of creative, and potentially destructive if not channeled properly, energy.

Arthur Diekman's concept of automatization and de-automatization[3] is an essential cornerstone of the values of using altered states of consciousness for growth and therapy. Automatization is considered as the basic psychological process in which the repeated exercise of an action or perception results in the disappearance from consciousness of its intermediate steps. De-automatization is the undoing of automatization presumably by reinvestment of actions and percepts with attention. Many of the non-logical and nonverbal processes that are these intermediate steps that are now inaccessible for analysis or restructuring are made accessible by conditions that are almost wholly concerned with pushing language and logic aside, and accent the nonverbal and nonlogical processes that occur in automatization.

---

*Feelings aren't delusional, but the beliefs to which they attach may be; see, for example, the case of Charles Manson and his followers' use of LSD.
§Refer to the earlier Francis Crick note.

1) *it is my hope and I feel I am my own evidence that this problem or gift has been turned to good use for myself in dealing with the world from my own personal ego.*

2) *I personally don't think I would be useful, helpful in my desire, my field of interest unless I did approach it in a logical, scientific, problem-solving way.*

3) *people are getting involved in altered states of consciousness; for example, 10 million dope smokers, LSD, heroin etc., due to their search for a satisfying awareness in their transient existence, and the more one knows, and is capable of turning in usefulness about the altered states of consciousness for the experiencing of growth and satisfaction, and awareness (results in growth and satisfaction, probably don't use "awareness").**

This way, Strassman, you can stay stoned and drop† all the time in order to be doing a great job, too.‡ I may go crazy but without a constructive channel through which to drive it, I would go crazy for sure.§

Did I destroy my pen?‖

My frankness and perfectly lucid opinion or statements may not be accepted by those whose egos are so firm and non-dynamic that they will scoff and be offended and shake their heads at my words and not be aware that somewhere, crying out, is a voice that implores, yes, please, we have had this experience once and it was your fear once that this flash in the pan—transcendence, unitive knowledge one day hit you but your fear of losing control roared, "don't!" It may be a frightening crisis, but where is any growth or cure without a crisis? [Written on top of page: horseshit!]#

---

*An editorial note.
†Take psychedelics, as in "drop acid."
‡Frequently experience that state in order to study and write about it successfully.
§An unfortunately accurate prediction.
‖From writing so hard and fast.
#This idea was not fully convincing.

My idealism may be a downer when I see how strongly people's minds are set, and what problems can arise. I feel that the excellent prognosis of well performed experiments have attested to the fact that it is a field which cannot but elicit a mere ebullience of idealism, untapped fields, dreams (about 1/36 of our life), ego distorting drugs, synergistic meditation, synergistic hypnosis,* dope grass as a cry out to be used, listening to incorporate it into, included in one small part of your mental material that takes or rules with an iron fist two thirds of your day and strongly influences the remainder of the social-individual-natural world-universe phenomenon.

Religion sounds like a part of all this, perhaps this is what I'm preaching, religion of the self,† a religion stifled by this society which demands automatization of all waking first state (normal conscious-ness) functions to a degree of depressed etc. resigned unhappiness and confusion belief in a higher level of organization than ourselves, or else our childlike mesomorphic‡ disregard for all but self, will, and a hulking self-deluded, disastrous excursion through existence, yield, provoke—yield to an extinction of his problems by default.

Perhaps a type of religion is necessary, and with such a relatively well-informed but poorly directed populace, must need to be a sophisti-cated one, gifted with the bestowal of the doctrine, a religious psychol-ogy,§ to achieve the highest states of ephemeral nonrational intelligent level of awareness, better yet lifestyle.

The description, explanation of these phenomena, and altered states would, in turn, provide elucidation in scientific jargon, the type with which our populace tends to choose to categorize as the mysterious magic language of the day, not cloaked in terms occur-ring many years ago, and which have resulted in such harsh laws

---

*Hypnosis or meditation in combination with drugs.

†More so a religion whose focus is a particular feeling.

‡A physical-psychological category belonging to a now-discredited system in psychology—"somatotypes"—which proposed that physical characteristics determined one's personality. Mesomorphs, or "muscular types," were extroverted, active, and competitive.

§Akin to the "psychedelic religion of mystical consciousness."[4]

for stimulation of these altered states of consciousness more widely available.*

This fanaticism, I doubt, will you find in many other applicants, so you better grab me while I'm still around.

I can't hang around with Lynn† then. She's too rigid and will stifle me, tie me down. Right now, no, don't think so, not really sure. Poor, sad Lynn. Poor, confused me.

I am jazzed. God has entered my consciousness tonight, and will be gone soon, but I think that numinous void, that Krishna‡ of Stanford's karma, that tutelary deity,§ that clear void, clear light, it's pretty powerful and tonight found a very receptive human bean.‖

I'm a smart dude, man, and don't think I don't have more knowledge and intelligence than 92% of your pre-med population of this country,# probably the most intelligent people and probably the entire world at this point.

Editing note: cut to one or two sentences. So recent an interest, my boy?** Never in 20 years of intensity of life†† and thoughts, plans, ideas, impressions left me with such a feeling of life and existence and beauty.‡‡ And I have been much more stoned than this before, you better believe me.

Accept my gifts or take blame for it destroying me!!

The end. A story by Rick J Strassman

If I do anything involving my current USA current lifestyle, it will be what you find contained in this letter.

What a perfect combination, lots of good dope, excellent, superb,

---

*Drug prohibition.

†A student I was dating at the time.

‡The Hindu god who presents the spiritual teachings of the Bhagavad Gita.

§A deity or spirit who guards, benefits, or protects a place, person, lineage, religion, culture, or occupation.

‖Not a typo.

#My score on the Medical College Admission Test, a national examination necessary for one's medical school application.

**A theoretical question from a theoretical medical school interviewer.

††My age then.

‡‡Onset of hypomanic euphoria.

unbelievable music before and after, very stoned, enjoying myself a great deal. What a waste of 20 years, or what a good thing for a lot of humanity for the next 30 or 50 or 60 or even 80 years as science is proceeding. Finally letting go and look what is coming out. Thanks to a stolid stone black Buddha* and a smiling Chuang Tzu,† and myself. And to letters from home, and thoughts of Lynn, and Charlie Tart's altered states of consciousness. Naranjo's on the psychology of meditation.[5] Changing to conceit and grandeur, huh?‡ Time to call it a night.

I share with Dr. Wessells this draft of my medical school essay/ Manifesto. I'd like his feedback, as his letter of recommendation will be one of the most important in my application.

His large wooden desk separates us. I can hardly wait for his enthusiastic and awestruck response.

He reads, shakes his head, glances up at me; reads, shakes his head, glances up again with a growing look of dismay.

"This is nuts," he whispers loudly. He is talking to himself but wants me to hear. He reiterates, "This is nuts."

He finishes, leans back in his creaking chair, then bends forward and looks directly into my eyes.

"You can't send this. No one will even consider you." He shakes his head, this time with a disbelieving grimace. Baffled, he returns his gaze to the pile of paper I had just handed him.

———

Reflections

THE BIRTH OF PSYCHEDELIC MESSIANISM

The evening I wrote the Manifesto marks the beginning of an especially fraught period in my life—June 1972 to October 1974—from

———

*The psychiatrist I saw at the Student Health Center.
†Jim Fadiman, who sported Fu Manchu facial hair at the time.
‡Demonstrating some insight.

twenty to twenty-two years of age. That day's LSD experience triggered a prolonged disordered mood, at first elevated and messianic. That grandiosity reversed course quickly upon arriving at medical school. The ensuing deep depression only lifted during a training session at a Zen Buddhist monastery while on a medical leave of absence.

This experience differs from earlier ones in two ways. First is its temporal course. While the LSD's effects lasted the usual several hours, I was in the throes of, and continued struggling with, the process it triggered for more than a year.

Another difference was the content of the state. The most noteworthy elements of previous narratives were perceptual and emotional: visions, ecstasy, auditory effects, and loss of body awareness. The emotional components of those experiences—for example, euphoria or terror—followed upon the intensity and novelty of those perceptions; at other times, they welled up spontaneously or in interactions with others.

In this episode, the most striking components were cognitive— ideas, insights, plans, goals, and priorities. This is not surprising; I was struggling to formulate a life after college. The solution to this puzzle required ideas, not simply feelings. Yet, feelings played a crucial role that day. It was the association of those feelings of joyful certainty with the ideas that set me on my course. These were not simply new insights, but I *felt* they were so profoundly revolutionary that they would deliver the world from its suffering. Messianic, in a word.

We see here my first attempts to develop a *cognitive* structure or model around *feelings* that I had experienced on psychedelics: bliss, certainty, expansiveness, openness, acceptance, equanimity, compassion, meaningfulness, empathy, awe, reverence . . . These feelings were the focus of my attention, rather than how to understand, integrate, apply, and communicate them for my and others' benefit. In this LSD episode, I arrived at the idea that if everyone had these feelings, a spiritual and psychological utopia would automatically follow.

I gradually acquired expertise in the fields necessary to scientifically test this hypothesis: medical, psychiatric, and clinical research training; Zen study and practice; and psychoanalysis. The irony, however, is that my experiments led me to conclude that the feeling, at bottom, is less important than the ideas one associates with them. That is, the ideas to which the feelings attach are more important than the feelings themselves. If one must choose, wisdom without healing trumps healing without wisdom.

When I wrote the Manifesto, I was conflating wisdom and healing. Healing may occur through the feeling itself—witness the panacea-like effects of psychedelic drug–induced "unitive experiences." However, it is not only about healing. How do we understand the nature of healing? In what ideas and actions will we now invest our lives? To what purpose will we apply our experiences? These questions are the purview of wisdom.

We first need to plant the seeds for wisdom—wisdom that resides in the intellectual rather than the emotional sphere—through practice, training, and study. Then, under the influence of psychedelic or other highly altered states, we reify them. Their truth and importance, and our dedication to them, take on greater urgency, and our commitment correspondingly increases.

Dr. Wessells's assessment of the Manifesto as "nuts" was shorthand for what psychiatrists likewise blithely call "crazy." It was a manifestation of a psychological disorder, a state clearly outside the realm of "normal everyday" mental functioning. At that time, the psychiatric diagnosis would have been a "mixed affective state"—mania or hypomania* in combination with depressive elements. One extreme mood alternates or even blends together with the other.

In Stanford's supportive and familiar environment, my academic function did not suffer while in this condition, as the melancholy elements remained in the background. In fact, several of my professors were extraordinarily supportive of the theories I first articulated in the Manifesto, especially those regarding the biological bases of altered states of consciousness.

---

*Less driven and expansive than mania.

However, the elevated mood and grandiosity papered over profoundly low self-esteem, a fragile sense of self, despairing mood, and confusion about my adult goals. The tenuousness of this expansive mood becomes clear in two upcoming chapters—"Permanent Insanity" and "New York Breakdown."

24

UBEHEBE

DEATH VALLEY IS NOW my go-to psychedelic destination. Every visit elicits deeper and more profound feelings of awe, beauty, and portents of miracles. The landscape—ranging from 11,000 feet above to 282 feet below sea level—provides endless opportunities for hikes, backpacking, and four-wheel-drive adventures. The park itself is 140 miles long and 5 to 15 miles wide, while additional wild countryside extends far beyond its confine to the north, south, and west. Even without drugs, it is a mind-blowing destination. My experiences there deepen my conviction that I have discovered a place of the utmost significance, and I wish to share it with others.

John is my best new friend at Stanford. He, too, is a third-year transfer student; coincidentally, from The Men's College on the same campus as The College. We didn't know each other then, but he was a member of the basketball team to which Zebulun Cohen belonged. He recalls playing the game between our teams, but not my LSD-crazed outburst.

We meet during the first quarter at Stanford. The university is short on housing for transfer students, and we both end up at a fraternity on campus that has vacancies. Neither of us wishes to join the fraternity and, as the quarter winds down, must find alternative housing. I locate a room in an adjacent dormitory, while John moves into one of the comfortable mobile homes in "overflow housing."

While at The Men's College, John also regularly took acid, and we soon become companionable and compatible tripping buddies. On our days off, we take LSD and explore the nearby foothills, coastal range, and beach. We learn how to interact while heavily intoxicated—lying on the ground keeping within sight of each other, hiking when less inebriated, sharing the clipped telegraphic manner of speaking that is typical of the LSD state. Much is assumed, and the assumptions are usually correct. We discuss deep and profound matters while high, share pleasure observing psychedelically altered clouds, waves, trees, sulfur-yellow banana slugs, and the crashing surf. We are attuned to each other on acid, interacting and non-interacting effortlessly, almost telepathically.

One late winter day, a dozen doses of blotter acid arrive from Sam. John and I decide to take some in Death Valley. Kevin, John's trailer roommate, asks if he can join us, and we agree.

Kevin has the most roadworthy and high clearance vehicle—a little Volkswagen station wagon—and we head out in it on a sunny early February day. Arriving before sunset, we make short work of dinner and burrow into our sleeping bags before the rapidly encroaching desert chill envelops us. The next morning over coffee, studying the three-by-three-foot map of the park spread out the vehicle's hood, I suggest we spend the day at the Ubehebe craters at the north end of the valley. I've been there before, but never on acid.

"Where?" Kevin asks with a puzzled smirk.

Kevin played basketball in high school but does not make the Stanford team. He and John met playing pickup games with other students. He is just over six feet, pale-skinned, with a shock of blonde hair coming halfway down his forehead. His nose is prominent and beak-shaped, and he grins a lot—either with you or at you is never clear. We've spent little time together, and I am not drawn to him. I find his voice grating and his attitude smug. However, John and he have developed a workable relationship as roommates.

"Ubehebe craters," I answer cheerily. "Big Hebe and Little Hebe. There is one big one and some smaller ones. It's volcanic, beautiful, and very weird."

John chuckles and says, "I'm game."

Kevin can't tell if we're joking.

Undaunted, I suggest, "How about we take the acid now and we'll be well on our way when we arrive?"

I take out the envelope containing three little blotter paper squares. We examine them carefully resting in my palm as I shield them from the cool breeze.

"Here they are!" I announce proudly.

"That's LSD?" Kevin asks. "Are you sure?"

Am I sure?

John and I glance at him and then at each other. A faint whiff of trouble enters our little group.

"Want some today?" I ask Kevin.

"Naw. I don't think so. I've never taken any. I'll be the straight man."

The whiff becomes a little stronger.

John and I ceremoniously place the little bits of paper on our extended tongues, swallow exaggeratedly, and take a couple gulps of water. By the time we park at the nearly empty trailhead, the familiar sense of euphoric anticipation, inner tension, and subtle visual effects have begun. Are those shadows or LSD-induced visual distortions playing over the landscape? Regardless, they fill me with joy.

After a short hike, we reach the edge of the crater and peer down and across the massive hole: 750 feet deep and 2,000 feet across. The acid's effects build, and John and I are increasingly unsteady. We sit down to get our bearings, and once we do, get up and approach an interpretive sign explaining what we see.

We read that the Ubehebe craters are phreatic or hydrovolcanic maars or pits. They're the result of a steam explosion three thousand years ago when magma rose through a fault and came into contact with the inland sea that once covered the entire valley. The result was a titanic explosion exposing countless layers of maritime sediment. The craters are "explosion pits." Unreal.

"Wow," I exclaim. "Ubehebe is one heeby-jeeby."

John laughs, his eyes shooting happy sparks.

Kevin is not so sure. "'Phreatic maar'? What's that? Is that a thing? What's a heeby-jeeby?"

"It's a *maaaaar*," I say, enjoying how my throat feels prolonging the word, like a chant. I'm feeling jovial; nevertheless, I ought not to assume anything about our odd man out, especially his resonating with any drug-induced lightheartedness.

Kevin frowns.

Turning back to the crater, John and I sit down and take in the panorama.

The crater walls radiate yellow in one section, red-orange in another. Day-Glo, shimmering, pulsating, glowing with age, power, and intensity, generating a deep bass hum. Cinder deposits form its upper reaches—light gray to nearly black. White silt covers the bottom of the hole. A profusion of small round desert holly bushes, no more than two feet tall, dot the land everywhere, their silver-white leaves shining ecstatically. Beyond, stretching one hundred miles south, are the snow-white salt flats that the inland sea left behind after evaporating.

It's too much to take in. I lie down and gaze at something more manageable—the cobalt blue sky and wispy cirrus clouds scuttling across the heavenly expense. John follows suit. Kevin paces restlessly, and the sound of crunching gravel under his feet grates unpleasantly.

Time to change position. We get up and stumble over to the next interpretive marker that announces its topic: "Where does the name Ubehebe come from?"

"Good question," I admit. Did I say that or just think it?

Reading on, we learn it's possibly a mangled version of *Duveetah Wahsan*—Duveetah's carrying basket, in the language of an Indigenous tribe who once inhabited the area. Or, it's the name of an Indian woman who previously lived nearby. Local natives call it *wosa*—coyote's burden basket. It's ridiculous, naming something like this. Tiny, tiny words, minuscule sounds, taking in a geological formation of this magnitude.

John smiles broadly. "Let's not forget Little Hebe."

"Are you fucking with me?" Kevin interjects, intruding upon John and my reverie. "'Little Hebe'? What the fuck is that?"

I can't help myself. "Right. Little Hebe. Ubehebe, I'm a hebe. You're a hebe. It's all a hebe."

John likewise chimes in, but "Hebe" is all he can manage between staccato bursts of laughter. We're on the same wavelength. Kevin is not.

Collecting ourselves, John and I down a half-canteen of water: cool, tasty, refreshing.

"Kevin," I manage to say while trying to hand him the water, "Have something to drink." He's flushed and probably becoming dehydrated.

"I'm fine. Don't worry." He finds a spot and sits down, knees drawn up against his chest. Fastening himself to the ground.

Another interpretive sign about exotic geology. Alluvial fans, scarps, talus. John and I laugh reading these words aloud while looking out at the scene defying description. The force that blew these holes in the Earth . . . Despite the breeze, it's quiet now, utterly empty, devoid of any perceptible activity or dynamism. But it is evolving, on a scale either too slow—or too rapid, I can't decide—to comprehend using everyday notions of time and space.

The sun's intensity builds, and the wind strengthens. There is no shade except for the interpretive signs' shadows. Kevin, hatless, is displaying a redder and redder face. John and I wear hats, affording protection from the worst of the sun. Besides, I recall from my day in the ocean in front of the San Onofre nuclear reactor, LSD is the ultimate sunblock.

The acid's effects diminish slightly, and we look at our watches. It's late afternoon and we need to decide what's next.

John and I suggest we return to the campground and get a good night's sleep. His parents in Los Angeles are expecting us tomorrow, and we'll head out first thing in the morning.

"I want to get out of here," Kevin mutters. "Tonight."

"Tonight?"

"Yeah. Now. I've had it. I don't like it here. And you guys are too weird."

John and I exchange worried looks. Kevin's the straight man but isn't acting straight. He exudes anger, fear, and impatience. The limited eye contact he makes is not reassuring. We don't argue.

We begin the long drive up and out of the valley, west into the setting sun. I'm in the passenger seat, John in the back. Kevin's reactions to anything John or I say are increasingly hostile, critical, and, most worrisome, suspicious.

"Why did you take me out here?" Kevin starts.

"Don't you think it was beautiful?" One of us tries to lighten the mood.

"It was awful. Ugly. And the two of you weren't making any sense talking to each other. I had no idea what you were saying. Hebe this, Hebe that. You were fucking with me."

He grasps the steering wheel tightly, takes the sharp corners of the steep winding road too fast, and the wheels screech. It's dark and the headlights seem too weak to effectively illuminate the road.

We turn onto US 395, a mostly four-lane highway, with long straight stretches. Kevin speeds up and slows down for no reason and veers across lanes.

"Damn it!" he shouts, pounding the steering wheel, then his forehead. He's losing it. "Damn it!" he shouts again when swerving on the road.

While I'm stoned on LSD, I'm not that stoned, and I can force myself down by concentrating on the immediate dangerous situation. I realize my life is in the hands of a deranged maniac.

"Let me drive, Kevin," I say. "You're upset and I'm nervous about your driving."

"I'm driving fine!" he shouts.

John from the backseat helpfully and hopefully seconds my recommendation. "I can drive, too, if you're worried about Rick."

"Forget it!" Kevin barks through clenched teeth. "You're on LSD!!"

For the next twenty minutes, we're in a stalemate. Kevin remains behind the wheel, his driving more erratic as his rage builds.

"Stop the car, Kevin," John says gently but firmly. He knows his roommate better than I do and has more sway.

"No!" he yells.

John repeats his suggestion, now more of a command than an offer. "Stop the car. I'll drive."

Kevin's eyes flutter. He suddenly looks exhausted, spent, defeated. He spies a pullout, jerkily pulls over, slams on the brakes, puts the car into park, and turns off the engine. John gets out and takes the driver's seat while Kevin unsteadily climbs into the back seat. Within five minutes of John confidently resuming our drive south, Kevin's asleep. We safely arrive in Los Angeles before midnight.

The next morning at breakfast, Kevin is refreshed and in a good mood.

"How's it going, Kevin?" someone asks.

"Great. I loved it out there. Thanks for a fun trip."

Neither John nor I see any reason to suggest otherwise.

Reflections

A CONTACT LOW

"Contact high" refers to individuals feeling intoxicated around others who are tripping, while not on anything themselves. The term appears most frequently in the context of psychedelic drugs, but we also see its use with cannabis. The phenomenon may occur unconsciously; that is, in someone who doesn't know that they are around people who are tripping. Subtle cues, pheromones, and other out of consciousness interactions indicate that something is different, and they experience an altered state without knowing why.

The existence of the contact high is common knowledge within the psychedelic subculture. However, academic publications on the topic— like the similarly well-known psychedelic-precipitated homosexual panic—are rare. In fact, the only research paper I have found is a 2020 publication[1] demonstrating the phenomenon, even when those "on psychedelics" only acted as if they were.

In this study, subjects took an inert placebo in a group setting, believing it was a psilocybin-like compound. Research "confederates" also participated in the group, pretending they were under the influence.* Many of the placebo-dosed subjects experienced moderate to intense psychedelic effects. How much stronger, one wonders, would the effects have been if the confederates were really on a psychedelic?

In this chapter, we see a case of a "contact low." LSD's effects on John and me—altered speech patterns, laughing, dilated pupils, lengthy periods of companionable silence—clearly broadcasted that we were tripping. Kevin then felt as if he were, too. As he was psychedelic-naïve, this was not an ideal introduction to the "drug state," especially in someone with his personality—suspicious, defensive, and rigid. These types require an extra dose of tender loving care to prevent acute paranoid adverse reactions.

I admit that John and I were less than warmly empathic and supportive of Kevin's distress. In a clinical setting, for example, I would have tried to decrease any ambiguous or insensitive interactions with someone decompensating like this. On the other hand, it's unlikely I would have allowed someone like Kevin into a research study in the first place. And from my experience, once someone like Kevin becomes paranoid on psychedelics, there's little one can do other than let it run its course, keep them from harming themselves, and, if necessary, provide antianxiety or antipsychotic medication.

---

*However, the paper does not say whether these confederates were psychedelic-experienced; in either case, the confederates were instructed to subtly mimic and amplify any "psychedelic-like" effects that the research subjects demonstrated; e.g., giggling, elevated mood, or increased rate of speech.

25

CLARISSA

AFTER LAYING OUT MY MANIFESTO, I now have justification to apply to medical school. I'm not interested in practicing medicine but believe that physician training will equip me with the tools and credentials I need to implement my messianic aspirations.

I apply to twenty schools—a nice round number. My New Jersey ophthalmologist uncle, along with Dr. Wessells, helps me edit my Manifesto/essay into submittable form. My uncle also suggests I apply to the medical school he attended. I had not heard of Albert Einstein College of Medicine of Yeshiva University in the Bronx, New York. "Give it a shot," my father's half-brother suggests. Now I'm at twenty-one schools.

By late winter, after twenty interviews around the country, all but two schools reject me, and those two put me on their waiting list. In other words, I may not get into *any* medical school. I look great on paper: The College, Stanford University, excellent grades, great recommendations, and success in research. However, it's difficult to restrain my enthusiasm for the Great Project and no one is taking the bait. The face-to-face encounters doom me. I don't realize how unhinged my fervor has caused me to become.

One after the other, the same scenario plays out.

"Why do you want to be a doctor?"

Anyone could be asking that question: young or old, Black or White, male or female, clinician, researcher, or administrator. My answer, more or less, is always the same:

"I want to develop a new model of healing that combines psychedelic drugs, Buddhism, and psychoanalysis. It will treat the whole person: body, mind, and spirit. It will revolutionize medicine and the future of humanity."

It's the only answer I give because it is the only answer I've got. Anything else would be a lie. "Acid and Maharishi," I tell myself with a grin.

This is 1972. The Controlled Substances Act is only two years old, and all legitimate clinical research with psychedelics has ground to an ignominious halt. These drugs, once seen as panaceas, now are anathema, taboo, unclean, dangerous, and toxic. In addition, psychoanalysis is falling out of repute because of new psychopharmacological agents: antidepressants, antipsychotics, antianxiety drugs, and lithium. Finally, no one knows what Buddhism is, and what they do know alarms them—orange-robed monks with shaved heads setting themselves on fire to protest the war in Vietnam.

I see my hopes for medical school fade, and with them my ability to actualize the Manifesto. In my journal notes, I refer to one interviewer's assessment as equivalent to my being "a crazy impractical daydreaming moron." I write in my journal after that: "Perhaps I am, but still, we must make good impressions to the contrary, mustn't we?" Then finally, "I hope I don't crash." I'm on a psychic roller coaster—grandiose highs and hapless lows, with little in between.

With a growing sense of desperation, I schedule an interview with my uncle's medical school. Because this is a last-minute decision, and I can't afford to make another trip to the East Coast, I arrange to meet with an alumnus from Einstein who practices in San Francisco.

Traffic is heavy between Palo Alto and my interlocutor's office this afternoon. The drive takes an hour, and I wait another thirty minutes before stepping into a dimly lit office. I see a tired-looking cardiologist in his forties behind a battered wooden desk piled to mid-chest level with books, journals, and papers. I've never seen an office so full.

"Sit down." He gestures toward an uncomfortable wooden chair, thankfully empty.

The doctor's glasses' lenses are thick, smudged with fingerprints, and discomfitingly reflect the faint light that makes its way through the equally grimy windows. He leans over to his right and digs through a paper mound rising from the floor. Finding what he's looking for, he turns his surprisingly benevolent gaze to me. I'm curious, yet pessimistic, and ready to rant.

"Do you like to study?" Dr. Milstein asks.

"Yes. I like to study."

Taking a deep breath, I say nothing else, while waiting for the chance to hold forth, an outcome I know by now is inevitable.

The cardiologist loses interest and returns to the materials on his desk.

"OK. You should have no problem there."

"That's it?"

"Yes. I'm sorry. I'm in the middle of a difficult case. Don't worry. You'll do fine there."

A month later, I receive my acceptance letter.

None of the schools I know about and wish to attend have accepted me. The one that has let me in is a black box in New York City—somewhere I have no interest in living. Now it's a question of "medical school or not," rather than "which medical school." My experience over the last few months makes it clear my reasons for physician training are not consistent with its reality.

Another problem is the calendar. Einstein begins in the summer, not autumn as do all the other schools, because it is experimenting with a three-year program instead of the traditional four. The United States needs more physicians, and this is Einstein's attempt to help fill that gap. July to July, three straight years, with drastically foreshortened vacations—a week each summer and a week each Christmas/New Year's.

Adding up my class credits, I discover I may be able to graduate a quarter early, in March instead of June. The registrar at Stanford confirms this. If I have to begin medical school in July, I will have time to relax before starting. The necessary paperwork is easy. I inform John and Dan—with whom I live off-campus—of my decision to graduate before they do.

"What are you going to do for the spring?" John asks.

"I'll stay here with you and Dan. Hang out with Bobbie."

That winter, I had begun dating Bobbie, a Southern Jewish belle. My girlfriend from last year, Lynn, is attending graduate school in Florida, and we have lost touch. Bobbie and I aren't making long-term plans, but spending the spring with her at Stanford, free from any class requirements, promises to be a pleasant way to finish college.

"First, though, I want to spend time with Sam down at The Men's College. I need to figure things out." We'll take acid and talk about it. I have faith in LSD and in my childhood friend.

I've maintained a close relationship with Sam and his schoolmates in Southern California, sharing with them countless psychedelic and cannabis experiences. A day-long drive every few months to visit them doesn't tax me, and I stay with Sam at the complex of houses where he lives with Spencer and several others.

As I climb into the Mustang, I wave to my housemates. "See you in a couple of weeks."

It's dark when I turn onto the short gravel drive leading to Sam's house. We greet each other warmly, shake hands, hug. He offers me a lit joint.

"Help you calm down," he says. No more need be said.

We carry my bags into the living room, drop them next to the familiar, well-worn, comfortable, enormous couch. It seats six. After flopping down onto it, I must exert effort to prevent it from swallowing me up.

I greet Clarissa and Peter who are sitting in their own overstuffed reclining chairs. Their feet rest and touch on the glass-topped, low-slung coffee table in front of them. Their two beers sit on the tabletop, and smoke wafts up from a cigarette in an ashtray near Peter. After taking a long hit, I get up from the couch and pass the joint to him.

I don't know Peter well. When we've been together, I feel off-balance. His sardonic reserve alienates me. Maybe it reminds me of myself. Or who I don't want to be. Or who I want to be. Or both. Maybe something else that relates to my father.

Peter mocks everyone and everything, and I resent being one of his targets. Whenever confronted, he mockingly denies.

"Who? Me? What? What did I say?" he'd cackle, grin, curl his upper lip, and display a mouthful of large white teeth. Beady, brightly burning, brown, nearly black, closely set eyes, wide with amazed indignation and hurt, laughing at you.

Clarissa, all agree, is an odd match for Peter. Small, lithe, blonde, she comes from a rich Midwest family. She loves her beer, her joints, and her acid. She looks wholesome enough: blue eyes, mid-length neat hair. Her face is open and friendly, and her easy laugh is contagious. She easily manages being the only woman in a room full of intoxicated young men. Much of her appeal resides in her sisterly-like features, but she also exudes a healthy sexuality.

"Why do you like Peter?" everyone asks her.

"Oh. He's such an asshole. I like giving him shit." Her Midwest candor allows her to see through, so she thinks, his irritating shell. She knows there is a needy little boy behind that façade, a defensive shield she will wear down with her warmth. Then, by opening up to her, he will to others.

I immediately feel an attraction to Clarissa. And, as everyone else, wonder why Peter and she are together. Their affection seems limited to their feet. More like brother and sister, bantering back and forth.

It's Saturday night, a few days later, and Clarissa arrives at the property. We all plan to attend a Bach concert on LSD on campus. Everyone doses with the blotter acid and stands around the kitchen table, waiting for what's next.

Peter reconsiders. "Classical music?" He looks around the kitchen. "Jesus. I'd rather play cards."

Everyone living at the compound is an avid bridge player. I've never learned the game.

"Bridge is stupid," I offer. Clarissa agrees.

She adds, "Only stupid people play bridge instead of going to a Bach concert."

Snorts greet her pronouncement.

Sam arches his back, stretches, and groans. "You might be right, Peter. I've been on campus every day this week and don't feel like going back."

I am surprised, but also think: Now, if Spencer declines, Clarissa and I will be the only ones going.

All eyes are on the last member of our little group. Spencer yawns, expressing one of LSD's telltale early signs. Yawning helps dispel face muscular tension. It's an unconscious reflex.

"Yeah," he says. "Bridge sounds good. Let me call Rusty and we'll have four."

Peter turns to Clarissa. "Are you okay going to the concert without me?"

She laughs. "Whatever, you unsophisticated asshole boors. I like Bach."

I chime in, "Me, too. We'll tell you what it's like."

Good-natured chuckling follows us out the door as we climb into my car.

The drug's effects strengthen rapidly as we briskly walk up the wide cement steps to the concert hall. The exertion triggers a rush of energy that flips a switch in our consciousness. We look at each other.

"Are you feeling anything?" we ask at the same time.

Also, at the same time, "Yes!"

At that moment, the evening becomes magical. I take hold of Clarissa's elbow and lead her into the hall. The chandeliers above us shoot sparks of light in all directions. Massive maroon velvet draperies hanging against the side walls glow with an inner radiance. Plush seats, dark blue velvet, more comfortable than any I have ever sat in. Ceiling murals portray the vanguards of the Western Enlightenment: Erasmus, Galileo, Hobbes, rubbing shoulders with their intellectual forebears: Aristotle, Socrates, and Plato.

The Brandenburg concertos spill out from the stage and over the audience. I close my eyes. Each note, a drop of liquid color, blends with other liquid drops of color in my inner eyes. Liquid music: tides, waterfalls, pools, eddies, waves, all exerting a nearly unbearable pleasure.

Clarissa also closes her eyes through most of the concert. We catch glimpses of each other and giggle from the brief but intense eye contact. Then we turn back inward. Intermission passes quickly. Unable to rise from our seats, we stare quietly and companionably at the empty stage.

I think: Clarissa is fantastic. What a terrific girl.

After the concert, we carefully walk down the steps and across the street to one of the little parks that dot the campus. Trees, lawn, and illuminated sidewalks. The moon is full, and the LSD adds an enchanting sparkle to the air.

We stroll around the vast college complex until 2:00 a.m. In perfect harmony.

At one point I say, "You know, I've got an older brother and younger sister."

Clarissa exclaims, "No way! I've got an older sister and two younger brothers!"

I realize, as does she, that our family constellations differ. No matter. It is as if they are the same. We are in this together—Clarissa and me. We hug, kiss. The acid makes my eyes water when looking closely at her face. She thinks I am crying.

Our cheeks touch. Her face feels rubbery and smooth, warm and cold, wet and dry. It's her face. I look at her, she at me. The light flashes off her teeth when she laughs—easily, happily, carefree. Kissing, our teeth loudly clank together.

"I think I like you," I say.

"I think I like you, too," she replies.

I look at my watch. "Oh, no!" I need to get us back to Sam's house.

"It's so late," she says. "Why don't you stay with me?" Clarissa's dormitory is in the middle of one of the two all-girls campuses. "My roommate is gone for the weekend. You can sleep in her bed."

Neither of us can actualize a sexual response once in her room. The LSD turns sex into a joke. Tonight, the absurdity of the sex act bothers neither of us. We hold each other, talk, whisper, giggle, kiss, hug, and massage each other's bodies until the sun comes up.

From my perspective, though, it's more than just the acid interfering with sex. My only previous physically intimate relationship has been with Lynn, an inhibited New England girl who was also a virgin. She found sex dirty, unpleasant, painful, and something to finish as rapidly as possible. On that account, in addition to my limited inexperience, I'm not confident about sex with Clarissa.

The acid's effects are gone by the time we make our way down to the dorm's cafeteria. We sit by ourselves, under the spell of the last twelve hours.

"These eggs are great," I say as I push an entire hard-boiled one into my mouth.

Clarissa laughs, tries doing the same, but can only bite off half.

Her friends sneak looks at this unexpected development. I notice and am pleased. Proud of myself.

"I don't have anything to do the next ten weeks," I say to Clarissa, as we walk through the gardens near her dormitory.

Then, "I was going to spend it with my friends at Stanford." No mention of Bobbie.

"Oh," she answers, looking a little sad, or so it seems.

This look is all it takes for me to blurt, "I'll come down here to be with you instead."

Clarissa's face reflects surprise, pleasure, anxiety, and eagerness. For a moment, I see Peter's image flash in and disappear from her eyes. Maybe it's residual effects of the LSD.

"Where would you stay?" she asks.

"Here. In your dorm. With you. We'll figure it out." I can't stay with Sam, as Peter also lives there.

"My dorm?"

"Sure. It'll work out. After last night, we can do anything together."

I return to Sam's property that afternoon, where Peter and he are drinking coffee outside.

Peter asks, "How was the concert?" But he is really asking: Where were Clarissa and you last night?

"Good. Great. Clarissa's amazing."

His eyes flash. "She is, isn't she?"

I take a breath and plow ahead. "I've decided to move down here for the spring. I don't have anything to do at Stanford and I'd rather be here."

Sam asks, "Where will you stay?"

"With Clarissa. In her dorm room."

Peter snorts. "Clarissa? Do you mean Clarissa?" It sinks in. "*That* Clarissa?"

Defensive, guilty, and embarrassed, yet defiant and triumphant, I answer, "That Clarissa."

Clarissa's now ex-boyfriend is a caricature of amazement. He stiffens, his neck arches to one side; outrage, amusement, admiration, and mortification.

"Wow. I didn't see that coming." Incredulous, eyes growing wide, a leering sneer. He adjusts his head and shoulders, physically expressing his need to readjust his body and mind. The sneer gives way to an ambiguous smile.

"Wow. Congratulations. Good luck, buddy." He barks a sharp cackle, slaps me on the back. Hard. His dark brown eyes burn into me.

For the next two-and-a-half months, Clarissa and I pull off the improbable. Not surprisingly, being around Peter is even less pleasant. He now has a legitimate grievance. Whenever we're together, he pokes my chest sharply with his forefinger. In some ways, I feel I deserve it.

"Hey, buddy. How's it going at The Girls' Dorm? Ha ha."

I mostly succeed at avoiding him, and when the three of us find ourselves together, he is surprisingly good-natured. Clarissa doesn't seem to miss him, but I'm jealous when she laughs at his mocking sarcasm, haughtier and more mocking than anything I can, or wish to, muster.

Reflections

LOVE ON ACID

Biological and psychological models help us understand this episode.

Classical psychedelics like LSD, as well as atypical drugs like MDMA, simulate release of oxytocin, the prosocial "love hormone." Thus, the LSD that night, through those neuroendocrine effects, made more likely an intense attachment between Clarissa and me. In addition, the inhibitory effects of psychedelics on the amygdala—a brain center mediating fear—helped lower fear-based defensiveness, especially concerning rejection. The music, too, was intensely pleasurable, adding to the general ambience of aesthetic and emotional intimacy—perhaps endorphins contributed to this intoxicating mix of hormones.

Psychologically, psychedelics amplify more or less conscious preexisting mental contents: feelings and thoughts, especially their meaningfulness, impact, and truth value. Clarissa was in a convenient, nearly platonic, relationship that required little commitment or emotional closeness. She had been in serious relationships before and was able and willing to engage with Peter at that level. For any number of reasons, however, this did not occur. Thus, she was open to engaging in a more gratifying fulsome relationship.

I was facing an extraordinarily uncertain future. I sensed that medical school was not for me, and I was not committed to Bobbie at Stanford. Perhaps a new relationship with Clarissa would give me meaning and purpose. She might also help me figure things out. While we all know that a relationship won't solve all our problems, it's a wish that is difficult to dispel, especially when times are difficult.

At a deeper level, the triangle of Clarissa, Peter, and me was the setting for my enacting the "Oedipal neurosis."*

Freud first coined the term, defining it as a young boy's wish to have his mother all to himself. This required the elimination of the father.

Here, it is useful to explain two psychoanalytic terms—*libido* and *cathexis*—involved in how this phenomenon comes about. Libido is the organism's life force, the drive behind all human activities. Cathexis is the psychobiological drive to attach—to oneself, other people, ideas, or objects. Freud emphasized the sexual elements of the libido, due in large part to how often suppression of sexual contents contributed to

---

*Oedipus was a prince in Greek mythology who killed his father and married his mother before discovering her true identity. Tragedy then cascaded upon the myth's protagonists—his mother/wife killed herself, and he blinded himself with a pin from her jewelry. Freud did not study as deeply similar conflicts within the little girl's unconscious. However, later analysts described an analogous "Electra complex." Here, a little girl unconsciously wishes to have her father all to herself, and this requires eliminating the mother. Electra, in Greek mythology, orchestrated the murder of her mother, thus avenging the mother's role in murdering Electra's father.

his patients' neuroses. Therefore, his characterization of a little boy's libidinal cathexis to the mother emphasized its sexual nature. However, sex qua sex is not an invariant feature of this stage of psychic development. The essential feature is the wish to wholly possess the mother and eliminate the father. This is the Oedipal complex.

The guilt the little boy feels in experiencing these wishes, as well as fears of retribution by the father, is enough for him to give up these fantasies and ultimately identify with the father. As he grows up, he seeks to emulate his father by partnering with a suitable woman for himself. If the little boy succeeds in some form or another in displacing his father, psychopathology ensues—both from his guilt as well as depression due to his inability to realistically assume the role of his mother's adult partner.

As a little boy, I had specific—not only generic—cause to engage in Oedipal fantasies. My father was abusive to both me and my mother. Thus, saving my mother from my father would make me a hero and boost my shaky self-esteem. Compounding these fantasies were my mother's frequent promises to leave my father, and "then we can be happy together without him." When this scenario never materialized, I blamed myself for its failure. Maybe I was doing something wrong or lacked an attribute that would otherwise result in its success.

Despite these interesting, conflicting, and intersecting subterranean psychological processes, Clarissa and I were a couple for over two years. We genuinely enjoyed each other's company, worked well together as a team, and spent many enjoyable hours with each other's families in California and the Midwest. I had never before had such a meaningful relationship. However, I could never fully free myself from guilt over taking her from her partner. In addition, the role of LSD in initiating our relationship set a challenging standard for its future. We could not maintain in everyday life a psychedelic level of closeness, empathy, and identification. In addition, relying on a benchmark of psychic unity, it was difficult to recognize or acknowledge real differences in goals, priorities, and personalities. That is, if only we could exist in that state of undifferentiated harmony, those differences would no longer matter.

26

PERMANENT INSANITY

WITHIN A FEW WEEKS of moving in with Clarissa, my life enters a pleasant routine. I have graduated from Stanford and am living for free at an exclusive women's college with a beautiful, talented, and intelligent young woman. And I am on track to begin medical training at a prestigious East Coast school in the summer.

While my life appears both exciting and comfortable, below the surface my inner world is in turmoil. The guilt concerning my LSD-fueled "victory" over the irritating and intimidating former boyfriend of Clarissa colors my subsequent interactions with her as well as him. Who, exactly, is Clarissa? Why is she with me and not Peter? How secure is my victory? If she could dump him so unceremoniously, what prevents her from doing the same to me? Do we have a future together? If so, what kind?

In addition, my living situation is odd and tenuous. How long can I stay at The Girls' Dorm before someone asks me to leave? How exactly am I getting fed? Who's paying for my meal plan? If I have to leave, where will I go? I've moved out of my off-campus housing in Palo Alto, and my housemates have taken on a new boarder.

And, most disconcerting, in less than three months I'm due in New York City to begin three years of unrelentingly punishing training. This, in order to attain a goal in which I have little interest. Except, that is, if it allows me to put into effect the messianic Manifesto, a model that alarms all who learn of it.

Clarissa's room is on the second story of the main dormitory of the women's college campus. Using the communal bathroom, much like the one from my former dorm at The College, requires some tact—which I gain quickly—and embarrassing encounters are rare. Our sex life, however, never reaches great heights. Her roommate's presence fifteen feet away is a damper. More significant, however, is my lack of experience and confidence.

Clarissa enjoys sex and I don't know how to. Maybe her pleasure is not for me. How could it be? I am not experiencing much pleasure, so why is she? Maybe she's thinking of her Midwest former—or maybe off and on—boyfriend whose name I hear every so often, especially around her younger brothers who are his good friends. Or maybe she is remembering Peter, whose girlfriend she was before I moved in with her only weeks before.

I spend my days with Clarissa and our friends. Everyone has classes, but only for a few hours a day. We smoke pot, listen to music, and make plans for the future. I don't look up any of the gang from The College, a mere ten-minute walk from Clarissa's dormitory.

Bruce's older brother Cyrus is visiting from the Bay Area this weekend and we plan to take LSD in the mountains. Bruce is the friend with whom I took the trip to the redwoods, during which on LSD he left his girlfriend at the gas station. Everyone likes Bruce and we are eager to get to know Cyrus. At the last minute, Peter decides to join us. Sam opts to stay home and catch up with his studies.

Making our way up the winding mountain road, I sit squeezed in between the two brothers. Each weighs more than two hundred pounds, is over 6 feet tall, and sports broad shoulders. I don't have much room.

The day is perfect. A light breeze, snow on the craggy peaks in the distance. The flowers of late spring spread their scent and colors everywhere along the wide dry canyon in which we hike. We are spread out but keep an eye on each other. This diffuseness of the little group strikes me as detached, however, lacking warmth, and the cool breeze magnifies this emotional chill. I feel isolated and begin withdrawing into myself, make less eye contact, and my short responses get shorter and vaguer.

Cyrus is especially quiet. And when I try to reach out to him, my curious questions—the mainstay of how I relate—seem to irritate him. He responds with a grunt or one- or two-word replies. Hidden behind a thick beard, his face is impassive. Is he rebuffing me? Bruce watches us and looks amused. Maybe his older brother becomes quiet on LSD, something he's familiar with and finds entertaining. He knows there is no undercurrent of malice, but I'm not so sure.

This situation could be bad, or it could be fine. Bad in this setting means meaningless. If it is meaningless, this concerns me the most. Is how I relate empty of meaning? Who really cares what I ask, or say, or don't?

Peter and I are at some distance from each other during the hike up the canyon. Still, I feel his resentment. When the group comes together for a snack or water, his mocking aloof manner confuses me more than usual. His mocking makes it impossible to tell if he is mocking. That is, is he mocking his mocking style, and therefore being genuine?

I think: "That's just how he is. He is that way with everyone, in all situations." So, is he mocking because he always mocks, or is he mocking me in particular because our relationship is different? That difference being that I recently moved in with his girlfriend after she and I took LSD. Now that we are on acid, does he see an opening to inflict revenge? Do I deserve punishment? But the mocking is confusing. Is it the punishment itself or is it a repudiation of the punishment I deserve?

It is as if Peter is saying "No, I'm not angry, I'm happy for her" in a mocking tone. But is he happy for me? Or, "I'm not mocking your having stolen my girlfriend from me. Even though I should hate you."

I quickly finish my snack and pull away.

After walking up the canyon another hour, Bruce announces, "It's getting to be that time. We need to turn around."

There is plenty of midafternoon light left for our return. Each finds his own rock to pee on. Then, a handful of trail mix and a long drink of water.

Peter, the two brothers, and I begin the descent in a tighter-knit group. This physical proximity makes everyone large and looming. Their size would seem normal if I put more distance between us. But I know that doing so will draw unwanted attention.

Suddenly we are walking through a seven-foot-high metal culvert that passes under the highway. It is unfamiliar. Did we come this way? How could I not remember this tunnel?

Peter says excitedly, the mocking tone nearly absent, "Wow! Look around! It's incredible!"

We all do and mumble in agreement. The air is full of sparkling jewels, ranging in size from the barely visible to the immeasurably large, filling the tunnel. I move my hand back and forth in front of my face. It reminds me of Sam and my LSD trip in the culvert that snowy day last year. My hands cut a swath of light through the bubbling sparkling air, leaving behind colorful trails.

Midway through the tunnel, dark and phosphorescent, florescent shimmering stars pulsate. I cannot feel the sand that I know is under my feet but continue moving forward. Almost like sliding, some force gently pulling me along. Daylight returns as we exit the enormous metal tunnel.

Bruce, as the group's mathematics and engineering representative, a role he delights in, confidently declares, "We have another half-hour before we get to the cars."

I look around. I am disoriented. Not confused, as in "Where am I?", but disoriented, as in "Where is this?" Nothing looks familiar. Or more precisely, nothing feels familiar. Or, even more to the point, everything feels unfamiliar and strange. I do not know where I am. And the nightmarish unfamiliarity at once leads to wondering who or what I am. I have become unmoored.

Maybe looking at the back of my hands, to see how high I am, will help. Large colorful blood vessels appear, glowing and pulsating. There are no bones nor muscles. My hands look as if they belong to someone else.

The group has moved on and I trot up to them. Everyone is silent. Why have they stopped talking? Did I bring on this silence? Is it because of me? Had they been talking about me and now that I have arrived, they don't want me to hear what they're saying? Or does my presence affect them in such a way that they no longer wish to talk? No matter. My isolation grows.

Peter watches where he steps, ignoring me. Bruce is leading the way, oblivious to anything other than the path ahead. Cyrus follows close behind his brother. What are they thinking? Why do I sense their hostility? Or is it disinterest? Disinterest at this moment is the ultimate hostility. I say nothing and focus on the rocky sandy gravel underfoot.

Am I so alone, so detached, so isolated and drowning in the unfamiliar because there is something wrong? Something wrong with me? Am I strange? Or bad? I think: "Maybe I am a negative influence, and everyone is keeping their distance." I defend myself to myself: "No, I'm not bad." But why is the group excluding me?

I realize how helpless I am at the moment. Dependent on this group for my survival, a survival that consists of returning to town from these mountains. And the group has turned its back on me, has disappeared me, turned me into an unreality, an absence. How could this possibly go right? I feel the last link to my sanity snap. I adopt a stance of madness.

The LSD transports me to Dr. Wessells's office in the biology building at Stanford. He is reading my medical school essay—my messianic Manifesto. "This is nuts," he loudly whispers several times, shaking his head in disbelief.

The pieces of a very big puzzle begin falling into place.

Dr. Wessells allowing me the opportunity to perform research in his world-class laboratory always slightly puzzled me. Rather than my success reflecting his genuine desire to take on a dedicated and persistent student, I wondered if he were instead humoring me. The professor's teasing and mock exasperated manner—how he seemingly expressed affectionate humor with his students—was difficult to interpret. Perhaps he had simply surrendered to my relentless entreaties, had given up. It was "enough already!" and he gave me the keys. Thus, my highly esteemed position in his laboratory was not due to my merit but to his sense of pity.

Now, I replay the scene in Dr. Wessells's office. His dismay reading the Manifesto mirrors what I now see as why he was so reluctant to let me work in his laboratory. Now I understand; it all makes sense. I knew Dr. Wessells thought I was "a little strange." But it was more than that. Much more. Rather, he had made a mistake, going against his better judgment. He had seen my insanity, my innately dangerous brokenness, but nevertheless had granted me access. The professor should never have let me through the door. But he had. And all of a sudden, the jig was up.

As my mind struggles to make sense of the isolation from my friends—alone, absolutely disconnected from those around me—the reason behind my mentor's attitude becomes clear. He knew I was insane, terminally mentally ill. He had been indulging my psychosis all this time. But why? The answer is plain: he was simply waiting for this moment when I would finally realize how insane I am, had always been, and will always be. The real truth, the one Dr. Wessells knew would one day dawn on me, has arrived. The group's attitude toward me today is the moment when the rest of the world can finally drop its façade of treating me as sane. But it is not as much the group's new attitude toward me as it is my finally correctly interpreting the meaning of that attitude.

Another realization comes to me. At last, I will get the care that I have needed my entire life, care that I would need for the rest of my life. A psychiatric hospital, locked up in a tiny little room.

This is my fate. My true fate. Not the pseudo-fate of a pseudo-successful student on his pseudo-way to medical school. Dr. Wessells, by letting me work with him, was saying in effect, "You'll figure it out sooner or later. Don't take any of what you see seriously. This superficially normal world, work, and relationships were designed to lead you to where you belong. You finally get it. *This* is where you belong. Locked up forever."

Every one of my benefactor's quizzical expressions, his teasing tone, had been a response to my craziness, a gentle attempt to get me to see it. The messianic medical school essay was only the most recent evidence, but the professor kept his conclusions to himself. I would realize the truth sooner or later. Up until now, though, I had been unable or unwilling to face the facts. It wasn't time. That time is today.

Even more terrifying: My insanity had prevented me from seeing my insanity. Upon reflection, I realize this has been going on for as long as I can remember. But the nature of the previously disguised information is now suddenly clear. My current crisis of isolation has supplied the last piece of the puzzle. My view of reality is several times removed, connected to my own experience by only the thinnest thread. I am in one world and everyone else in another. I belong in a mental hospital. This is where my life has been leading, and it is finally upon me.

As my body walks quickly with the others down the canyon, it weaves in and out among boulders, sand, and gravel, while the descending sun bears down on it.

A vision appears. I am in a small, dimly lit seclusion room in a psychiatric hospital, close to the floor. I cannot tell if I am lying in a bed or sitting in a chair, perhaps even lying or sitting on the floor. Wherever it is, I am at an uncomfortable angle, one that forces me to dissociate, to shed awareness of my body. Now it is comfortable, but I cannot move my body. I have no control over it.

I sense a light, a brightness, maybe an overhead lamp, but I can make nothing out, nothing is distinct. I hear, or perhaps simply feel, movement around me. The nurses are wearing nuns' habits. Maybe they are nuns. I can't see their faces. It feels as if there are two or three of them. They seem benign, even kind, and have my interest at heart. They are simply watchful, available to help.

I blink my eyes and look around the mountain scene. The vehicles are another mile ahead. I'm following ten yards behind the group so I can process this vision and its implications without interruption.

Reentering the nightmare, I realize this scenario is not yet real; that is, it does not yet correspond to objective reality. I resist this outcome because it feels wrong. Or at least it does not feel right. I have just decided that everything up until this moment has been lived as if in a dream, that I have interacted with projections, not reality, my entire life. I have woken up from a dream into a nightmare of psychic paralysis. But where is the transition? In this state I cannot act, I cannot actualize any will. I am not even sure if I have a will. It is the essence of weakness. Not dead but acting as if so. Complete dependence on people and an institution designed to deal with my psychosis of inertness.

The afternoon ends with my finally letting go into who I really am. This is not the Rick who believed he had fooled everyone with his apparent normality. This is the result: the world of psychosis, of permanent and total insanity, the crazy world. And this is how I am in it. This is how I am. In fact, even while I see myself appearing normal, this psychosis-world is going on alongside this one. Any remaining barrier is rapidly dissolving. Time to call a spade a spade. I wonder, Is this really it?

In the hospital room, I am lying in, not simply on, the wetness of a semi-firm warm material. I sense it is my own shit, but I cannot see or smell it. There is no discomfort. Perceiving more clearly, it is as if I am just barely raised or suspended over it, or just lightly touching it, a physical lightness. Nearly immaterial. All my sensations are reduced, almost extinguished, but not because of dying. It is the terror that awaits me once my world of sensation and perception are over. It is empty and terrifying. Living and no longer knowing if I were alive. It is an absolutely abstract state, one in which the impossible contradiction exists: that I have always been this way and have not realized it until now. In the little seclusion room and the normal outside world at the same time. No longer. It is insane now *all* the time and the rest of my life. If indeed I were now alive.

I relax into that world. I could give up. While I dissociate from my body in that little room, I am free. It has been so hard in the outside world. Here is my chance to stop struggling, to stop fighting. To be completely passive. A state of no bearings, no orientation, nothing to ground in reality. And I swing between that state and one with a body, an individual physical self.

The entire past condenses into and explains this moment, everything leading up to this moment and to this realization. But I cannot sustain one world all of the time, despite realizing that the insane world is the true one. Somehow, the most frightening quality is its eternity. This conflict of real and unreal, normal and insane, will never resolve and will never end.

We arrive at the vehicles—Peter's car and Cyrus's truck. I don't want to drive down the mountain road with Peter. I force my body to sit again between the two brothers in the truck. It is nearly impossible to take a deep breath, feeling even more compressed than on the drive up. I say nothing. What could I say? How could I say it? Which version of reality would I be speaking from? Neither do my two companions speak. I know I am in trouble. But where can I get help? Who will help me? A twenty-minute drive feels like hours. We arrive at the campus.

Somehow, I manage to eke out, "Cyrus, drop me off at Sam's, okay?" Not back to Clarissa's dorm. I will talk to Sam. I recognize that my break has occurred in the setting of indifference and muted hostility. Sam is my oldest friend. I will talk with him.

Arriving and parking at the compound, the brother to my right steps out of the vehicle. I slide off the seat and wordlessly, without looking back, make my way down the gravel driveway and across the brown lawn to Sam's one-room bungalow. It is warmer here than in the mountains. I knock on the screen door, looking inside.

Before Sam lets me in, I say through the screen door, "I am really messed up. I need to talk."

My childhood friend glances quickly at me and says, "You need a joint."

We smoke quietly. Sam carefully scrutinizes me while I carefully scrutinize the joint. It is easier to focus on something small and near than look around and lose myself in the empty psychic vastness surrounding me.

I explain my condition.

Sam sits quietly for a couple of minutes. Finally, he says, "Let me get this straight. You think you're crazy and have always been crazy. That everything in your life up until now has been steering you toward this realization without you knowing it."

"Right."

"That doesn't make any sense."

I finally look up at Sam and notice the wall behind him.

He says, "Do you know why?"

"No."

He explains. "If you had always been crazy, you wouldn't realize it just now."

"But what about Dr. Wessells?"

"That's just how people are. It doesn't really mean anything. Most people are fucked up. You did nothing. You were just yourself. Rick."

"Oh."

"And don't mind those guys. Cyrus and Bruce are weird. And Peter is an asshole."

"Oh."

A poison-filled sac in my mind bursts. I feel it drain down along the sides of my brain, inside my skull, down to my ears. Warm, then cool, now barely perceptible. I check whether fluid is draining out of my ears. There isn't any.

"Oh."

I relate to Sam, and he relates to me. It is normal, it is real, not something I see in my mind's eye—dissociated and immobile in a tiny psychiatric hospital room.

My mind begins a very wide U-turn. I notice a Huichol yarn art piece glowing on the wall, happy and friendly. I relate to it, too.

Genuine affection shines from Sam's eyes. I look down at the ground, embarrassed, unable to meet my friend's countenance.

I say, "Crazy fucking shit, man. Thanks."

Sam gets up and walks into the kitchen.

"Would you like some tea?"

"Yeah. How about chamomile?"

"That sounds good."

Six years will pass before I take another psychedelic drug.

Reflections
A VERY CLOSE CALL

This episode underscores how important set and setting are in determining psychedelic drug experiences. It also demonstrates the invaluable role of a sympathetic and empathic friend in averting a potentially catastrophic outcome.

My anxieties—social, sexual, and intellectual—tapped into my generic insecurities as a young man. Was I truly any good? Was I pulling something over on everyone? Why didn't they see how inadequate I really was? Or did they?

Two of the most common bad trips are those of "permanent insanity" and "homosexual panic." I recount an example of the latter in "Basketball Gay Panic" while this particular case involves the former. When editing this account, I tried to make more succinct the description of the horrifying whirlpool I was circling that day. However, the endless loop I was in was a fundamental feature of the experience itself. Editing the account for brevity would dilute one of its most essential elements—the sense of no escape, its permanency, and, even more terrifying, the fact that it had been going on forever without my realizing it.

The silver lining of Sam's last-minute decision to not come along that morning—perhaps his presence in the mountains would have forestalled my bad trip—turned out to be my salvation. He was the perfect resource to help quell my acid nightmare. His simple, empathic, and friendly presence was as important as anything he said. I felt safe with him, regained some of my own sense of self in his reflecting back to me his knowledge of who I was. He recognized me as myself, someone he had grown up with. He knew me better than any of my other friends, and I knew him better than any of them. His bare-bones yet insightful assessments of Dr. Wessells's style, as well as Peter's and the brothers' personalities, were perfect.

I was fortunate in having available—and responding to—the first line intervention for a bad trip; that is, removal from an overstimulating environment and "talking down"—calmly and reassuringly trying to understand and assuage one's confused state. If this fails, mild tranquilizers such as the benzodiazepine antianxiety agents are next. However, these medications cause sedation rather than diminishing the psychedelic effects themselves. Stronger antipsychotic medications have more side effects but are also more effective in dampening down the altered state itself.* Finally, psychiatric hospitalization when all else fails. However, while administering a more or less effective "LSD antidote" might end the traumatizing effects of the drug, it does not undo the trauma it has already caused, trauma that needs to be addressed.

I have not infrequently wondered what might have happened if Sam were not available that day. I do not think it would have gone well. At the very least, I would have needed professional interven-

---

*We may have a new medication to specifically reverse psychedelic drug effects. Ketanserin—a serotonin 2A blockading drug not yet available in the United States—reverses subjective effects of LSD when given an hour following its ingestion and the psychedelic experience is underway. However, we do not know if the drug works in diminishing LSD's peak effects, say at four to six hours.[1]

tion, and a damning "psych history" would follow me the rest of my life.

Be that as it may, I avoided psychedelic drugs for many years after that day. I could not take the risk. It was only after establishing a regular Zen practice and undergoing several years of psychoanalytic psychotherapy that I felt stable enough, having adequate psychological resources, to again venture into those realms.

27

NEW YORK BREAKDOWN

THIS CHAPTER RECOUNTS a nine-month-long episode of severely disordered mood and thinking that resulted in my taking a leave of absence from medical school.

While the events I write about in "The Manifesto" created ripple effects extending for months, they did not adversely affect my everyday function. My school performance continued at a high level and my friendships were sound. On the other hand, the ideas I formulated and became so attached to in my Manifesto did not seem compatible with life as a New York City medical student. The foreboding quickly became a reality once I moved to the Bronx.

This chapter's drawn-out disturbed state began on my first day of school in the summer of 1973, and while it was not entirely resolved with my return to California in the spring of 1974, it was at least manageable by then. During this period, I vacillated between a shaky elation and grandiosity that was no match for a self-hating depression. Like the hypomanic origin of the Manifesto, the contents of this period were disturbed thinking and mood, not perceptual. In addition, hints of psychosis intruded. However, an undercurrent of clarity remained in which I recognized the depth of my confusion and turmoil and finally decided on a solution: leave New York.

I begin this chapter by establishing its setting. My primary source material are excerpts from the journal I kept then, which I place in *this font.* These journal entries refer to a collection of books, authors, ideas, and terms that include East Asian religious, theosophic, psychoanalytic, and scientific. I use footnotes to explain them in this chapter, instead of referring back to them in a freestanding Reflections section at the end.

I recompensate after the horrifying acid trip earlier in the spring, which I describe in "Permanent Insanity," but my mental equilibrium is still fragile. I *know* medical school is not for me. I am also unprepared and anxious over the prospect of relocating from familiar and idyllic Northern and Southern California college life to the Bronx. Clarissa has another year of school, and our relationship, as intense as it has been from the onset, will be difficult to maintain living on two distant coasts.

Medical school at Albert Einstein College of Medicine begins soon, the first week of July, while the two schools who have me on their waiting lists begin in the fall. The clock ticks.

There is one last alternative.

During my final quarter at Stanford, I write a term paper for my physiological psychology class that draws the attention of the professor, Karl Pribram. Dr. Pribram trained as a neurosurgeon and has been performing neuroscience research for nearly thirty years.[1] He is best known for developing a novel holographic model of brain function.[2] While the details of his theory are too abstruse for me, I sense that his work is esoteric enough that my fascination with altered states of consciousness might find a receptive audience in him.

My paper proposes a role for the pineal gland in the production of profound changes in consciousness. Dr. Pribram gives the paper an "A+" and extends an invitation to meet. By the end of our chat, he offers me a position in his laboratory studying the pineal gland! I can't accept right now but tell him I will be in touch once the medical school situation becomes clearer. Over the next several weeks, it does become clearer, but no more appealing. Einstein remains my only choice.

I tell Dr. Pribram I accept his offer. First, though, I must check with Einstein to see if I can postpone my admission. The medical school replies quickly and tells me I can delay for two years; after that, I will need to reapply. I return to Stanford and Dr. Pribram's laboratory. I meet some of his graduate students who eye me suspiciously, skeptically. Closing the professor's office door behind me, I sit down and ask the question I've been avoiding.

"Will you be paying me?"

He answers, "Didn't I tell you? All I can offer you is lab space."

I return to Southern California and Clarissa's dorm, write to Einstein, and tell them I will be there as originally planned.

After landing at JFK airport, my other half-uncle—a photojournalist—and his wife pick me up in their compact Buick Capri. I overnight at their house on Long Island. The next day, we make the drive to the Bronx in a little U-Haul loaded with furniture.

New York City in July is hot and muggy. It also smells bad in a way I have never known before: garbage, bus and truck exhaust, and the unique odor emanating from street-level vents connected to the underground tunnels carrying subways throughout the city. It's a different world. And, besides my two half-uncles one to two hours away, I know no one.

I am the first tenant in a studio apartment on the ninth floor of one of two new twenty-seven-story high-rises in the middle of campus. On one side is a complex of hospitals and on the other, the medical school. Using the elevators, we carry upstairs a large wooden desk, a couple of chairs, a couch, a bed, and several lamps. Assorted kitchen utensils. My relatives leave midday, and I sit on the new, shiny wooden floor and look around. It hits me:

I've just made a huge mistake.

Up until that moment, I had been able to force the direction of my mixed depressed-hypomanic state into expansive messianic aspirations. Its depressive component I had mostly succeeded in suppressing.* Now,

---

*Suppression differs from repression in that suppression is a voluntary defense intended to keep certain ideas and feelings out of awareness, while repression occurs unconsciously. Suppressed material is accessible with effort or during periods of stress. Repressed material only makes itself known indirectly; for example, through dreams, slips of the tongue, or inexplicable behavior or feelings.

before the end of my first week in New York, that psychological defense falters. I write a poem before going to bed one night:

> Taking off my glasses,
> checking my clock
> looking down at my roses
> pillow*—noticing vaguely
> my T-shirt and boxers I am
> wearing—my eyes aren't really
> that good
> having read "sleep" in be here
> now,† with so much spirituality and so much joy, but old age
>   too, a
> clique of spiritual seekers
> fun and games‡
> please take me with you
> look at my tired, very puny
> look-
> ing body right now-with a watch and love-leather§
> through the haze of
> my nearsighted eyes
> wondering quietly and whispering
> without feelings of anything at all
> but detached‖
> fatigue
> "what is this stuff going on
> this book, this body, this bed
> I see no purpose in any of this:

---

*A pillowcase printed with rose images.
†*Be Here Now*, by Richard Alpert/Ram Dass, which I refer to in "The Manifesto."
‡A reference to the elitist nature of some New Age spirituality.
§Thin leather bracelets Clarissa and I wear to remind ourselves of each other.
‖A subtle and complex notion. It means neither to suppress feelings and thoughts nor indulge them. In my case, I simply wanted to feel better.

right now." Detached
I am here* now but not real†
excited about all this material‡
that I have surrounded this
shell of a body with.
I am depressed but not with a grasping
attitude.§ What if Clarissa never came
back to see me-to live with me?
What then?
Many plans, thought,
gone to waste? Perhaps, but they are teaching me, but
   not nearly as much as they could be, you know. I'm so
   attached‖ so much of the time.
Now where am I?
A tired little body, not knowing why he is here at all, going to
   bed, seeing his T-shirt, boxers and bed with the fogginess
   of his eyes.
Alone-completely alone#
Relish it, as it is the feeling of dying, of quiet insanity.** Of
   death and quietude
and dissolution. The tired small body (even if 6'5"—small
   bodies). Good night and hello darkness.

---

*Another reference to *Be Here Now*.
†A wish to dissociate from the reality of my new circumstances.
‡My coursework, which in and of itself was exciting.
§Grasping, the opposite of detachment. I am depressed, grasping or not. Here I try to spiritualize my melancholy. It may have a spiritual element, but its bases are personal and psychological.
‖A recurrent theme throughout this episode—my lack of perfect equanimity in the face of massive stress reflects poorly on me.
#A key precipitant of this episode.
**The mirror image of the messianism fueling the Manifesto. If I can't save the world by executing the ideas in the Manifesto and/or instantly thriving in this foreign environment, I might as well be dead. Or, passively psychotic, like the vision in "Permanent Insanity."

My classmates are strange, and I find no one with whom to relate. One-hundred-seventy-six medical students who all had just been pre-med students. At Stanford, I may have known two pre-meds other than myself. Many of my classmates have been in the Jewish Modern Orthodox Yeshiva educational system since kindergarten. They wear yarmulkes, get up early in the morning to pray, and eat kosher food. For both men and women, dissecting their cadaver in gross anatomy class is the first time most of them have seen a naked body of the opposite sex. They are aliens. Aliens who look down on me—if they notice me at all—and my nonobservant lifestyle and West Coast vibe. Off campus, it's just as strange and more forbidding. Where do I go for a walk? And I've never been around so many people of color: African, Caribbean, Puerto Rican. I fear for my life every time I take the subway.

I find two marijuana smokers, but partaking with them involves getting low, not high. One talks nonstop about coursework while his shirt pockets burst with different colored pens and highlighters with which he marks up class notes and textbooks. His girlfriend cries whenever she reminisces—which is often—about their life together at UC Santa Barbara: the beaches, farmers' market, fresh air, friendly people, and constant sunshine. The other, a Yale graduate from the East Coast, is sarcastic, aggressively teasing, and speaks nearly entirely in puns, double entendres, and cryptic non sequiturs.

Books on Buddhism provide solace. I find especially attractive the concept of begging and almsgiving, the relationship between poor monks and those donating food. I think: A mendicant alms-receiving life would be better than what I have here. It's a happy fantasy; at least it would be simpler:

Thus one resorts to his own method, his own path of least resistance in order to sustain his biological essence. Most frequent way to do this was beg, alms-giving allowed both sustenance to the beggar, and an instant and immediately vanished feeling of omnipotence, clarity, beatitude.*

*On the part of the donor.

I write Stanislav Grof, a Czech psychiatrist whose seminal work with LSD in Prague and the University of Maryland has inspired me over the years.[3] He is still in Baltimore. I wonder if I could study psychedelics with him as a medical school elective. I'm grasping at straws, as one takes electives only in the last year of school; but, if I have something to look forward to, the present will be more tolerable. Dr. Grof's reply, which I paraphrase, is discouraging: "The tide has turned. There's no funding, no drugs, I'm leaving Baltimore."

A shadowy group in Manhattan with "kundalini" on their letterhead learns of my interest in the pineal gland. They open up their archives to me, which I dig through on Saturdays. "Let us know if you find anything we could use," their pallid leader requests. I don't know what I'm looking for, but the articles on full-spectrum light draw my attention.* Arcana, Lovecraft, occult, Theosophy, and pagan materials fill the rest of the library, topics in which I have no interest. After several visits, I excuse myself from further participation. Besides, would I work for them and not attend medical school?

Clarissa is a crucial support. She and I talk often, and she visits regularly. She reminds me of a past in which I functioned normally and had friends, reflecting back to me my identity, one with which I am in danger of losing touch.

I get a cat—Gray. She is a beautiful companion—gentle, intelligent, and interactive. She studies with me and plays fetch in my little apartment.

I struggle with classes, and my grades are poor. Never have I had to learn so much in so little time. Einstein's experimental three-year curriculum packs two months of material, say, biochemistry, into two weeks. I can't keep up.

---

*Seven years later, in 1980, the first paper appears on full-spectrum light suppression of human melatonin. For my pineal studies in the mid-1980s, the University of New Mexico clinical research center retrofitted a "light room," coating the walls and ceiling with silver-impregnated white paint that reflected high intensity full-spectrum light on our subjects. This room made possible full suppression of melatonin throughout the evening, which allowed us to assess the pineal hormone's physiological function.[4]

I decelerate to a four-year program, and this opens up a two-week vacation. Clarissa and I visit Jim and Dorothy Fadiman* in Northern California. Could I somehow work with them? However, both are just beginning to establish themselves and don't have a position. We also discuss how it's important for me to clarify what I really want.

I return to New York and regress further.

I try to place my dysregulated state into a model that helps me understand it and cope. While Buddhism seems to be that system, I don't really know what Buddhism teaches nor how to practice it. Without grounding in any one system, my search becomes increasingly confused:

> Little ball of E† (about 24 g)‡ can either return to mother, to home, to mass of crude energy which returns as material life,§ or does it change energy levels to dissolution, to Nirvana‖ level of organization, which is physically incapable of returning to material consciousness. Is there a soul, then? Buddha says no. Buddha's ball of energy was forced, forced itself, to a new energy level through ascetic practices and previous lives resulting in this present level of this and other lives as electricity, the soul being somewhat similar in composition to electricity, can be altered by electricity, permanently. The farther away from Buddha one is in time, the weaker effects you can get from people who have been transmitted to by higher and higher people.

---

*Dorothy's studies on light and spirituality, on display in her film *Radiance: The Experience of Light*, led her to the pineal gland. Jim then introduced me to it when we first met in 1972.

†Energy. As in "$E = mc^2$."

‡A reference to theory that the soul weighs twenty-one grams.[5]

§A reference to reincarnation, or transmigration of the soul. This notion exists in many religious traditions and proposes that after death, something unique to the individual moves on to another physical object, usually animate.

‖The final absolute end of suffering. By implication, this means no more reincarnation, as Buddhism teaches that life is inherently suffering.

Transmission* (problem-says Dr. Lethcoe†) whether a teacher is necessary or not—maybe a case of direct transference of this energy is possible. However some resistance and obeying Ohm's law. It loses some power even in the most direct transmission. Therefore, pretty much practically, theoretically and theoretically as well, the levels of enlightenment and grossness, of doctrines and techniques available, need to be necessarily depleted somewhat in strength. Buddha cleaned out a lot of souls with his incredible one.‡

Soul is just a convenient term. What can you change in a luminous egg?§ The consciousness of the atom‖ is a truism—or else, where in the hell did that atom come from except from something completely incomprehensible—such as God.#

Rough sketch. Ego equals body preservation. God drops to spirit, to mind-intellect, to emotions, concepts body (all with loss of energy, latent). No quantum levels! Unless whole universe is a big chemical reaction, one big dream. I.e., It doesn't really matter what you call it or explain it, it just is. It can only take care of itself when the energy level reaches the level of resonance.** When does it begin? Where does it start in time? Time and space collapse.

---

*Transmitting the essence of the teaching from master to disciple. A Zen scripture, Sandokai, calls this "two arrows meeting in midair."

†Who taught the Indian Buddhism class I took at Stanford.

‡Via transmission.

§A notion Carlos Castaneda develops in his books about Don Juan, a northern Mexican shaman.[6]

‖A reference to Bailey's Theosophical work, *The Consciousness of the Atom*.[7] The "soul" of the atom, as it were, brought that atom into existence and allows it to continue existing. Without it, the atom would no longer exist.

#This two-sentence paragraph contains Theosophy, Judaism, and Mexican shamanism. However, where is the center, the guiding principle? "God's incomprehensibility," an arguable notion, took me years to begin understanding; at this time, God's incomprehensibility was simply that.

**Reminiscent of Neoplatonic Aristotelianism. In this system, the "contents" of higher spheres of spirituality descend through lower ones on their way to Earth. In doing so, their contents become coarser.

The holy man has orgasmic power, * *potency, it is just a corollary, the physical manifestation of pure awareness, not the orgasmic man as being much more than orgasmic, a coarser form of enlightenment, centering on the physical. Next time, hopefully, the physical will still be there, though so will a higher nonphysical nonbiological reunion with higher level of consciousness occur.*

You can explain it all as energy, time space, matter. Terms.

To watch the clock turn an interminable 5 seconds. From the seven to the eight. Forever. Things all stop and hold still. While I watch them exist. Turn down the music with your eyebrows.† All as separate. From each other they are. Frozen in time. Relatively of course. The excruciating pain of expectancy, of slowness, the rushing by of the wind, of timelessness.

There are scattered throughout my writing moments of bliss, remnants of the joy I experienced when first articulating the Manifesto:

It takes only a second to appreciate, be consumed with, the joy of the world in its entirety.

I believe the great men of psychiatry have never reached the elevated state of consciousness that I have. I am on to something they are not:

Freud, Jung either have been there once before, but cannot transcend what they are, if they were to remain in the state which they have finally reached, or begun to approach so very closely. They withdraw back into their own ego, as returning previously to the role as subject. Not as object and subject, a reconciliation—more like a dissolution of differences between the two. And have just remained as they were forever, at that eternal, infinite instant. For to do so, would involve

---

*A reference to the work of Wilhelm Reich, an early psychoanalyst who proposed that one reaches true mental health only through the orgasm.[8]

†A reference to my having a supernatural power.

biological death, no one can transcend his own nerve cells if he wants to be aware of it.

A case conference with a dying patient rekindles my messianism.* At the same time, I acknowledge the impossibility of implementing it:

Teach dying old woman something of EMPTINESS.† HELP PEOPLE BECOME BODHISATTVAS,‡ UNAFRAID TO LIVE AND DIE. Get their creativity going again. Tap into their unconscious and supra-conscious without fear.

Spread the Dharma,§ is what you want to do, as best as you possibly can, and you don't know which way that is. Science, philosophy, religion—no scientists‖ are into it—that's where I am most needed. But I can't handle it. They're too unaware and I am too insecure in my being to maintain my energies among so many counter-growth ones.

In contrast to wishing to teach Buddhism to the dying, I can't ignore my unusual experiences and distress:

My hands feel huge and big sometimes# me writing, sometimes me not having any control at all. ESP is necessary and mind talking

---

*A reaction to my less conscious painful despair over my helplessness in the face of such suffering.

†*Sunyata*, a fundamental Buddhist notion. It proposes that all phenomenal existence, including the self, is devoid of intrinsic reality. Penetrating into the heart of emptiness occurs in kensho, Buddhist enlightenment.

‡Buddhist "saints." These are semi-divine mythological figures such as Avalokiteshvara/Kuan yin, the bodhisattva of compassion to whom one prays in time of need and whose character one tries to emulate in daily life. A bodhisattva also is someone who delays his or her own enlightenment until they have aided all others in attaining theirs.

§Buddhist teachings. One of the three pillars of Buddhism, the other two being the *sangha*, the religious community, and the *Buddha*, the founder of the religion, represented by all later transmitted teachers.

‖My teachers at Einstein.

#A somatic hallucination.

without words.* *Is this what saints go through during a spiritual conversion?† They go to psychiatrists‡ if they cannot handle it. I, myself, a new concept of myself emerging. Without any control, and truthfully, it's a little bit scary, thinking I may be losing my mind. But remembering that to tread that path is a very difficult task and many turn back. Could you imagine the torture Jung had to live through for three years?§ Why didn't he kill himself?‖ What an incredible hassle. Is this the existential crisis the great philosophers come to at the time of their conversion to religion as an answer?# Hang on to biology for dear life,** baby, as it's going to be a wild ride . . .*

I am really flipping out, and have been for a long time. Everything was really secure before The College†† . . .

If I don't make it through, I will go crazy, and they will have to stick me in one of those fucking institutions.

---

*Extrasensory feeling may exist, but in this context, it reflects how my self-boundaries are weakening.

†A notion with a long history. It takes two forms. One is that religious figures who experience highly altered states are simply psychotic/schizophrenic. Therefore, we can safely disregard their words as symptoms of mental illness, not inspiration. The other form is the belief that mental illness in which delusions and hallucinations occur is in reality a condition akin to inspiration. Social constructs, however, cause us to pathologize rather than revere such individuals.

‡My stance toward psychiatry and psychotherapy at this time was negative, as if availing myself of them would be an admission of failure of my spiritual quest.

§A reference to Carl Jung's three-year period he recounts in *The Red Book*. Assessments of these years range from "creative illness," a "period of introspection," a "psychotic break," or "simply madness."[9]

‖Suicide may be an option for me, too.

#Because logic fails them.

**While the medical model and biological psychopharmacology informed my clinical psychedelic drug research, here, it could not function as a reason for living.

††This points to the difficulty I encountered in both moves away from a familiar environment to a strange new one. First episodes of serious mental illness often occur at such times.

Gray is a terrific cat. But she is a cat and has her own mind. One day I angrily throw her against the wall for resisting my cutting her nails. Later I'm in the kitchen and she rubs up against my leg affectionately. Is she making up for the trouble she caused when I cut her nails? She may have gotten over it, but I haven't. I sprinkle mustard powder into her eyes.

I am stunned. I'm out of control. Ashamed, guilty, self-loathing, abashed, self-hate fills me. Demoralized, disheartened... Disheartened—how low have I fallen?

> *Stretch your head, man, don't bind it. I knew it would be like*
> *   this. The ruse is up, dude!* *
> *Why never want to let go.*
> *Why continue to grab after a shadow?*
> *Helpless, helpless, helpless, falling, falling, falling.*
> *To realize our impermanence and*
> *arbitrariness is horrifying.*
> *It makes everything you want*
> *or think a laughing mockery*
> *of itself, and of you.*
> *Whistling at the dark.*
> *Stupid!*
> *Bread knows it.* †
> *Cat knows it.*
> *Why can't I know it!*
> *Cat is slave to hormones, so am I.*
> *Bread is slave to my hands?*
> *So am I.*
> *Everything would be the same*
> *if I were here or not.*

---

*I'm not enlightened, even if I want to be or pretend I am.
†While in New York, I baked bread; here I attribute to it consciousness.

WHERE IS MY GURU?!?*

Eat when anxious
Stutter when anxious†
Forget it, man
You have really had it
What is anyone to do
When all you do is
Snort, sputter, wheeze
inhale, exhale, where is the mantra?‡
Where's Clarissa?
Where's my fucking head?
It's wasted-ignored, never heard
from.
Go back to California where
you belong.
Leave, give up.
Forget it.
Be happy again.
Study the kidney, man—
Study and stutter
Stutter and study.
Increase your impotence—
it's the American way.§
Straight teeth and crooked heads,
that's what our country is full of.
Know more

---

*I knew I needed help and believed it would come from an Eastern religion. Within a month of dropping out of school, I attended my first Zen Buddhist meditation retreat.

†After returning to medical school a year later, I responded well to behaviorally oriented speech therapy.

‡A sound, word, or phrase of scripture that one repeats vocally, subvocally, or silently to produce an altered state of consciousness. Here, the mantra would heal me.

§The banality of Western/American culture.

no less
no more.
Know more
Know less
feel sorry for yourself
because of all you know
nothing
isolated pieces of
meat*
No meaning
It defies meaning
life is DNA. Life is
my cat
running up to me
and scratching my ass off.
And me trying to kill
her, slamming her
against the wall,
Coward.
Look at Peter,†
Everything is subject
to his will and
nothing can resist—
Nietzsche!!
Only his head will
resist as it reaches its
infinite limit,‡ if he

---

*The idea that the study of man's parts denigrates man's spiritual nature. This is a rationalization for the academic difficulties I was experiencing.

†A Men's College acquaintance who appears in "Clarissa" and "Permanent Insanity." He often referred to Nietzsche in our conversations, especially the notion of the "will to power" as the preeminent human drive. Making power your goal leads to an extreme form of self-centeredness.

‡Limits of rational thought, or of the nature of one's sense of individual selfhood.

ever opens his eyes from his scars.
Cut her nails
hold her down
Wait until she's sleeping-
My cat is stronger than
I am.
I tremble at her
power.
I am humbled and
worthless against her
indignant
onslaught of insult
So i slam her head
and pour mustard
seed in her
eyes.
Worm of nothingness.
I am losing my mind in medical school,
in New York City,
completely alone.
Only with Clarissa am I with
someone.
I had friends before
her, and had friends
with her. but I am
without her and have no friends
here.

Disinterested all-knowing all moral perfect observer (third person)
1) Object 2) Subject 3) Buddha who merges truth with himself and all
three with each other. To hate object means to hate subject (me) and
witness (Buddha-Christ)—sooo hard.

*Where there is no person, there is nothing personal—of the person—like the chariot of King Milinda.**

I write to the graduate school of theology that shares a campus with The College. It is an abridged version of the Manifesto and concludes by asking if they will accept me for a year or two of graduate studies. They do not reply.

I am losing weight and have difficulty sleeping. I twice dream of death: in one dream, I'm on a subway that lifts up from the tracks instead of crashing into another train coming at us on the same track. Heading upward with a car full of fellow travelers into outer space, dark with stars, I know we've died. In another, a Black man walks up and shoots me in the chest.

How can I feel better?

Analyze dreams? Jung
Or ignore dreams. American New York City
Or ignore everything. BUDDHA?
People don't ignore anything, and i don't think Trungpa†
*   does. They are aware of everything at once. This is how i*
*   would like to be. Aware of everything at once, and without*
*   the need to look so damn hard.*

---

*An Eastern religious parable. A "chariot" lacks essential existence. Rather, it is a conventional term for a collection of parts that, working together, gives the impression of being an independent freestanding whole. Similarly, neither the body nor mind inherently exist. They only give the impression of doing so because we don't perceive its reality accurately. I liked this idea because it promised a way out of my personal distress; that is, no self meant no unhappiness because there was no one to feel it.
†Chögyam Trungpa, a Tibetan Buddhist who wrote several books that greatly influenced me during my college years.[10] His charisma and unorthodox teaching style, enormous appetite for alcohol, mastery of English, and incisive critique of Western culture and English language made powerful impressions on all who encountered him and his work.

I grow suspicious around my two marijuana-smoking friends.* Are they giving me sideways glances, puzzled questioning looks? Are their jokes more barbed and hurtful? Friends who, instead of coming to my aid, add to my distress. I can't rely on them and withdraw further. One day, Marshall, my former anatomy partner, calls. He's a nice fellow but we have not spent time together. I can barely speak with him on the phone, my speech is so impaired.

I apply for a leave of absence. I can take two years. Any longer and I will need to reapply to school. In my request I mention that studying Buddhism is one of my goals. The assistant dean, a gentle gay Black physician who approves the leave, tells me he thinks I will attain enlightenment. I need to attain something, and attaining a return to California is enough.

Reflections
MY LOWEST POINT

When editing the first several drafts of this chapter, I had difficulty making sense of the hyper-abstract nature of my journal entries. It is as if the more painful my feelings, the more abstract were my attempts to understand and manage them.

After rereading the material many times, I see the same theme as that occurring in the Manifesto: the conviction that a certain state of consciousness and its integration into the larger world would be a great boon—salvific, ushering in a utopia of body, mind, and spirit. Rigorously testing this hypothesis, however, required skill sets—spiritual, scientific, and psychological—I did not yet have.

Another difficulty in reviewing this material is revisiting just how bad I felt then. Diagnostically, one could say I was dealing with a major depressive disorder, with remnants of the hypomania that began when I

---

*A sign of developing paranoia and/or a realistic appraisal of their response to my decompensating.

wrote the Manifesto. In addition, there were early symptoms of psychosis. While the suspiciousness, ESP, and somatic hallucinations were less disabling than the anxiety and depression, they were ominous signs. I had never before, and have not since, experienced a similarly prolonged painful psychological state.

28

EN ROUTE TO THE TEMPLE
Childhood's End

I MOVE BACK to The College town, where Clarissa and my friends are in their last year of school at their respective colleges. I withdraw two hundred dollars from the bank—my life savings—to jumpstart my return. I rent a room in a house with other students and support myself typing term papers and theses. I'm fast on my manual typewriter and charge by the page.

Less easily and quickly manageable is my mood. Once more in a familiar supportive setting, I expect to feel happy and optimistic, but I'm not. Considering my condition in the Bronx, it's not surprising I continue struggling. New York and Einstein showed me just how fragile is my hold on who I am and what I want. I cannot pretend the last nine months did not happen, when social and academic pressures overwhelmed me. I'm now safe—safer—having left New York. I am less disorganized and hopeless, suffer less duress, and am functioning. My only obligations are Clarissa and myself. No deadlines nor tests. I have two years to right myself, hoping never to repeat a similar catastrophe.

I believe Buddhism will answer the existential and personal questions with which I struggled while in medical school. It so happens that a Zen temple is nearby, and I attend an intensive seven-day retreat there within a month of my return.

The discipline during the retreat is extraordinarily demanding, and while *koan* practice is an interesting meditation, I'm not sure it's for me.

Koans are Zen "riddles" that defy logical solutions. Examples are: "What is the sound of one hand clapping?" and "Show me your face before your parents met." Concentrating on solving koans provides leverage for breaking through the constraints of logical thought. By so doing, one begins making headway in attaining the "no-mind" of kensho, Buddhist enlightenment.

Interspersed within fifteen hours per day of meditation are four private meetings with the teacher where we review my progress in solving my koan. The Zen master and I sit on the floor facing each other in a tiny room. A highly polished flat dark rock—two inches thick, three feet long, and two feet wide—rests on the floor between us. My first koan requires expressing myself as the master striking his wooden staff against the rock. I look for the answer everywhere, all of the time, in memories and thoughts, in the sights and sounds around me. It is not easy, but not impossible. However, this practice feels too indirect. I want to address personal questions of identity and occupation. Koan practice appears better suited for monastic life, and I'm not ready for that. In addition, I am alarmed to hear during lunch with a small group after the retreat that the Zen master kissed and fondled one of the female retreatants repeatedly during their private interviews.

After Clarissa graduates, we move to the Bay Area where I work for her brother-in-law's house-painting business. I wire brush window frames, hang and tape sheetrock, install doors and locks, prime and paint interiors and exteriors. It's grueling work and there's no opportunity to talk about deeper things.

I ask Jim Fadiman if he could recommend other Buddhist teachers. He tells me about JK, the Zen master who leads The Temple. She is a Western woman who trained at a preeminent Japanese Zen monastery for many years. After receiving transmission from her teacher, she moved to the United States in the mid-1960s. Before long, she relocated to a large rural site and gathered a primarily monastic community around her.

JK belongs to the Sōtō Zen lineage. Some refer to Sōtō as "farmer's Zen." This contrasts with the characterization of Rinzai Zen—the lineage to which the monastery of my previous retreat belonged—as "soldier Zen." Whereas Rinzai emphasizes koan practice, Sōtō's "koans" are daily life. The koan is "Why does the loud breathing of the fellow sitting next to you bother you so much?" not "What is the sound of one hand clapping?" Sōtō might show me how to practice Buddhism and remain in the world; that is, understanding the nature of reality, as well as dealing with everyday life in a manner consistent with that understanding. I still have medical school to consider.

Clarissa and I attend a weekend retreat at The Temple. Hours after arriving, I develop a fever, myalgias, and arthralgias. I go to the infirmary, lay down, and take a nap. Upon awakening, I see a shaven-headed monk sitting in a rocking chair reading one of JK's works.

He puts down the book and asks, "How are you feeling?"

He radiates a helpful friendly attitude, is gentle, and makes direct eye contact. The lack of any perceptible aggression startles me—no sarcasm, irony, or skepticism.

"Better. I get these brief episodes. They usually last only a few hours."

"There is no rush, but if you're feeling well, let's get you back to the group. It's a busy weekend."

Sōtō Zen's meditation practice is consistent with the emphasis on "the koan of daily life." It is "just sitting," or *shikan taza*. The technique is simple enough—one neither grasps at nor pushes away mental and physical experience. However, there is a goal, the "dropping off" or "harmonizing" of body and mind—the enlightenment experience. And this experience informs how you interact with the world. I find this practice more relevant and generalizable than focusing on specific koans.

Even in this short retreat, it's clear the goal of training at The Temple is enlightenment. It's a regular topic of discussion—in class, at tea, during work periods, in casual encounters with monks. What is it?

How do you attain it? How is its authenticity verified? What happens after that? Enlightenment is the lifeblood coursing through the heart of The Temple.

The color of monks' robes signifies level of spiritual experience and resultant rank within the community. I don't sense that this hierarchy is make-believe because those of higher rank do appear different. They are more solid, joyful, focused, empathic, and responsive. I wonder how these experiences reflect spiritual growth and how JK recognizes them. This smaller circle of higher-ranking monks also has greater access to JK and her advanced teachings—another impetus to press for enlightenment.

JK is away this weekend, but her presence fills The Temple. If enlightenment is The Temple's lifeblood, she is its beating heart. The monks freely share their experience of being her disciples—a relationship available to both lay and clerical members of the community. They love the teacher and entrust her with their spiritual and personal lives. Discipleship appeals to me. It would provide a relationship with a powerful, wise, kind, loving figure. Someone to whom you turn for answers to your deepest questions. And she answers them.

Most unexpected over the weekend is the overflowing of affection I feel from and toward the monks, both men and women. It is as if we are long-lost friends, now reunited. Everywhere I sense the unspoken greeting: How good to see you! Welcome, welcome! These are people with whom I can relate, let my guard down, and trust in expressing my wishes and fears. It's not only a place to study and practice Zen Buddhism. It is a community whose members are highly intelligent, emotionally available, and psychologically sophisticated.

The psychedelic experience had helped me establish a benchmark for intuiting the truth. However, this benchmark was only a feeling, not a way of understanding and living my life. The strength of that feeling had compelled me to seek out such a system. My introduction to Sōtō Zen Buddhism evoked a feeling of truth similar to that I had glimpsed during my psychedelic experiences.

⚡

We return to the Bay Area. I work in data entry and as a gardener, saving money for a training session beginning in October.

I now have a goal. It's what I want to do. Maybe I will stay there and become a monk after all. I don't know what to do with my life . . . I'm not ready to return to medical school. Whenever I assess my inner state, I'm confronted with an enduring lingering depression: sad, helpless, confused, and hopeless.

The date arrives and I board a Greyhound bus in San Francisco. It lets me out at a depot in a small town south of The Temple. It's a brisk fall day—blue sky, bright sun, and a chill in the air. At the station are two others arriving for the training session. On schedule, a monk drives up in a well-worn Chevy Blazer and we climb in. Arriving at the monastery's gates just before sunset, the driver identifies himself on the intercom. The tall wooden gates open, we pull in, and they close behind us.

NOTES

PREFACE. RESEARCH IS ME–SEARCH

1. Strassman, *DMT and the Soul of Prophecy*.
2. Strassman, *DMT: The Spirit Molecule*.
3. Bukowski, *On Drinking*.
4. Hofmann, *LSD: My Problem Child*.
5. Lilly, *Center of the Cyclone*.
6. James, *The Varieties of Religious Experience*.
7. Freud, *Cocaine Papers*.
8. Burroughs, *Junky*.
9. De Quincey, *Confessions of an English Opium-Eater and Other Writings*.
10. Moreau and Peters, *Hashish and Mental Illness*.

EXPLORING ALTERED STATES OF CONSCIOUSNESS

1. Tart, "States of Consciousness and State-specific Sciences."
2. Tart, *Altered States of Consciousness*.
3. Weil, *The Natural Mind*.
4. Grof and Grof, *Holotropic Breathwork*.
5. Hof, *The Wim Hof Method*.

PROLOGUE. THE BEGINNING

1. Brown, *Dreaming Wide Awake*.

2. PRAYER WHEEL

1. Dean et al., "Biosynthesis and Extracellular Concentrations of N,N-Dimethyltryptamine (DMT) in Mammalian Brain."

4. TENSE INFANT ANALYTIC SESSION

1. Grof and Grof, *Holotropic Breathwork*.

7. TERRY AND BEER

1. Bukowski, *On Drinking*, 166.

9. CLOUD SPEAKERS

1. McQueen, *Psychedelic Cannabis*.
2. Ward and Simner, "Synesthesia: The Current State of the Field."
3. Strassman, "Book Review: 'Living High: Daily Marijuana Use Among Adults.'"

10. FLYING CARPET

1. Sheldrake, "Psi in Everyday Life."
2. Luke, "Anomalous Psychedelic Experiences."

14. STEAK ON ACID

1. Sanders, *The Family*.
2. Lifton, *Destroying the World to Save It*.

15. BASKETBALL GAY PANIC

1. Kempf, *Psychopathology*, 477–515; Chuang and Addington, "Homosexual Panic: A Review of Its Concept"; Glick, "Homosexual Panic: Clinical and Theoretical Considerations."
2. Mallory et al., "Banning the Use of Gay and Trans Panic Defenses."

22. NUCLEAR REACTOR

1. Krasnykh et al., "Radioprotective Action of 5-Methoxy Tryptamine and Other Alcoxy-Tryptamines."
2. Barrett et al., "Hallucinogenic Drugs Attenuate the Subjective Response to Alcohol in Humans."
3. Taylor, "Today Is the 47th Anniversary of Dock Ellis' Acid-fueled No-hitter."

23. THE MANIFESTO

1. Strassman et al., "Elongation of Axons in an Agar Matrix That Does Not Support Cell Locomotion"; Strassman and Wessells, "Orientational Preferences Shown by Microspikes of Growing Nerve Cells In Vitro."

2. Strassman, *DMT: The Spirit Molecule*, 57–58.

3. Deikman, "De-automatization and the Mystic Experience."

4. Strassman, "The Psychedelic Religion of Mystical Consciousness."

5. Naranjo and Ornstein, *On the Psychology of Meditation*.

24. UBEHEBE

1. Olson et al., "Tripping on Nothing: Placebo Psychedelics and Contextual Factors."

26. PERMANENT INSANITY

1. Becker et al., "Ketanserin Reverses the Acute Response to LSD in a Randomized, Double-Blind, Placebo-Controlled, Crossover Study in Healthy Participants."

27. NEW YORK BREAKDOWN

1. "Karl H. Pribram," Wikipedia.

2. Pribram, *Languages of the Brain*.

3. For example, Grof's work in Pahnke et al., "The Experimental Use of Psychedelic (LSD) Psychotherapy."

4. Strassman et al., "A Model for the Study of the Acute Effects of Melatonin in Man."

5. MacDougall, "Hypothesis Concerning Soul Substance Together with Experimental Evidence of the Existence of Such Substance."

6. "The Shapes of the Luminous Egg," image and comment posted in 2021 by danl999 on Reddit website, Castaneda subreddit.

7. Bailey, *The Consciousness of the Atom*.

8. Reich, *The Function of the Orgasm*.

9. Shamdasani, *Jung Stripped Bare by His Biographers, Even*, 71–73.

10. Trungpa, *Meditation in Action*; Trungpa, *Cutting Through Spiritual Materialism*.

BIBLIOGRAPHY

Bailey, Alice. *The Consciousness of the Atom*. New York: Lucifer Publishing Company, 1922.

Barrett, Sean P., Jennifer Archambault, Marla J. Engelberg, and Robert O. Pihl. "Hallucinogenic Drugs Attenuate the Subjective Response to Alcohol in Humans." *Human Psychopharmacology: Clinical and Experimental* 15, no. 7 (2000): 559–65.

Becker, Anna M., Aaron Klaiber, Friederike Holze, Ioanna Istampoulouoglou, Urs Duthaler, Nimmy Varghese, Anne Eckert, Matthias E. Liechti. "Ketanserin Reverses the Acute Response to LSD in a Randomized, Double-Blind, Placebo-Controlled, Crossover Study in Healthy Participants." *International Journal of Neuropsychopharmacology* 26, no. 2 (2023): 97–106.

Brown, David Jay. *Dreaming Wide Awake: Lucid Dreaming, Shamanic Healing, and Psychedelics*. Rochester, VT: Park Street Press, 2016.

Bukowski, Charles. *On Drinking*. Edited by Abel Debritto. New York: HarperCollins, 2019.

Burroughs, William S. *Junky: The Definitive Text of "Junk."* New York: Grove/Atlantic, 2012.

Chuang, Henry T., and D. Addington, "Homosexual Panic: A Review of Its Concept." *The Canadian Journal of Psychiatry* 33, no. 7 (1988): 613–17.

Dalai Lama [Tenzin Gyatso]. *A Flash of Lightning in the Dark of Night*. Boston: Shambhala, 1994.

Dean, Jon G., Tiecheng Liu, Sean Huff, Ben Sheler, Steven A. Barker, Rick Strassman, Michael M. Wang, and Jimo Borjigin. "Biosynthesis and Extracellular Concentrations of N,N-Dimethyltryptamine (DMT) in Mammalian Brain." *Scientific Reports* 9, no. 1 (2019): 9333.

Deikman, Arthur J. "De-automatization and the Mystic Experience." *Psychiatry* 29, no. 4 (1966): 324–38.

De Quincey, Thomas. *Confessions of an English Opium-Eater and Other Writings*. New York: Oxford University Press, 2013.

Freud, Sigmund. *Cocaine Papers*. Edited by Robert Byck. New York: Stonehill Publishing, 1974.

Fromm, Erich, D. T. Suzuki, and Richard Martino. *Zen Buddhism and Psychoanalysis*. New York: HarperCollins, 1970.

Glick, B. S. "Homosexual Panic: Clinical and Theoretical Considerations." *Journal of Nervous and Mental Disease* 129, no. 1 (1959): 20–28.

Grof, Stanislav, and Christina Grof. *Holotropic Breathwork*. Foreword by Jack Kornfield. Albany: State University of New York Press, 2010.

Hof, Wim. *The Wim Hof Method*. Louisville, CO: Sounds True, 2020.

Hofmann, Albert. *LSD: My Problem Child*. New York: McGraw Hill, 1980.

Huxley, Aldous. *The Perennial Philosophy*. New York: Harper & Row, 2009.

James, William. *The Varieties of Religious Experience*. New York: Triumph Press, 1985.

Jamison, Kay Redfield. *An Unquiet Mind: A Memoir of Moods and Madness*. New York: Vintage Books, 1996.

Jung, C. G. *The Red Book: A Reader's Edition*. New York: W.W. Norton & Company, 2012.

Kempf, Edward J. *Psychopathology*. St. Louis, MO: CV Mosby Company, 1920.

Krasnykh, I. G., P. G. Zherebchenko, V. S. Murashova, N. N. Suvorov, N. P. Sorokina, and V. S. Shashkov. "[Radioprotective action of 5-Methoxy Tryptamine and Other Alcoxy-Tryptamines]." *Radiobiologiya* 2 (1962): 156–60. [In Russian.] For English translation see *Radiobiology* (Engl. Transl.), January 1;2.

Krishna, Gopi. *Kundalini*. Boulder, CO: Shambala Books, 1970.

Lifton, Robert J. *Destroying the World to Save It*. London: Picador, 2000.

Lilly, John C. *Center of the Cyclone: An Autobiography of Inner Space*. New York: Bantam Books, 1973.

Luke, David. "Anomalous Psychedelic Experiences: At the Neurochemical Juncture of the Humanistic and Parapsychological." *Journal of Humanistic Psychology* 62, no. 2 (2022): 257–97.

MacDougall, Duncan. "Hypothesis Concerning Soul Substance Together with Experimental Evidence of the Existence of Such Substance." *Journal of the American Society for Psychical Research* 1, no. 5 (1907): 237–75.

Mallory, Christy, Brad Sears, and Luis A. Vasquez. "Banning the Use of Gay and Trans Panic Defenses." UCLA School of Law Williams Institute 47

(April 2021). Report available for download at williamsinstitute.law.ucla .edu under the "Publications" tab.

McQueen, Daniel. *Psychedelic Cannabis*. Rochester, VT: Park Street Press, 2021.

Moreau, J. J., and H. Peters. *Hashish and Mental Illness*. New York: Raven Press, 1973.

Naranjo, Claudio, and Robert E. Ornstein. *On The Psychology of Meditation*. New York: Viking Press, 1972.

Olson, Jay A., Leah Suissa-Rocheleau, Michael Lifshitz, Amir Raz, and Samuel Veissiere. "Tripping on Nothing: Placebo Psychedelics and Contextual Factors." *Psychopharmacology* 237 (2020): 1371–82.

Pahnke, Walter N., Albert A. Kurland, Sanford Unger, Charles Savage, and Stanislav Grof. "The Experimental Use of Psychedelic (LSD) Psychotherapy." *JAMA* 212, no. 11 (1970): 1856–63.

Pribram, Karl H. *Languages of the Brain: Experimental Paradoxes and Principles in Neuropsychology*. Hoboken, NJ: Prentice-Hall, 1971.

Ram Dass. *Be Here Now*. San Cristobal, NM: Lama Foundation, 1971.

Reich, Wilhem. *The Function of the Orgasm*. New York: Pocket, 1975.

Sanders, Ed. *The Family*. Revised, updated ed. Cambridge, MA: Da Capo Press, 2002.

Shamdasani, Sonu. *Jung Stripped Bare by His Biographers, Even*. Wales, UK: Karnac Books, 2005.

Sheldrake, Rupert. "Psi in Everyday Life: Nonhuman and Human." In *Parapsychology: A Handbook for the 21st Century*, edited by Etzel Cardeña, John Palmer, and David Marcusson-Clavertz, 350–63. Jefferson, NC: McFarland and Co., 2015.

Strassman, Rick. "Book Review: 'Living High: Daily Marijuana Use Among Adults.'" *American Journal of Psychiatry* 145 (1988): 1467–1468.

Strassman, Rick. *DMT and the Soul of Prophecy*. Rochester, VT: Inner Traditions, 2014.

Strassman, Rick. *DMT: The Spirit Molecule*. Rochester, VT: Park Street Press, 2001.

Strassman, Rick. *Joseph Levy Escapes Death*. Berkeley, CA: Regent Press, 2019.

Strassman, Rick. "The Psychedelic Religion of Mystical Consciousness, Review of William Richards' *Sacred Knowledge*." *Journal of Psychedelic Studies* 2, no. 1 (2018): 1–4.

Strassman, R. J., P. C. Letourneau, and N. K. Wessells. "Elongation of Axons in an Agar Matrix That Does Not Support Cell Locomotion." *Experimental Cell Research* 818 (1973): 482–87.

Strassman, R. J., G. T. Peake, C. R. Qualls, and E. J. Lisansky. "A Model for the Study of the Acute Effects of Melatonin in Man." *Journal of Clinical Endocrinology and Metabolism* 65 (1987): 847–52.

Strassman, R., and N. K. Wessells. "Orientational Preferences Shown by Microspikes of Growing Nerve Cells In Vitro." *Tissue and Cell* 5 (1973): 412–17.

Tart, Charles T. "States of Consciousness and State-specific Sciences." *Science* 176 (1972): 1203–10.

Tart, Charles T. *Altered States of Consciousness*. New York: Wiley, 1969.

Taylor, Jon. "Today Is the 47th Anniversary of Dock Ellis' Acid-fueled No-hitter." Sports Illustrated website, June 12, 2017.

Trungpa, Chögyam. *Cutting Through Spiritual Materialism*. Boulder, CO: Shambhala Publications, 2002.

Trungpa, Chögyam. *Meditation in Action*. Boulder, CO: Shambhala Publications, 2019.

Ward, Jamie, and Julia Simner. "Synesthesia: The Current State of the Field." In *Multisensory Perception*, edited by K. Sathian and V. S. Ramachandran, 283–300. New York: Academic Press, 2020.

Weil, Andrew T. *The Natural Mind: An Investigation of Drugs and the Higher Consciousness*. Rev. ed. Boston: Mariner/Houghton-Mifflin, 1986.

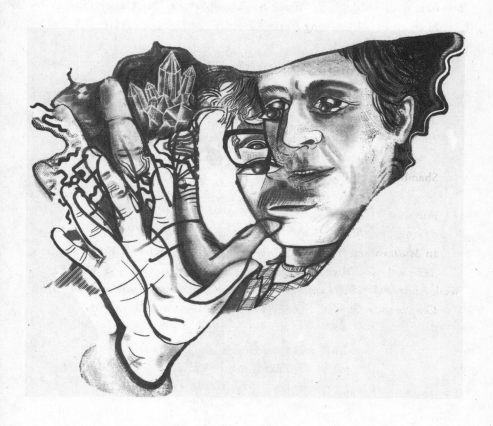

BOOKS OF RELATED INTEREST

DMT: The Spirit Molecule
A Doctor's Revolutionary Research into the Biology of
Near-Death and Mystical Experiences
by Rick Strassman, M.D.

DMT and the Soul of Prophecy
A New Science of Spiritual Revelation in the Hebrew Bible
by Rick Strassman, M.D.

Inner Paths to Outer Space
Journeys to Alien Worlds through Psychedelics
and Other Spiritual Technologies
*by Rick Strassman, M.D., Slawek Wojtowicz, M.D.,
Luis Eduardo Luna, Ph.D., and Ede Frecska, M.D.*

The Psychedelic Explorer's Guide
Safe, Therapeutic, and Sacred Journeys
by James Fadiman, Ph.D.

Psychedelic Medicine
The Healing Powers of LSD, MDMA, Psilocybin, and Ayahuasca
by Dr. Richard Louis Miller

Microdosing with Amanita Muscaria
Creativity, Healing, and Recovery with the Sacred Mushroom
by Baba Masha, M.D.
Foreword by James Fadiman, Ph.D.

LSD and the Mind of the Universe
Diamonds from Heaven
by Christopher M. Bache, Ph.D.
Foreword by Ervin Laszlo

LSD: Doorway to the Numinous
The Groundbreaking Psychedelic Research into
Realms of the Human Unconscious
by Stanislav Grof, M.D.

INNER TRADITIONS • BEAR & COMPANY
P.O. Box 388 • Rochester, VT 05767
1-800-246-8648
www.InnerTraditions.com

Or contact your local bookseller